AF575240

Glitch: Designing Imperfection

Editing and Curation: Iman Moradi, Ant Scott
Additional Curation: Joe Gilmore, Christopher Murphy
Design: Qubik / Fehler
Typefaces used: Taz III

Library of Congress Control Number: 2008929885

Printed and bound in China by Asia Pacific Offset

10 9 8 7 6 5 4 3 2 1   First edition

Mark Batty Publisher
36 West 37th Street, Suite 409
New York, NY 10018
www.markbattypublisher.com

ISBN-13: 978-0-979666-6-8

Distributed outside North America by:
Thames & Hudson Ltd
181A High Holborn
London WC1V 7QX
United Kingdom

Tel: 00 44 20 7845 5000   Fax: 00 44 20 7845 5055

www.thameshudson.co.uk

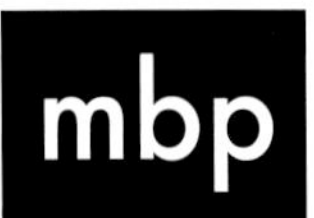

Contents

Contributors

alorenz
Daniel Althausen
Cory Arcangel
Scott Arford
Christophe Behrens
Michael Betancourt
Enrico Bravi
brianelectro
Brusa
Alessandro Canova
Miguel Carvalhais
Kim Cascone
Yve Choquard
Curt Cloninger
Derek Collie
Roger Cosseboom
Taylor Deupree
Dextro
Manuel Dilly
Jeff Donaldson
Paul Emery
eNo
Fairchild Semiconductor
Adam Farcus
Jerome Faria
Fehler
Benjamin Fischer
Scott Fitzgerald
Tim Fox
Tina Frank
Nik Gaffney
Iris Garrelfs
Joe Gilmore
Mathias Gmachl
Vasco Godinho
Brent Gustafson
Alex Horber
Will Hurt
Eddy Joaquim
JODI
Tim Johnson
Daniel Julià
Jason Kahn
Mario Klingemann
Karl Klomp
Rainer Kohlberger
Jan Robert Leegte
Lia
Dimitre Lima
LoVid
David Lu
Rob Lycett
Stephan Maich
Hamish McDougall
Chad McKinney
Meta
Iman Moradi
Michael Norris
O.K. Parking
Alex Peverett
Norbert Pfaffenbichler
Per Platou
Andrea Polli
Nicky Proniewicz
Kristiano Pronin
Paul Prudence
Tim Redfern
reMI
RetroYou
Johnny Rogers
Billy Roisz
Michael R. Salmond
Ant Scott
Mike Scullen
Steven H. Silberg
Sincretic
Megan Sproats
Daniel Stanciu
Ralph Steinbrüchel
Telcosystems
Luciano Testi Paul
Dan Tombs
Kentaro Tsuji
Ben Ullman
U-Sun
James Warfield
Marius Watz
Kate Wintjes
Akihiko Yoshida

Acknowledgements

With thanks to all the contributors and interviewees without whom this book would not have been possible.

We are grateful for generous support and guidance from Derek Hales, director of the Digital Research Unit based in the School of Art, Design and Architecture at the University of Huddersfield.

Iman would additionally like to thank his parents and Alison for their unwavering support.

Ant would like to thank Kenneth Knowlton.

Joe would like to thank William Jones and Niels Bohr at 1,024 for their continued support.

Chris would like to thank the University of Ulster for supporting his time on trips to Leeds and Joe's visit to Belfast.

Foreword

Per Platou
Old Bitch Bay, June 2007
www.liveart.org

In 1995, after many years running a tiny, much too eclectic record label, I decided to apply for membership to UKS (the young artists' society in Norway). The original work I submitted was a cassette tape with recordings of different types of office trash, chairs, shelves and old Siemens computers being crushed in an industrial garbage compactor (yes, it was my night-time job; I had to feed the kids). From my point of view it was a kind of identity prank. After working with so many musicians with far bigger egos than skills, not even to mention sales potential, I wanted to prove that I could be an "artist" too.

"This will knock their brains out," I thought about the tape, but I was wrong of course. After a long waiting period my application was turned down without any reason, and in a moment of rage and disappointment I filed an extremely angry and vicious complaint, venting all my contempt for the snooty art world, stating elaborately that they had missed their only chance of revitalizing their rotten, bourgeois and corrupt system. Two days later I received a kind letter of acceptance, and after a few months I was asked to join the board.

So there I was, knowing nothing, but with a rapidly growing self-awareness as a "conceptual artist" inspired by ... well, I knew the names of Marcel Duchamp and Andy Warhol (mainly through the Velvet Underground). But this was 1995 and suddenly came the internet, and then came Netscape, and then I stumbled over a totally weird webpage that repeatedly caused my Mac to halt, shiver violently and eventually crash. "My first virus!" I exclaimed happily and emailed it on to everyone I knew. The web address was jodi.org and some years later I would come to know the couple behind it as one of a handful of truly radical net.art pioneers, fucking with my computer and my understanding of art.

The net.art movement (with the very important dot) was all about resistance toward the slick neo-liberal dotcom-hype that dominated so much of the late 1990s. Its mythological origins state that the term originally was a technical mistake, and a quite interesting one.[1] And here, far too early, comes the moral: Aren't the mistakes always more challenging, more interesting, more touching than sickening success stories? Just look at the American avant-garde film movement from the 1950s and 1960s; one name that stands out is Stan Brakhage, the hardcore eccentric filmmaker who always "destroyed" his shots in the developing process by adding mysterious chemicals, food, insect legs or whatever. His "mistakes" became an art form influencing what today is seen as mainstream visual old-skool glitch aesthetics used in everyday jingles for MTV and ads for Jaguar cars. The same can be said about the electronic glitch music movement that started in the late nineties and manifested itself through the Viennese label Mego.

So what is a "glitch" anyway? Well, it stems from German and Yiddish and means to slip or slide, but in everyday use it's a spurge of electrical current, or a little electronic hiccup. And when glitch music came along it felt extremely contemporary and relevant for all us who had experienced fucked-up CD players or a "live" computer crash. When my partner Amanda Steggell and I conducted our first internet-fuelled dance performance *M@ggie's Love Bytes* in 1996, the computers on stage crashed several times and things went extremely bad, technically speaking, but this very fact left the audience in awe, and one critic even spoke about "the incredible drama created by what seemed like stone-age technology."

It didn't take much to understand that the tension was created by what went wrong, and not what we had rehearsed for months in a dance studio. "Failure is success" we deducted cleverly, and a couple of years later we deliberately fake-crashed a Mac during a new performance ... resulting in a yawning audience. The crash wasn't real and somehow one could subconsciously feel it.

Fast-forward to 2002 when we decided to arrange a small symposium in Oslo to investigate if the concept of glitch could be transferred from music to other art forms, like visual glitch or social glitch (which is today often filed under "relational aesthetics"). Submitting "glitch + art" to

Alta Vista in those days resulted in very few hits, but the one on top was significant: a fresh new visual glitch diary called beflix.com by a young Englishman named Tony Scott. He investigated the visual phenomenon of computer glitches and during what must have been his first public presentation ever, he stunned the Oslo audience with several extremely beautiful screen grabs of computers or software crashing, snapped at the exact moment of their death, so to speak. And Tony was totally hardcore, no fake glitches would ever be allowed in his garden. Since then I have been convinced that one can (and should) allow for various kinds of random actions/events in art-making, technically or otherwise, but the conclusion remains: It is impossible to deliberately make a mistake.

A short time ago, I conducted a series of "public confession sessions" in Oslo under the label "Reality Check," where artists were encouraged to discuss art projects that had failed miserably. At first it was hard to get anybody to speak up; however, a few brave souls stood up, and the event soon became a massive success with hordes of fellow artists, curators, press and delinquents turning up, crying and laughing with the miserable (heroic) ones. It was without a doubt the biggest success in my infamous curatorial career. The outcome, however, was highly dubious; after a few sessions, artists were calling me day and night, literally begging me to be on the show, with the most unbelievably boring projects. Eventually, after one too many nightly phone calls from drunk, miserable, incredibly dull artists who tried to convince me that they were "totally losers," I decided to quit the whole show, to let the true failures, the hubris die with dignity and not be buried with the average common artcrap.

So for the love of all the true-life glitches out there, it is my sincere hope that this glossy coffee-table book of beautiful errors fails miserably.

1. net.art – the origin.
http://www.nettime.org/Lists-Archives/nettime-l-9703/msg00094.html

Introduction

Iman Moradi
Lecturer, School of Art, Design and Architecture, University of Huddersfield, UK

"A glitch image hits you right between the eyes."
Ant Scott

Definition

The visual glitch is an artifact resulting from an error. It is neither the cause, nor the error itself, it is simply the product of an error and more specifically its visual manifestation. It is a significant slip that marks a departure from our expected result.

Glitches usually arise from mistranslations that are facilitated by a loss or breakdown in our communication signals. They are the imperfect and unexpected results of such malfunctions, which have no apparent purpose to their existence in the setting of perfect processes.

On the other hand, visual glitches are quite often fleeting artifacts that momentarily offer a glimpse into the inner workings and complexities of storage, display and communication technology. In doing so, they sometimes become an unintentional feedback mechanism, a last chance for us to know that technology has malfunctioned.

From a visual composition standpoint, glitches are incongruously linear, complex, sharp and occasionally blurred. Fragmentation, linearity, complexity and repetition are the more common meta-qualities of visual glitches. Together with the quality of being unexpected, they make the visual glitch an unashamedly amorphous entity that pleases or annoys.

Contemporary Context

Due to our never-ending pursuit of signal perfection, higher definition, increased clarity and fidelity in consumer electronics, audio and visual, glitches are eliminated in a matter of milliseconds. At other times, they completely steal the limelight and become centrepieces of attention – however unwanted – such as an ATM video display glitching.

Visual glitches are rare in standard occurrence and yet paradoxically, they are quite easy to provoke, which makes them ideal for being appropriated, used as a medium for artwork or even elevated to the status of a genre. Imperfections in diamonds are affectionately called "inclusions." Outside of art and design, however, glitches don't get off the hook so easily – they are branded as bad reception, undesirable fuzz, static or interference.

As a complete contrast, however, to some, visual glitches have become the rare diamonds and objects of fetish and desire. It is not unusual for the qualities of fetish objects to be exaggerated as they are framed, or placed on a platform for discussion. Thus the fetishization of the visual glitch can result in challenging and questioning common taste in the best examples, or simply demonstrating a lack of aesthetic awareness in others. Consequently, fetish glitches are not necessarily glitch artworks, but their appropriation as artworks is quite common. The appreciation of the glitch can also be perceived as an attempt to explore or facilitate the fetishization of technology itself.

Popular culture is saturated with images of visual interfaces distorting and glitching. The glitch has become a prop or direct metaphor to assist the narrative. It is a touchstone for conveying heightened danger, or fear of the unknown.

Process

For the glitch artists, the process of creating visuals is an involved process, which stems from an understanding of their tools: computer hardware (storage media, memory and display technology) and software (operating systems, image processing libraries, file storage and data transmission protocols). Fundamentally though, everything boils down to principles of composition, color and personal taste, which are immutably non-specific and timeless. Aesthetic considerations therefore govern the way glitch artists crop, compose and even provoke the generation of these images. (Scott refers to a tweaking of his colors in print, a process that borders on the insanely meticulous and some others have documented lengthy processes and outcomes in creating visual glitches.)

In *The Pattern on the Stone*, W. Daniel Hillis defines the essence of digital technology as the process of restoring signals to near perfection at every stage, and he goes on to link this to the concept of keeping a complicated system under control. The visual glitch is a blatant display of lack of control on the part of digital technology and in a reverse kind of way it symbolizes our dominance over it.

In forcing a visual glitch, there is an element of unpredictability that makes experimentation worthwhile and rewarding.

Less commonly, the qualities of pure visual glitches are also studied and mimicked by adept designers, who create what can be termed as "glitch-alikes." These directly share the visual characteristics and makeup of pure glitches found in their original habitats, but are actually synthesized and faked.

This Book

We certainly live in machine-inspired human cultures of perfection, where the clarity of a signal becomes a marketable asset or bankable commodity, and in which static, undesirable detritus and failure are not usually options. Nonetheless, throughout the course of creating this book, we have heard artists, designers and audiences of media-arts events discuss at length what is so special to them about the glitch.

In the works featured in this book, which are from artists and designers worldwide, there is a lot of meaning attributed to these semi-unordered bits and bytes – to the conceptual value of those losses and unexpected surprises. For one contributor it could be their state of mind and personal neuroses playing out in the digital canvas. For another, the playful nature of design accidents or their assertion of dominance over our less-than-intelligent machines. Yet to others, using the glitch as a medium harks back to a time when imperfections were tolerated and are now retrospectively enjoyed as qualities. In a sense we are cherishing the little idiosyncrasies that are absent from the soulless machines churned from the production lines.

The glitch therefore has metaphysical presence, and many philosophical allusions have been made over its nature and origin during our correspondences with contributors. Does the glitch serve as a constant reminder for the human capacity to err? Does it comfort us by humanizing the machine?

To the glitch artists who strive to get their work shown in galleries and the designers whose work graces the covers of glitch albums and features in vodka advertisements, these provoked, designed or otherwise captured and framed glitches hold as much significance as traditional mediums.

Aside from appreciated aesthetic qualities, the utter complexity of some images, juxtaposed with their spontaneity and sometimes short life, is a status unique to glitches and systemic chaos in nature. From a media history standpoint it is also interesting to anthologize aspects of media such as glitches, for they may be forgotten when our signals become more perfect and our glitches less visual.

Some attempts have been made to categorize the aesthetic qualities of glitches and understand where they sit, or even ask the question whether glitches are a genre, medium or sub-medium in the pantheon of art forms. On the whole, though, it is my belief that the glitch should remain largely uncategorizable and orphaned in the face of changing technology. Its lack of function, or unwanted function, sits well within the realm of glitch art and design already, where it is used as a medium that adequately conveys persuasion and subversion in the same visual frame.

Whether or not you accept glitch art as a valid art form, glitches themselves are too short-lived, unless captured and displayed.

Interviews

Angela Lorenz

Graphic Designer
Berlin / Vienna
www.alorenz.net

How do you create your designs? When you're listening to a new CD/LP for a cover design project, what sort of initial synaesthetic images pop into your head?

This is not what usually happens. Images in my head, I mean ... unfortunately I'm not a synaesthete (that would be cool!).

The only time I remember having a very clear visual idea of how the cover would look, I had that "vision" while taking a shower, not while listening to the music. That was the kid606 *ps i love you* CD/LP on Mille Plateaux – the cover image is a 1:1 replica of that initial idea. But with most other projects it didn't work that way, also because the design isn't always based on the music itself.

How do you reconcile initial spontaneous images with your currently available tools and design processes? How much compromise is involved?

In the example above (kid606), no compromise at all. But that is the only example I can think of. Other than that, how I start to work on something largely depends on the project – the designs are not always about the music itself; it's often the title or the concept or the working process of the musician that I'm working with. Like, for example, the Full Swing EP (orth03) by Stephan Mathieu: the design works along the same lines as the audio, it's about enlargement and about defining an almost arbitrary starting point and taking it from there – I did the same thing with that image that Stephan did with his audio samples. Constructing something out of next to nothing. It's also about authorship – this image has no author really; it's the result of a file conversion failure (hence arbitrary), and Stephan also says that the samples he's used are so tiny and insignificant it only matters in principle but not in practice where they come from.

What do you understand by "glitch aesthetics," and would you say your work exhibits glitch aesthetics, even if it doesn't necessarily contain "errors"?

Not all of my work, but some of it for sure. Probably the interesting part of it. For me it's not so much the glitch aspect that's interesting but the generative aspect – letting the unexpected happen and using it. That's what computers are for, in my eyes, and that's why I find that approach important: our own imagination is very limited, and our aesthetic standards are skewed, so human-generated design is often very predictable. We copy. We stick to what we consider the right way. We do it like we've done it before. Computers obviously have no idea or opinion about aesthetics, let alone beauty. They're unbiased. A machine will relentlessly output *every* option, including what we call a "glitch" if you've set it up that way (sometimes it helps to be a bad programmer!) and you get to see things you'd never have considered yourself. This is like spontaneous mutation with regard to evolution, I think. Humans would not exist without it.

In my eyes there is no such thing as an error from the point of view of the machine: it runs or it crashes, and giving an error message is just part of the process. The only thing that could actually be considered an error would be a crash, but since that happens outside the limits of the system it can't be observed from inside so it doesn't exist either.

Do you find the technological experimentation an enjoyable and necessary part of your design process?

Yes. Absolutely.

If there were some piece of software that churned out endless new visual ideas with a recognizably "alorenz" theme, would you change your current style, and why?

Seeing as that's exactly what I like to do – writing things that churn out endless new visual ideas – I don't think so. Style is a dead end. I sincerely hope I haven't arrived there yet.

You've previously talked about this word "Zufall," meaning something between "accidental incident" and "fate." Is it the same as "serendipity"? Please explain the significance of this to your work.

Serendipity. Thanks for the word. I wasn't sure what it meant so I just looked it up – beautiful! Very appropriate too, as I wasn't expecting to expand my English vocabulary today. But no, it's not quite the same thing – what I was on about with "Zufall" was that it carries a sense of fate in itself which is a kind of paradox since the general meaning (how it's normally used) is exactly the opposite: coincidence. "Zufall" – can literally be read as "your lot in life" – "das Los, das einem zufällt," as Alfred Andersch has pointed out beautifully:

The name of the person buried here was Luise Zoufal, she had lived from 1878 to 1924, and under her name and the dates the words were incised: MINE HAS BEEN A GOODLY LOT.

Of course Anna failed to understand why I was still laughing. I tried to explain my unexpected merriment.

"She believed in her lot," I said. "She thought her life was goodly. And on top of that her name is Zoufal – 'chance!' – Zoufal!"

(...)

"I don't see it that way," she said hesitantly, when we had almost reached the gate. To me it's as if she meant to say: "I've drawn the winning ticket in the lottery." And pausing at the gate, she added thoughtfully: "I wish I knew why she thought her life was goodly. Funny word: goodly."

When we were back on Karl-Marx-Platz and had closed the gate behind us, I tried to prove to Anna that the inscription on Luise Zoufal's tombstone was a quotation from the Bible and that the word must therefore be interpreted as a synonym for the word "fate."

"Maybe," she said. "But she thought her fate was a ticket she'd drawn in the lottery of the God she believed in. That's certainly what she meant. She knew it was chance, but she thought this chance was her fate. To her they were one and the same thing." [1]

This is where I'm coming from, as far as I'm aware. I don't think this is a personal thing in that it would have special significance to my work in particular – it's much bigger than that, one of the big unanswerable questions, or complex of questions, of mankind, isn't it? The tension between the ideas of free will and predetermination, the quest for meaning, the desire for a goal and a structure: this is why people have constructed religions since the beginning of time.

Regarding my work I think I already somewhat explained the significance above: what we perceive as a glitch or random occurrence, with regard to digital arts, is obviously predetermined by how we set up a system and within that system every possible outcome is equally valid. The glitch only exists for us. Personally, I don't think randomness exists on any level – for us it does, because we're trapped inside the system we live in, and we like to think that there's no rhyme or reason to things we don't understand so we label them randomness, Zufall, fate or whatever... but to me this is just the same as declaring a hailstorm the wrath of God.

Why do you think there aren't as many visual glitch artists and designers as there are glitch musicians?

I've often asked myself a similar question – Why is graphic design so far behind? If you look at how music has been developing in the last, say, 40 years (particularly digital or electronic music, but probably other kinds as well – I don't know much about what's going on in New music, jazz, improvisation etc.) ... and other forms of expression as well, I get the feeling that graphic design is really lagging behind, at best picking up certain "trends" several years after they've become static.

I guess one of the reasons might be that graphic design is so dominated by the marketing industry that sometimes people don't even see that there might be a difference ("I'm a graphic designer." – "Oh, so you work in advertising?" – I mean if someone tells you he's a musician you wouldn't ask that question, although music is being used in adverts just the same). So I never worked in advertising, but from what I see every day there doesn't seem to be much room for experimentation there ... "glitch aesthetics" just don't have that sort of commercial value.

On the other hand, the David Carson rip-off style that was so popular in the 1990s (in advertising as well, at least here in Germany) is also a kind of "glitch" by your definition, isn't it?

Glitch and its relatives simply presume experimentation I would say, both on an aesthetic and a technical level, and that's just not so common in graphic design as it is in music. Of course there *are* a lot of great designers whose work seems to prove the opposite, but if you look at the profession in general, the goal seems to be making things "look nice" and ... yeah, that's about it. Almost every electronic musician I know is quite an expert in what technology he uses, and how, be it hardware compatibility issues or spectral analysis or whatever ... not because they're all nerds, but because you need to know this stuff in order to do what you're doing. And because it's interesting. With designers it's more like, "I'm the creative here, the technical issues aren't my problem." I worked in pre-press for a while and this mindset seems to be all too common. Just try to explain to a designer where that PostScript error is coming from ... What I just want to say is, in order to make glitches, or any other kind of unexpected or unintentional result a part of your language, you have to understand it first, and with a lot more designers than musicians that's just not the case.

Another thing is, when there's a designer, 99% of the time there's a client as well.

You are interested in forms of activism. Does the glitch's subversive nature, being a fault or error, have anything to do with why you've chosen it as a perfect expressive medium to work with?

I don't think there's a subversive nature in any kind of medium. I don't consider myself a glitch artist or glitch designer or whatever.

Political activists (the ones that I know, at least) tend to be very conservative when it comes to aesthetics, and for a reason – they want to address the broad public with their issue, not some kind of small avant-garde circle that might be attracted by innovative design experiments. I don't mean to say that they think (or I think) that the broad public is too stupid or unimaginative to understand anything else than bold or underlined, just that that's not their main concern – clarity comes first.

I don't believe in subversion in the art world – it's too often just a feeble excuse for not even trying. People allegedly developed a high culture of subversive communication in the GDR, but 1. I've never lived there, 2. this culture is dead now (from what I can tell), 3. it wasn't artists who developed it, but people. I guess this kind of thing exists under every dictatorship or censorist regime, but I wouldn't say it's tied to one medium or other (if it were that easy it wouldn't be subversive).

Why should glitch be subversive? I mean, is there any evil oppressive art police that says errors are verboten? I find errors often interesting, not because they're errors but because they generate results I myself wouldn't have come up with.

Be it that bug in *procedure#09* which led to the "6.45KB" series, or the conversion error that let the Full Swing EP cover image happen or the beautiful results you get when you feed a video beamer (or monitor) with screen updates at 200 Hz – they're all "errors" from our point of view, but from the point of view of the computer there's nothing wrong with it. It's either possible or not (and if not it doesn't *happen*, because it'll have crashed already), quite Wittgensteinian actually – "the world is all that is the case."

Actually, come to think of it, there is no such thing as an error for a computer ... there is a bunch of rules, and whenever anything happens it happens inside that system, even if it's not what you intended.

1. Translation: © Doubleday 1970. Alfred Andersch: Efraim's Book. Manheim, Ralph. Published: New Directions 1994. (Original: Alfred Andersch: Efraim. Volk und Welt Verlag (Lizenzausgabe), Berlin 1990; © Diogenes Verlag, Zürich 1967)

Johnny Rogers

Media Collage Artist
Baltimore, USA
www.johnnyrogers.ws

What does glitch mean to you?

Well usually a glitch comes to be outside of the user's intentions. In a universe of broken symmetries, a small rebellion of this type earns my respect. I can read the visually manifested glitches with my eyes, and they look really cool! It's refreshing to watch our human-centric hand vanish while the digital pulls back into the beautiful, beautiful landscape.

A lot of your earlier work is monochrome photography, but then it became purely 1-bit, black-and-white for a time. Was that a conscious response to working with glitch imagery?

I don't think it was a response to my glitch imagery specifically. It certainly displays the aesthetics I was really interested in at the time. The 1-bit is attractive conceptually and visually. Also, the economic benefits of photocopies played a role in this.

You've made a lot of large-format photocopy prints of bold, blocky glitches, such as in your "Deconstruction" series. What is it about making big physical prints that you like, in a world where digital art is increasingly screen-based?

Well, I actually quit making prints for the most part around 2003. Though I do still admire the effect of cool prints, the waste, cost and space factors are unattractive to me. The internet is my primary means of distribution.

In your "Fuck Information" series of exhibitions, viewers were invited to obstruct parts of the glitchy images by sticking colored dots on them. The images are obviously carefully composed with an eye to aesthetics; are you also saying, "fuck aesthetics"?

Were you conducting an experiment to see what happens when a glitch is glitched again by the stickers?

Long ago I was fairly deep into photographic media and history. This eventually changed. By the end of my first semester at SFAI (San Francisco Art Institute) I was so bothered by precious, priceless, pixel perfection, and purist photo poppycock that, in an effort to set my style and do what seemed radical, I started making all my work dry erasable and presenting it with sticker dots and markers. I wanted to embrace reproducibility and play, while giving a shrug to the final product. I actually wouldn't call the work glitch art. In fact all of the "Fuck Information" stuff was the same single pin-hole photo I took back in 1994 when I was 11! Think of it more as 1-bit quantum dithering.

You've made glitch videos and stills from old games consoles such as the NES (Nintendo Entertainment System). How do you make them glitch? What is interesting about using these machines – a sense of childhood nostalgia?

Well I don't usually *make* them glitch ... a NES will do that just fine on its own. The "NES Glitch Compilation" is documentation. There indeed is some spooky nostalgia lurking behind all this as it goes. I certainly try to represent where I'm coming from. Having one's nostalgia primarily tied to consumer media has its weird effects.

Who are you communicating to in your work?

Anything outside of my conscious self, like anyone who cares or happens to look. Though I'd note that all this stuff is probably inherently fine-tuned to those born in 1983.

Which is more interesting to you: the process of finding and making a glitch, or the eventual visual results?

I think both would have to ultimately end up perfectly balanced and identical in interest.

Kim Cascone

Composer, Sound Designer, Writer
San Francisco, USA
www.anechoicmedia.com

Why do you think the glitch in visual arts lags behind the development of the audio glitch?

If you look at the history of personal computers from the 1980s onward you'll see that music and audio applications had entered the market before photo retouching and video editing applications. This was due primarily to the limited power of CPUs. While the CPUs circa the 1980s could handle MIDI or non-real time rendering of audio they were still not able to meet the demands of video/image editing.

So, the tools for commercial audio/music creation appeared first. Then professional tools were gradually developed for the graphic art industry as CPUs became faster.

But even after Photoshop appeared on the market the application was slow unless you had a top of the line Mac. For example, doing a Gaussian blur took forever – so it was mostly professional designers who could afford these top of the line computers and began using applications like Photoshop. But due to all the downtime – mostly waiting during processing – designers weren't able to experiment freely since machines were tied up rendering.

Also, the financial hurdle of buying top of the line Macs prevented many visual artists from experimenting "off the clock." In other words, when an artist was working on a $10,000+ rig they were focused on recouping a material investment and had little time for undirected, free-form experimentation.

Because of this, there seemed to be less experimentation in the digital visual arts at first. But in the 1990s we saw Photoshop start to be used in many creative ways – one such was by artists creating rave flyers and CD covers.

Another factor in the early experimentation with computer technology by electronic musicians was that many of them built and/or hacked their own hardware and so were already used to a more heuristic approach. In general there was more of a DIY approach which facilitated interesting results.

Because of this artists explored the boundaries of software and computers and eventually developed an aesthetic based on bugs and/or failure.

For example, I used to have a bug in my Ensoniq EPS sampler where it would randomly play all the samples still lying around in RAM – even if deleted from the sound bank I had set up. It was an interesting effect which I would try to recreate by turning the machine on and off very quickly but was too intermittent. It was things like that which piqued my interest in applying software bugs to creating music.

But real-time audio still required a lot of processing power and Macs were not capable of this in the beginning. There were some brave applications that attempted to do this but I can remember waiting forever while my little SE-30 Mac processed my sound files in Sound Designer or Turbosynth.

As a result of this slowness most people used computers for controlling external synthesizers and samplers via MIDI and using outboard effects to modify samples and load them into a sampler.

Once hardware and software became cheaper and more accessible much content reflected a deeper problem that formed along two axes: a lack of knowledge of technology and little knowledge of art history. It seemed most people learned the technology but nothing about aesthetics or composition. Like the old adage: Those who forget history are doomed to repeat it.

Bedroom artists acquired these tools in order to express their ideas but often-times repeated worn tropes.

Also, prior to the internet, it was more difficult to gain access to this knowledge but there is no excuse today with web sites like ubu.com to come up to speed on the history of experimental music.

And also prior to the internet there was no easily accessible medium in which to distribute one's work. Indie music had college radio, cassettes, vinyl and CDs to proliferate content.

While that was a barrier to entry many musicians couldn't hurdle it was even more difficult for visual artists and was a factor in the slow development of experimental, digital visual art.

Does the bulk of glitch imagery demonstrate a failure of aesthetics rather than being artistic compositions?

I wouldn't diagnose the bulk of glitch imagery as having a "failure of aesthetics" because that reflects a very subjective position. But I would say the bulk (or glut) of content is attributable to an intersection of consumer capitalism with technological aesthetics layered on top of the lack of a filtering or self-editing mechanism.

The drive to create in individuals today has become a manufactured desire; a forced need for recognition and celebrity rather than a genuine need to express oneself. This has driven the corporations who create new markets at any cost. They do this by instilling false needs in consumers through advertising, which in turn incites desire. The need to create is more ego-driven than it ever was in the past due to being fed images of success and wealth.

One becomes "creative" by consuming affordable (and sometimes free) digital tools, listening to MP3s online, learning to mimic style (from industry magazines like *Future Music* and *Electronic Musician*) then posting content to a website.

Now anyone with Garageband and internet access can become a minor celebrity on MySpace, complete with sexy snapshots of scantily clad "friends" adorning your page. It's like *American Idol* without any judges.

Corporations manufacture this brand of desire, i.e., "stardom for hobbyists," in order to develop and exploit a market. While it is not bad for people to be creative and derive pleasure from it, there is added pressure to gain approval for their content. This is what drives the desire: the desire to be accepted and admired. This is a panacea for the lack of personal power in a consumer society; e.g., "If my work is consumed by others, then I am somebody."

So many people's motivation to make art comes from a manufactured and manipulated set of needs, not from any desire to explore ideas and aesthetic problems. It's like the idea of playing electric guitar in a rock band in order to meet girls has been proliferated by media.

Also, most of the aesthetic is developed through mimicry. In our age of light-speed immediacy people don't want to spend years working through abstract aesthetic issues and develop a unique voice; they want to make content and be recognized for it.

It isn't a failure of aesthetics so much as it is shallow mimicry driven by alienation that is part of the self-destructive mechanism of consumer capitalism. Without more knowledge about art and music history we are hurtling unchecked toward a homogenized culture of consumer generated content – a famous-for-fifteen-megabytes culture.

To pick up on your point about filtering, in visual glitches what you start with, the raw material, is essentially digital garbage.

This raises an interesting question: What is the difference (to the viewer or listener) if I create an image that resembles a glitch versus capturing an actual glitch and using it in a piece?

Iman Moradi brackets these as "glitch-alike" versus "pure glitch."

While some artists start with actual software garbage or glitches others merely replicate the effect of a glitched file using plug-ins and patches. To the viewer or listener there is no difference since they are unaware of the history/origin of the artifact. This becomes a problem on the axis of mannerism versus accident or reproduction versus original. But in the world of pop spectacle producers rely on the illusion of content via mannerism. Audiences have been weaned from being able to determine the originality of an artifact. We don't question whether the reverb on a voice is a real acoustic space or an electronic effect. We don't question whether the song on the radio was recorded with all the musicians playing together ... we don't realize the bass player uploaded her track from an internet cafe in Paris, the vocals were heavily edited, pitch corrected and electronically doubled, the drummer is nonexistent i.e., the drum track is a patchwork of loops constructed from various sessions and drummers, etc.

So we consume idealized artifacts that rely on a crafting of effect: a simulacra of content conjured through style. The effect of a glitch is to subvert the listener's expectations. A glitch is cognitively reacted to as a rupture in the continuum of an idealized artifact and originated as a subversion of the smooth and technically perfect surface of digital audio. Glitch is a critique on what audio purists thought of as a benchmark of pristine audio; a quality that only those with expensive gear could afford to enjoy.

Oval recorded a piece on their first CD titled "The Politics of Digital Audio" that I thought philosophically framed the device of glitch quite well, but the politics of glitch seemed to elude most music writers and critics. Glitch then became part of the lexicon of the underground in digital media and quickly turned into another stylistic effect in electronic music. Because we all knew these artifacts of malfunction and now had permission to use them in works.

Plug-ins came along that re-created this simulacra of accident, and were downloaded by producers hungry for fresh ear-catching sounds. The proliferation of glitch had little to do with innovation and more to do with a competitive consumption of style. I think this is why glitch got used up in a sense. Artists moved on quickly after depleting the genre via the use of glitches and went looking for the next cool plug-in that would make them sound unique.

So much of pop culture is based on this cycle of use and discard and why glitch never fully made it out of that ghetto.

With sufficient filtering, can this collection of garbage be transformed into art? "Filtering" suggests there's some human thought and control happening. In other words, starting with generic glitchy material, does deliberate selection produce a body of art that is as personal to the artist as brush marks in a painting?

A collection of glitched files could have been made in any number of ways and because they are introduced to the viewer/listener without origin or history the files are a stored phenomenon – not accidents themselves but documents of accidents.

Files containing malfunctions are something a beta-tester would collect while testing software.

An artist wishing to work with actual glitches would accumulate a database of bugs, i.e., symptoms or behaviors that exist outside the set of expected behaviors intended by a software designer. These bugs are problems to be traced and solved in order to conform the product to a specification. So merely collecting a folder's worth of glitched files might or might not be considered glitch depending on how much of a purist you are.

Some artists would rather induce failure while exploring the edge boundaries of the software in real-time, using the inherent bugs to create unexpected sounds. But a collection of sound files should be considered part of an artist's repertoire – they are valid statements, gestures and vocabulary in the creation of a composition. For example: a sound designer builds a sound library so she can use them later on. This library reflects a personal aesthetic and the sounds collected are used much like brush strokes or colors.

Do you agree it's important to draw a distinction between randomness and glitchiness? Do you think of glitches as being created by essentially deterministic yet highly complicated mechanisms?

I don't agree. A glitch is an accident, a malfunction, and most accidents are not deterministic since they are unexpected. While failure can be deterministic, accidents are not. Determinism implies intent. Accidents imply randomness. However, I don't think there is a distinction between randomness and glitchiness.

In your work, are you aware of a subjective difference in the outcome when using random data as inputs, as opposed to deterministic yet random-looking data, such as the digits of pi?

Most random numbers are generated via an algorithm called a "Pseudo Random Number Generator" (PRNG) so they are not truly random – they are deterministic. Also pi is random in a certain statistical sense and seems as random as the output of a PRNG. We can make a PRNG that is completely indistinguishable in its output from a true RNG. But the PRNG is deterministic whereas the true RNG is not. And although pi is deterministic no one has yet to find any meaningful patterns in the fractional part of pi so for all intents and purposes it can be considered random.

Is random data too random to be pleasing to the ear? Does glitch data work better, and does that carry over into the visual domain?

Due to human survival traits we tend to hunt for patterns in visual data more than sound data. Sound data is used to alert us, it warns us. If we seek patterns in sound it usually needs to correlate to some visual data.

Again, randomness in visual data is subjective: a texture of foliage hiding the camouflage patterns of a predator animal. One needs to be trained to see this quickly in order to ensure survival. Yet it is hard to perceive natural sounds in a similar manner. We cognitively separate sounds into threads and identify them separately. With visual data this is more difficult at times. Our parsing of visual data is done differently for survival reasons. Glitch is a subversion of expectation. We expect a portrait of a woman to be visually cohesive but when we see a rupture in the visual organization of that data we experience it as a systemic malfunction.

If we were to send a glitch image to a newspaper to reprint it would be rejected due to its imperfection. The editor expects something standard and to her this is obviously a faulty data file. You can subvert expectations in any file format based on its intended function. A photograph of the woman is a literal reproduction of a physical object and not an interpretation using techniques in modern art. The axis of intention versus expectation exists in any mechanical reproduction i.e., accuracy of reproduction. In sound you have the same thing. Is this sound an accurate representation of an oboe or flute or violin? Are there artifacts from the conversion from the analog domain to the digital? How faithfully does it reproduce the original? If an artist was looking for an unusual effect for that instrument then the glitch is a welcome accident that can be a solution in an aesthetic problem. Otherwise it is rejected.

In your 2002 monograph *Post-Digital Tendencies in Contemporary Computer Music* you say, "... the revolutionary period of the digital information age has surely passed." Music has been post-digital for some while now; has its revolutionary period passed, too?

Not at all. There are two problems here. The first being the definition of the term "revolutionary." The next problem: Which elements must be present for an artistic genre to be considered revolutionary?

The term "revolutionary" implies that an abrupt change has taken place within a continuum. A "punctuated equilibrium," to borrow a term from genetics. This rupture manifests itself as a severe pushing or transgression of boundaries to the point where a restructuring or reordering occurs. Therefore, after glitch appeared it didn't take long for its adoption and proliferation to render it mainstream. Glitch started to make its appearance in pop culture such as dance music and film credits. Subgenres sprung up around it (Click-House, Microhouse, Clicks and Cuts, etc.) and so a visual aesthetic also developed around it. As a result the frustration of digital malfunction, which we are now familiar with, entered the lexicon of stylistic devices and hence became an expected device in certain genres as used by certain artists. Once it was depleted of its stylistic currency it was no longer potent as an act of subversion. Whatever "revolutionary" content glitch might have contained was drained from it. So I suppose you could call the current era "Post-Glitch."

This is a familiar cycle for artistic devices: underground breeds a meme that is then appropriated by the mainstream, sanitized and then fed back through mainstream media for general consumption. For a genre or a device to be considered revolutionary it has to somehow remain vital or situated in the underground while offering limited access to mainstream outlets. In order for this to work though these mainstream outlets have to have some cache in order to use the device with some authority. Good examples in pop music are Björk and Radiohead – but if the mainstream has full access to this device, i.e., able to fully co-opt it and drain it of its vitality, then it becomes depleted of its revolutionary content. The signifier becomes free floating; severed from its original signified and because of the lack of history this effect has become more pronounced, more ubiquitous.

Very few pop artists are able to use these devices because they must (by proxy) belong to the culture which spawned the device in the first place and are able to use it in an intelligent way. They don't deplete it of its cultural value as might be the case if someone like the Black Eyed Peas or Hilary Duff were to use it in a Coke commercial or something. So for glitch the revolutionary period is still struggling to be located but I don't think there is one. The genre has no recognizable center. No handle. It keeps moving, shape-shifting. It blurs when it's recognized and then only sharpens for brief periods. It is not a genre so much as a tactic of subversion that has become a fashion statement.

And if we accept that where music goes, the digital visual arts follow, what can we expect next? Established cutting-edge electronic music acts have been dusting off their old analog gear; can we expect artists to go back to their canvas and darkroom?

No, but there are artists and filmmakers who are combining analog and digital techniques in interesting ways. Michel Gondry, Rob Tyler to name a few. Besides there is nothing saying that a post-digital aesthetic could not be located in analog electronics. Any system has functional boundaries that can be subverted.

Ant Scott

Media Artist, Mathematician
Bournemouth, UK
www.beflix.com

What do you consider a glitch?

To me it represents an error condition. Computers just act in a deterministic way for the most part, although you can get high-energy elementary particles from outer space, which can interact with the processor and flip a bit. But nonetheless, if the software doesn't do what you expect it to, that represents a glitch because it's a deviation from what the programmer wanted. Of course, it's the programmer's fault, but we prefer to blame the machine and say it glitched.

So, I think of glitch as being the outcome of some machinistic process, and if you restart the machine in exactly the same way, you'll get the same glitch. But that's just my interpretation, because of the way I go about making glitch art. The thing about randomness, in visual terms, is that it's a homogeneous mash, just noise. Whereas, although glitch images might be quite dense and complicated, there will probably be some overall structure or rhythm on a larger scale, which is the shadow of the computer following orders in a logical, orderly way. Stuff that's purely random isn't so interesting to me.

How did you get into glitch?

In 1970-something, when I was little, my dad brought a calculator home from work. It was pretty advanced for those days because it had an electronic on/off button. With it switched off, I pressed several buttons at once, and odd symbols appeared on the yellow LCD display. I thought that was amazing, and a little scary because I thought I'd broken it.

The main point was in 1984, when I had a Dragon 32 home computer, and I learned how to write a program in assembly language to display the memory as colored pixels on the screen, I remember thinking just how beautiful it looked. Not glitch as such, but glitchy-looking, sort of pixellated and disjointed. I still have that code on tape, and recently exhumed both the Dragon 32 and the tape to make further explorations.

What is it that you do in your work? Does that sit well with the notion that it is forced? Is it a real glitch?

For a while, my favorite method to make glitches was to load corrupted game files, called ROMs, into PC-based arcade game emulators. The idea is that if the game code is wrong, you stand a chance of seeing some nice glitchy graphics, which I would freeze-frame at the most interesting points and save for subsequent cropping.

But the method I've always come back to is data visualization, converting numbers into pixels and displaying them in a rectangular block. The data comes from either files I have lying around on my PC, such as crash logs, temporary files used by the operating system or the data in the RAM, which is back where I started in 1984. It's quite self-contained and inward-looking I suppose – everything comes from rooting around in the dregs of my PC. I'm not concerned with any meaning or context associated with the data, it's what it looks like on screen that is my primary concern. I like to change the colors, which is the most time-consuming part, like equalizing an audio mix – bringing parts forward or pushing them into the background.

Recently I've been making photographic prints directly from the computer screen, letting glitchy animations from my VJ software expose the paper and leave soft analog trails. It's important to me to make these tangible prints, because they're the final statement of my intent. When images are still in the digital domain, they can be endlessly tweaked with powerful software, so in a way they're less valuable, because a final decision hasn't been made yet. I think it's more fun to make a final, bad, decision than to make no decision at all.

Data visualization isn't real glitch, but it has buckets of glitch aesthetic, and the process of finding good images involves luck and technological experimentation, which are both part of the game of finding real glitches. I'm more motivated by the aesthetic outcomes than the process of creation.

Where do you draw inspiration from?

I have a macabre interest in disasters that have been caused by technological failure, such as the Challenger space shuttle explosion or the Chernobyl nuclear reactor explosion. The effects of seemingly insignificant glitches in the operating software for a nuclear plant, rocket or medical equipment, for example, can propagate, get magnified and either destroy the system itself or harm its users.

I find it fascinating that so many critical real-world systems are reliant on ephemeral software that nobody can prove will work correctly under all conditions. There's an internet email forum called RISKS that is all about this.

So anyway, when you look at a pictorial representation of computer memory, with all the messiness and dense, complicated structures, it is sobering to think that it's precisely this sort of digital mash that an airplane relies upon to stay up in the air.

What are you trying to convey through your works?

Nothing. They are perfectly meaningless, but they might make you feel something. The colors I choose are predominantly synthetic and sort of half-clash. I went through a phase of using what I call my "radioactive colors." These are very particular slightly dirty oranges and acid greens/yellows, cool blue greys and some other colors, to give an overall nightmarish impression of a post-nuke reality. Because I don't actually draw or construct the glitch material at all, changing the colors is my main artistic input.

People see different things in them – flowers, people, buildings, reflections and so on, precisely because they are devoid of any premeditated intent.

I tend to find that people who are outsiders to the digital arts scene are the most receptive to the images, and can view them without the psychological baggage of knowing where they come from.

Do you think glitches are a fad? Is there a post-glitch aesthetic?

I think "fad" is a loaded word, but it's a phase, and there's nothing terribly wrong with that. Irrespective of whether glitch still is, or ever was, cool and interesting, I personally still very much like art with straight lines, blocks of color and repeating patterns – a lo-fi digital aesthetic of sorts. It's quicker just to say "glitch" though.

The glitch aesthetic is very much allied with a particular era of technology, and looks the way it does because of the way current processors are engineered, how data is organized to be processed efficiently and because visual output devices are mostly raster-line based. I think it's only when one or more of these aspects changes radically that digital trash will take on a markedly different visual character.

O.K. Parking

William van Giessen, Joost van der Steen
Graphic / Interaction Designers
Arnhem, Netherlands
www.ok-parking.com

Please outline your working ethos and history as a graphic design studio – your experimental glitch research and the commercial side. How did this way of working come about?

During our study at the Academy of Arts in Arnhem (Netherlands), we worked together on several projects. These projects were mostly assignments that we had to make for our study courses. But we also did some early experimental research together in our spare time, in the field of glitch, chance and error. After a while we used these glitch experiments in our graphic design projects. Because we had the artistic freedom we could spend a lot of time to develop our vision and way of working toward implementing glitch in usable, functional graphic design projects. At first, it was in a pure visual aesthetical way, but more and more we became fascinated by the concept of chance and error and how to use this in a conceptual way in graphic design.

O.K. Parking has two faces, one is the commercial graphic design studio; the second is the autonomous, artistic, experimental self-initiated glitch projects side.

When making commercial graphic design projects the client most of the time isn't very pleased with glitch images. Sometimes it can work out great, but mostly the concept of glitch is more interesting and usable. The result doesn't have to show the (extreme) visual language of glitch, but it can be made out of glitch-experimenting and concept.

When starting a new design project, do you look at your portfolio of experiments to see what would work best? Do you start new experiments with a specific project in mind?

Whenever we start a new commercial project we first think about if glitch is possible. Nine out of ten times it isn't. When it is possible, we look in what way, visually and/or conceptually. Then we start with new experiments. Each project/client is unique, so it deserves (we strongly believe it needs) a unique approach to the project. Mostly, new experiments are based on new ideas. But it's also possible that we had new ideas during previous glitch experimenting that we can develop and use for a project. Or there are possibilities to take existing glitch experiments (which fit the project) and develop and research it more and take it to the next level.

For our self-initiated glitch projects, we often work from just messing things up (technical devices, hard/software) and the ideas that come along. We often find (or buy) old/used material that serve as a starting point. First we see what happens when we glitch it. If we like it we go on with it, to make an installation out of it or use it in a commercial project if we have the chance.

If we use the glitch in a visual way (in our own projects) we're not going to change the images. Not the color, not the size, nothing. We let them be actually the way we captured them. Yes, if needed for print we make it CMYK/300dpi but we always make sure the image will be as close to the real one. We keep in mind that (for commercial projects) it has to be reproducible. (Although in the producing/printing process there's a lot of glitch fun to do!) The fingerprint of the software and hardware is important to us. So we will never change colors or something of the glitch visuals.

What has been the most fun experiment you've done to make glitches?

William: "SPRAAK: With SPRAAK" ("SPEECH" in English): We made an installation piece in which we were searching for a more interactive way of chance and error. It isn't a visual glitch piece but more a conceptual approach toward chance and error. When we tried speech recognition software for another project, it seems all of them were buggy. They didn't work the 100% they should do. We really liked this because when we talked, our words were recognized quite badly. We thought about it and came up with the idea of making the software mistakes visual. The first "SPRAAK" installation was in a bar. We made a table with two microphones on it. The chitchat of people sitting at the table was captured by the buggy speech recognition program, and made visible by projecting the words flying out of the people's shadows. The visual words fly above, where they end up in a word cloud with all the words said in the conversations spoken earlier. People not sitting at the desk (standing a bit away) don't know what the conversation is about. When they join, interactive confusion starts ...

Joost: "PLOTTER": When we were plotting several graphic design projects, some of them were printed very glitchy. We looked in the files of the one that went wrong. We discovered that the plotting machine cannot handle certain things. They always seem to randomly glitch the image coming out of the plotter. With "PLOTTER" (a large canvas print) we only used the things that could go wrong, making a unique, random, unforeseen canvas print. We only did it once but if the same file is being printed again the eventual image would turn out completely different. We didn't expect a machine could make something this beautifully glitched!

Given the dual nature of your work, are you equally interested in both the process of making new glitches and the aesthetic outcomes?

The process of glitching is the most important. A little glitch or accidentally discovered faults can lead to an interesting new project. These projects can be used or be meaningful in a commercial assignment, visually or conceptually. The pure aesthetic in a work is only interesting for a short amount of time. More interesting is using the glitch as a concept in a whole project

The experimenting itself, with devices/materials, is the most interesting. Doing so we experience the world of aesthetical glitch, wonderful images and unforeseen results. When we're busy with the glitching process it's like entering a new (or lost) world. The eventual result itself is not the most important part in the process. The research is the part we enjoy and get knowledge from. We write down what we do and what kind of results came out of it, and save it for later when we think we could use it sometime.

Where did you first encounter glitches?

We first encountered glitches when we had computer crashes or were using malfunctioning devices. The things everybody runs into from time to time. We discovered that we could use glitches instead of resetting them or trying to fix it. We started to save them (often screenshots or snapshots with a digital camera). The next step was actually looking for glitches. We started to use accidental glitches in our graphic design work as part of the process. It seemed to us quite obvious to do because it was a natural part of it. The next step was making glitches on purpose with all kinds of devices in all kinds of ways. Behind the perfect world of soft/hardware an even more beautiful and inspiring world comes alive.

In what ways do you consider the software and hardware to be your co-creators?

We consider software and hardware to be our tools to give shape to our ideas. Just like a painter needs paint and tools to put his idea on canvas, we use technical devices or buggy software to "paint" our ideas in our graphic design work. Of course, each tool has its own characteristic way of expression, and each piece of software or hardware has its own fingerprint, which shows up when you glitch and use it. In this way, you can say it acts as a co-author or co-creator. But, the "master" shows his talent in the way he uses it. When he goes beyond it. With glitching you know what probably could happen, in what sort of way, with a certain kind of material you use. But then there's always an unforeseen element. This makes it exciting and challenging to push it to a higher, conceptual level in our work.

Who are the target audiences for your glitch graphic design work?

Everyone who is interested in it! We don't have a specific group of people in mind. Although we really like to show it to people who are completely unfamiliar with the glitch idea. They are the ones that get the most enthusiastic about it, rather than notorious art lovers!

Do you think it's important to document glitches as a record or fingerprint of current technology?

The materials we use are from old computers to new webcams. Each device from a certain period of time has its own characteristic visuals. It's very nice to see that each device creates different visuals. We don't think it's necessary to really record these fingerprints because it automatically happens. Contemporary machines will be old next, and the glitching is something that happens all the time (if you're hunting for it or you aren't).

1

001.001
001.002
001.003
001.004
002.001
002.002
002.003
002.004
003.001
004.001
004.002
005.001
005.002
005.003
006.001
007.001
007.002
007.003
008.001
008.002
008.003
008.004
008.005
008.006
008.007
009.001
009.002
009.003
009.004
009.005
009.006
009.007
010.001
010.002
011.001
012.001
013.001
013.002
013.003
013.004
014.001
015.001
015.002
015.003

016.001
017.001
017.002
017.003
017.004
018.001
019.001
019.002
019.003
020.001
020.002
021.001
021.002
022.001
023.001
023.002
023.003
024.001
024.002
024.003
025.001
025.002
026.001
026.002
026.003
027.001
027.002
028.001
028.002
028.003
029.001
030.001
031.001
032.001
032.002
032.003
032.004
033.001
033.002
034.001
035.001
035.002
035.003
035.004

036.001
037.001
038.001
039.001
039.002
039.003
039.004
040.001
041.001
042.001
043.001
044.001
045.001
045.002
046.001
047.001
048.001
049.001
049.002
050.001
050.002
051.001
051.002
052.001
052.002
052.003
053.001
053.002
054.001
054.002
054.003
055.001
055.002
056.001
056.002
056.003
056.004
057.001
058.001
059.001
060.001
060.002
060.003
060.004

061.001
061.002
061.003
062.001
062.002
062.003
062.004
062.005
062.006
062.007
062.008
062.009
062.010
062.011
062.012
062.013
062.014
062.015
062.016
062.017
062.018
062.019
062.020
063.001
063.002
063.003
064.001
064.002
064.003
064.004
064.005
064.006
065.001
066.001
066.002
066.003
066.004
066.005
066.006
066.007
067.001
067.001
067.003
067.004

067.005
067.006
067.007
068.001
069.001
070.001
070.002
070.003
070.004
071.001
072.001
073.001
073.002
073.003
074.001
074.002
075.001
076.001
077.001
077.002
078.001
079.001
079.002
080.001
080.002
081.001
082.001
082.002
083.001
083.002
084.001
085.001
086.001
086.002
086.003

Akihiko Yoshida
BinSick05 - 06
Video Still
2005

086.001

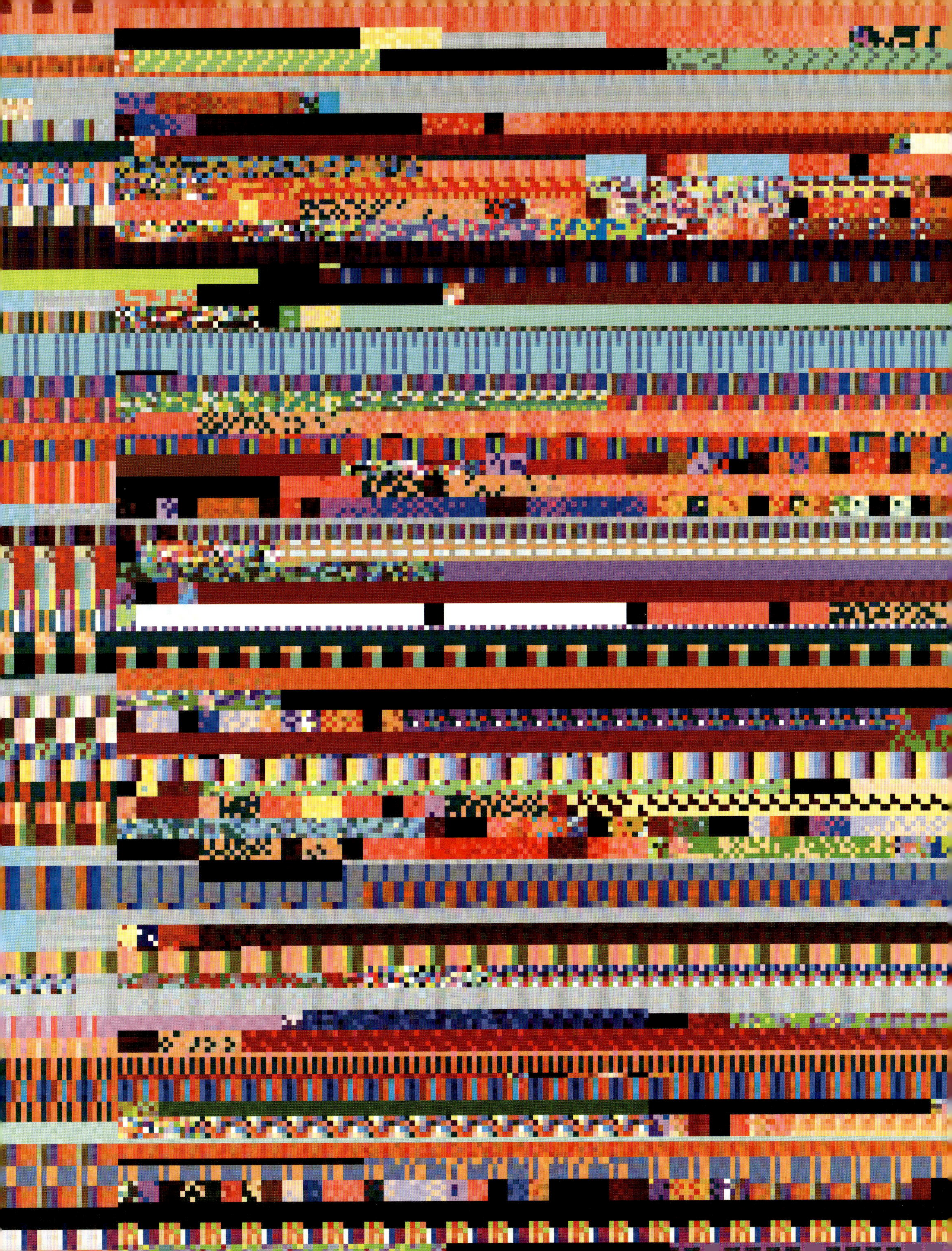

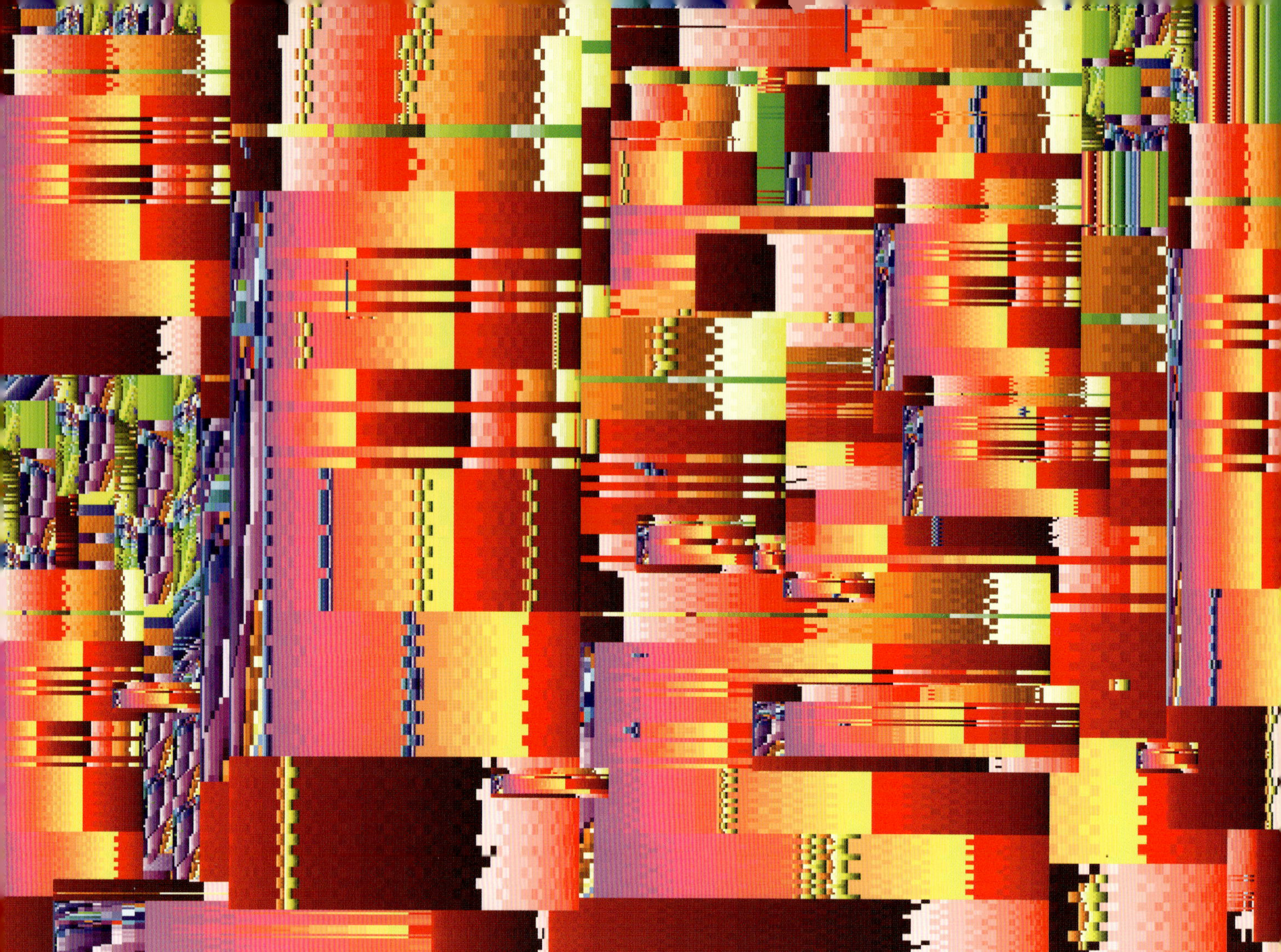

Alex Peverett
NEW61B
JPEG
2000

055.001

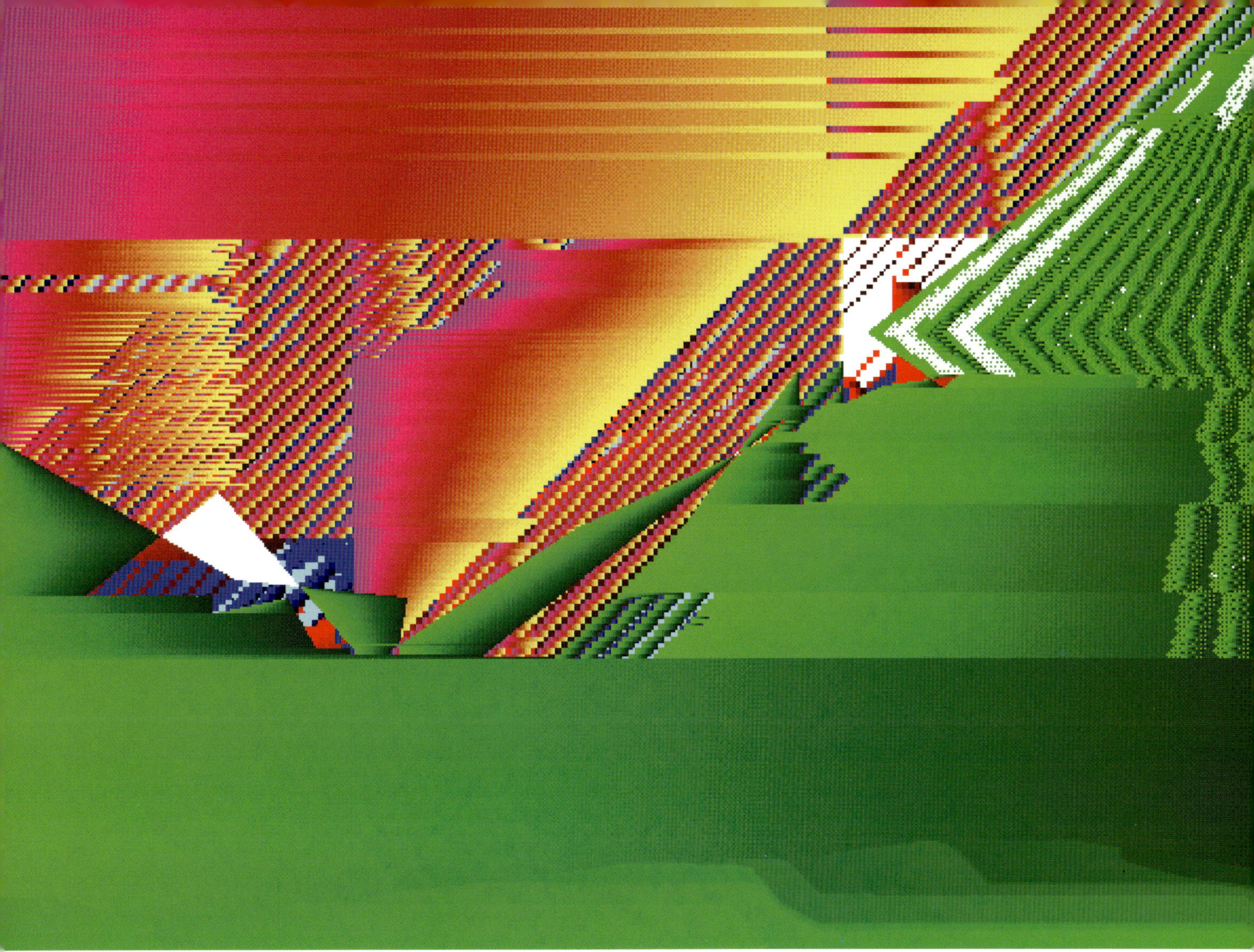

Alex Peverett
Virga
JPEG
2000

055.002

Dimitre Lima
Glitch Me I'm Clean (overleaf)
JPEG
2006

044.001

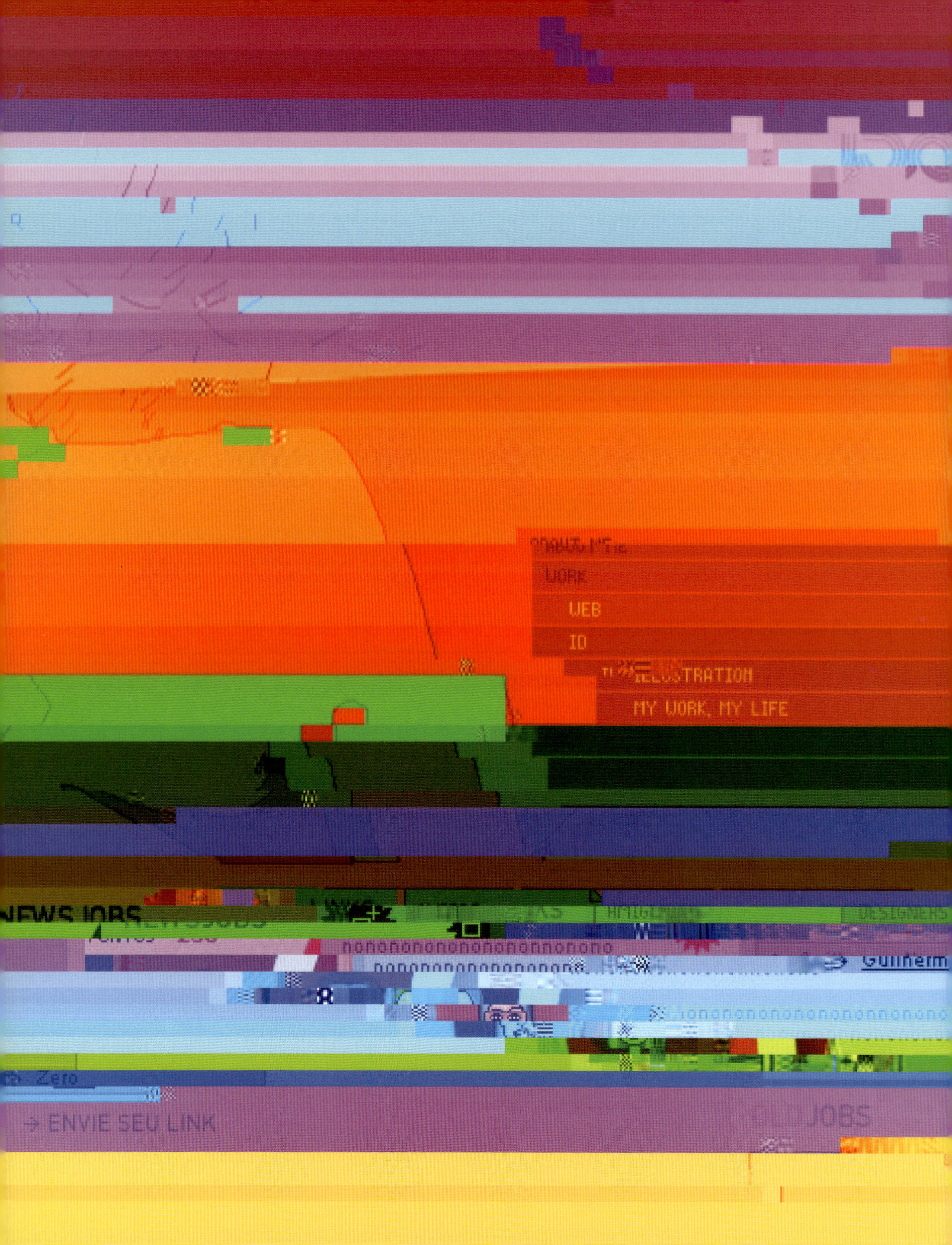

WORK
WEB
ID
MY WORK, MY LIFE
NEWS JOBS
DESIGNERS
Zero
→ ENVIE SEU LINK
JOBS

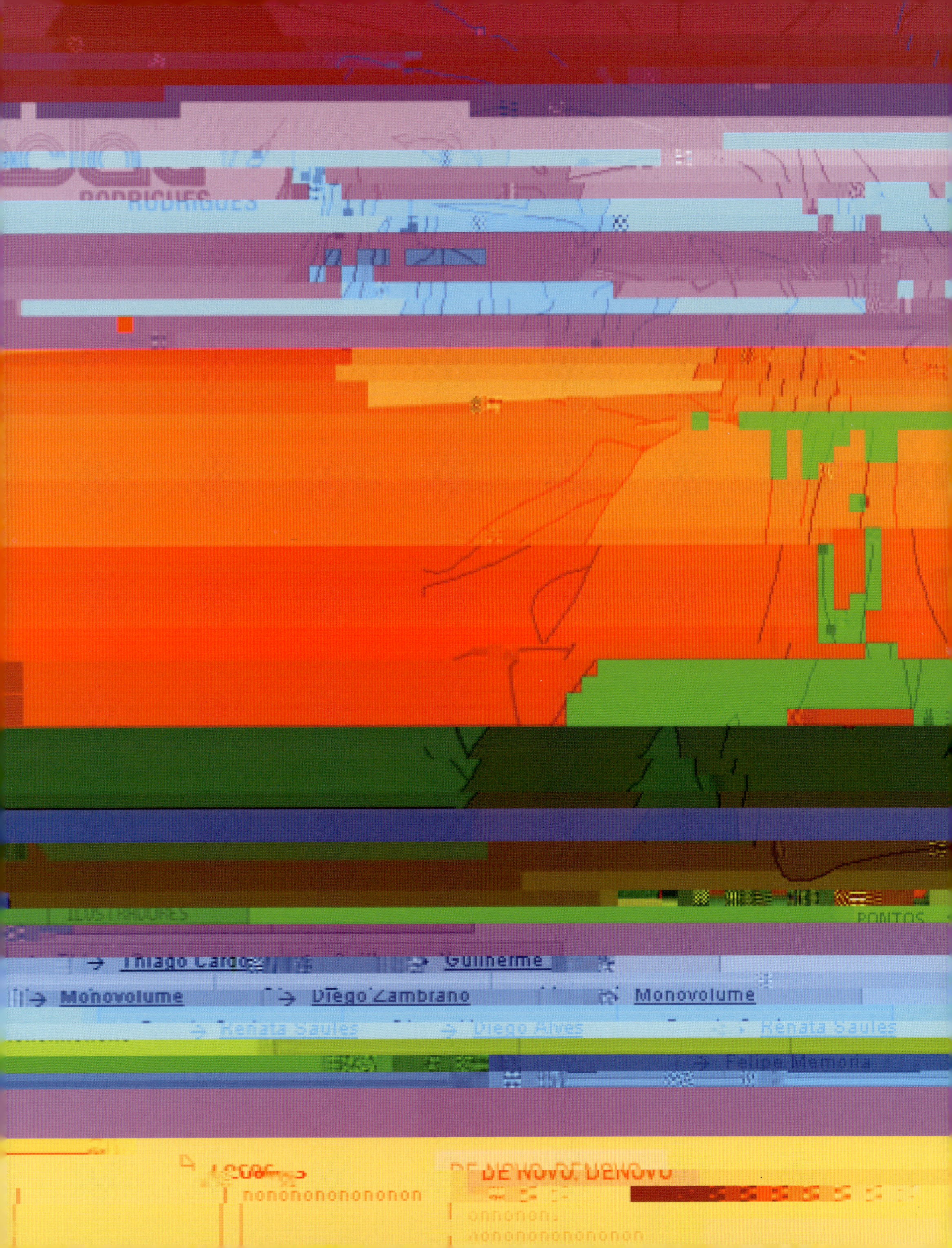
RODRIGUES
Guilherme
Monovolume
Diego Zambrano
Monovolume
Renata Saules
Diego Alves
Renata Saules
Felipe Memoria
DE NOVO, DE NOVO
nononononononon

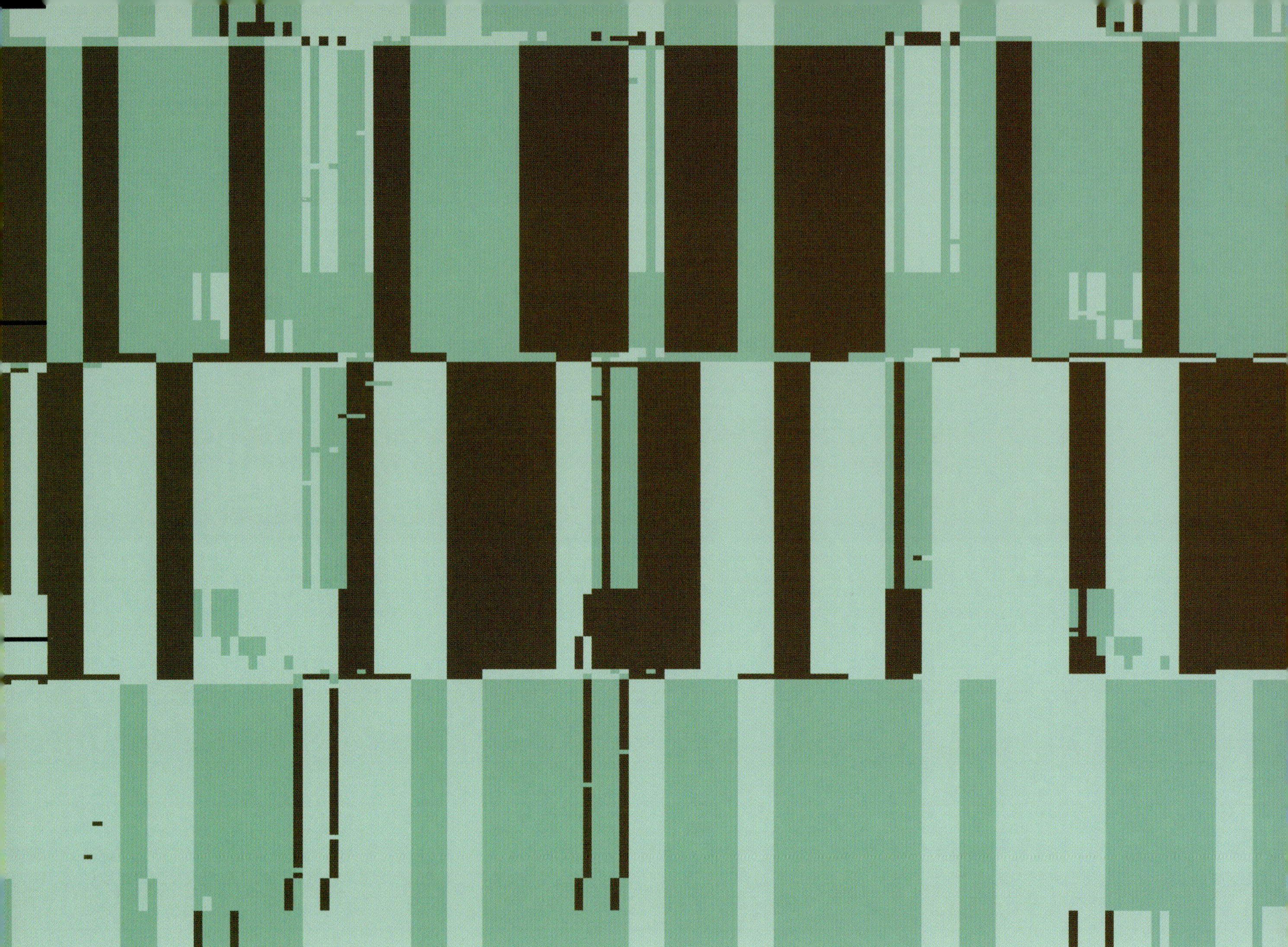

brianelectro
Untitled 79
Screenshot
–

008.001

brianelectro

Untitled 19, 291, 28, 259, 214, 260

Screenshots

–

008.002
008.003
008.004
008.005
008.006
008.007

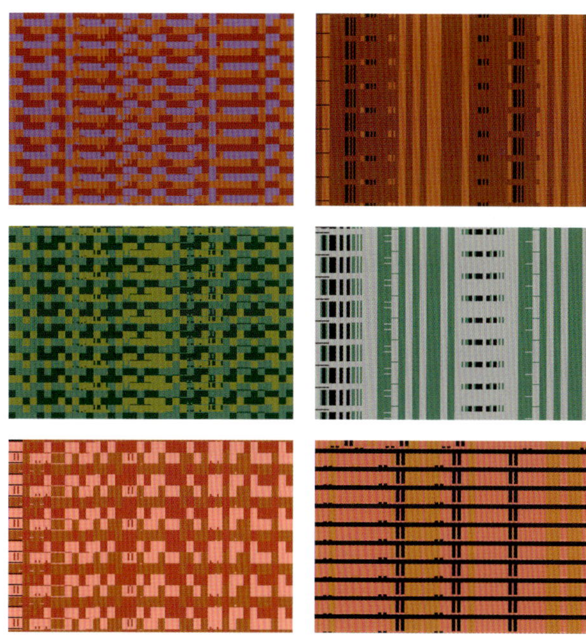

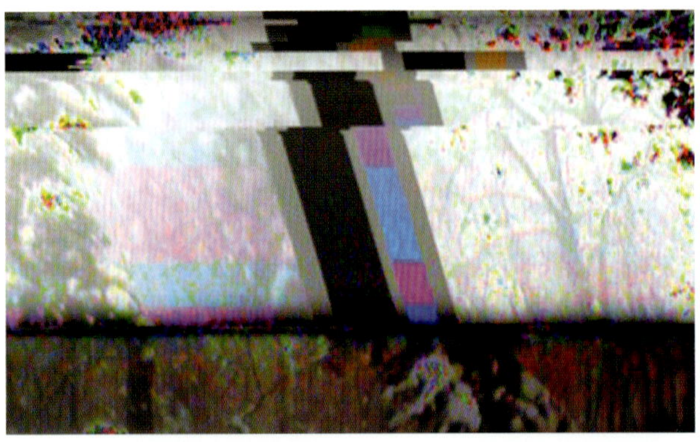

Megan Sproats
Neige 2
Video Still
2005

073.001

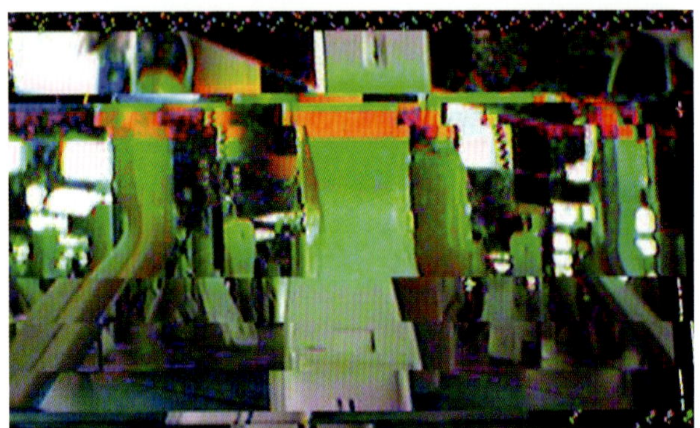

Megan Sproats
You Need a Visa 1
Video Still
2005

073.002

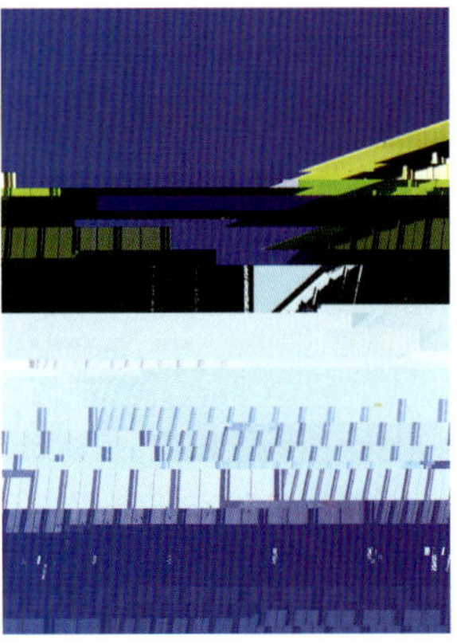

Eddy Joaquim
Shed Take #2
JPEG
–

033.001

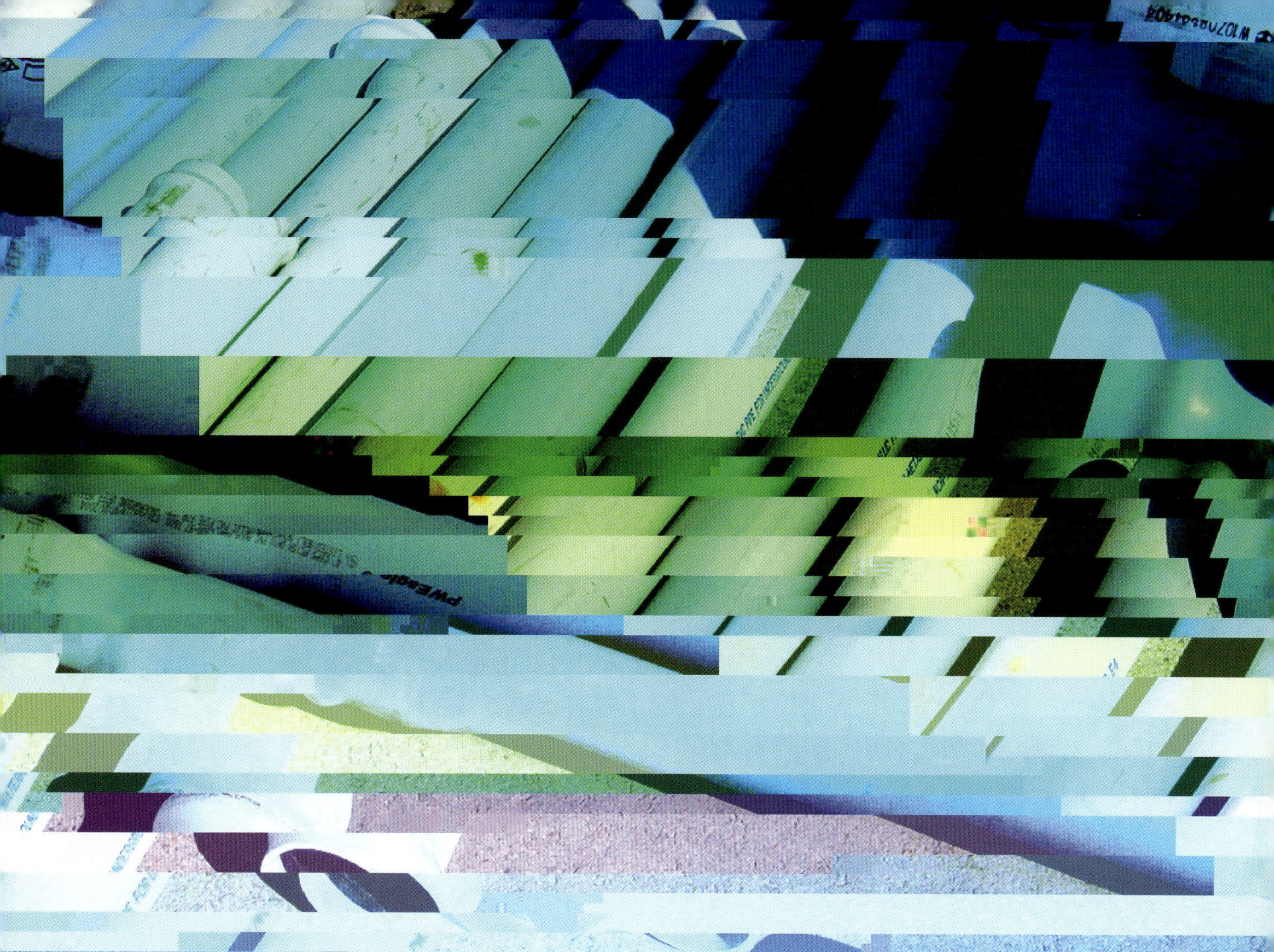

Eddy Joaquim
Pipes Blue
JPEG
–

033.002

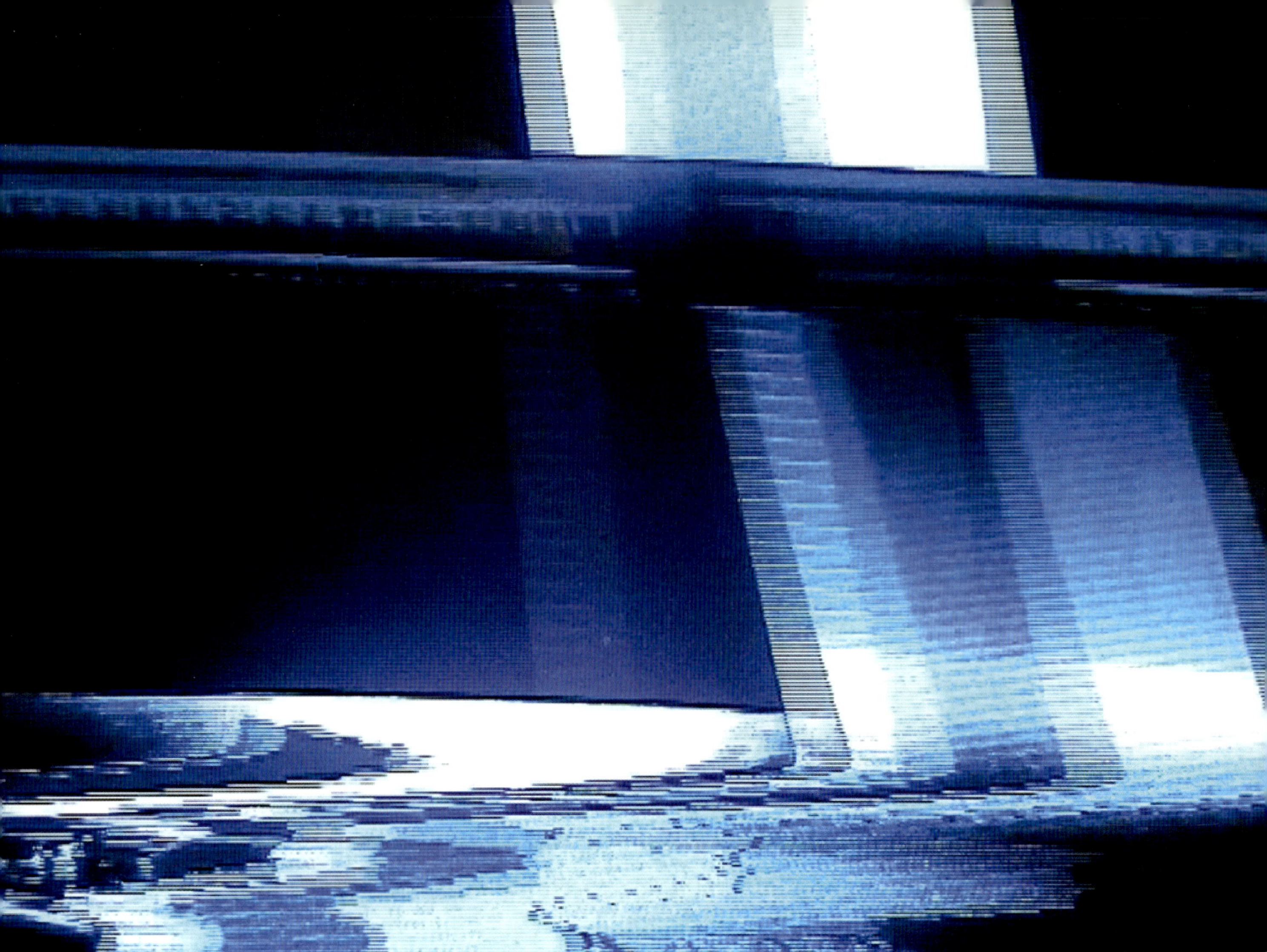

Tim Fox
Untitled
Video Still
2005

025.001

Steven H. Silberg
Pipeline
JPEG
–

070.001
070.002
070.003
070.004

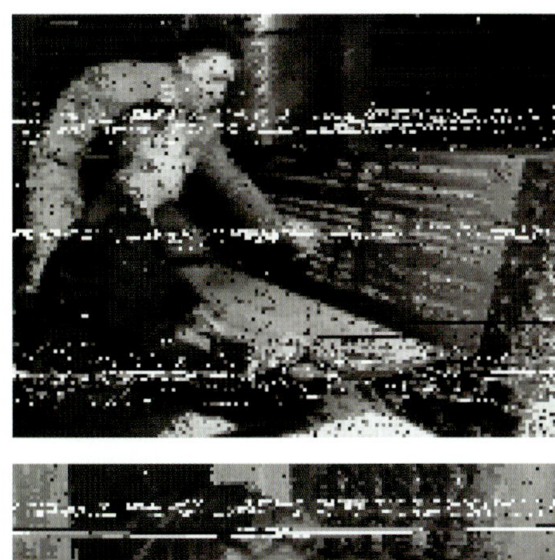

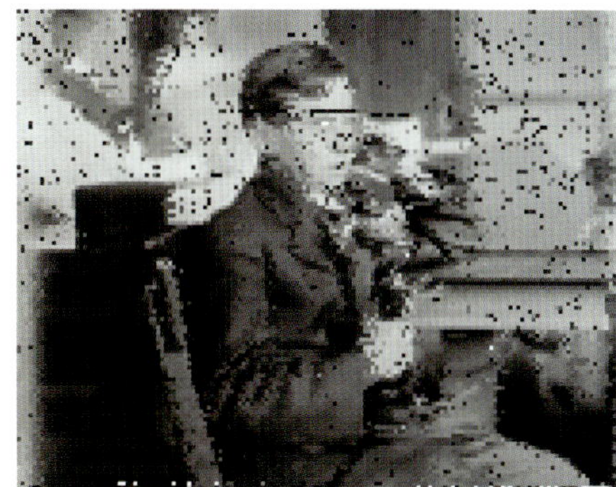

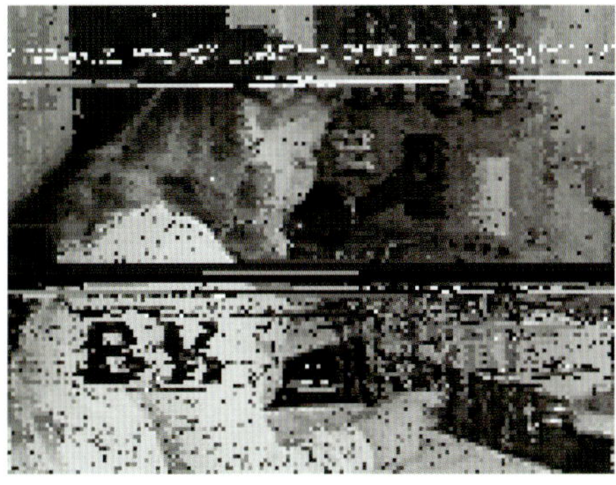

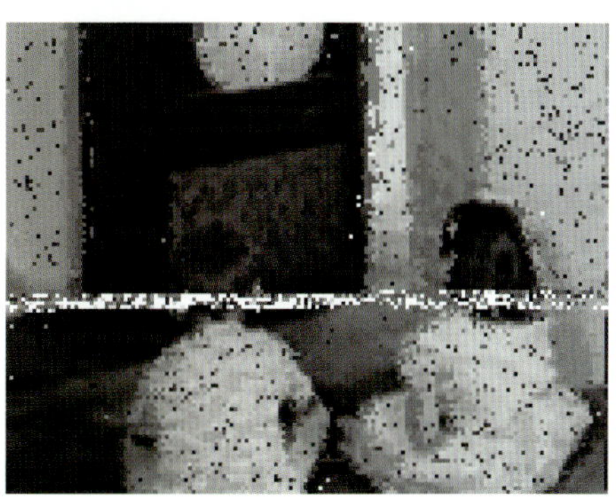

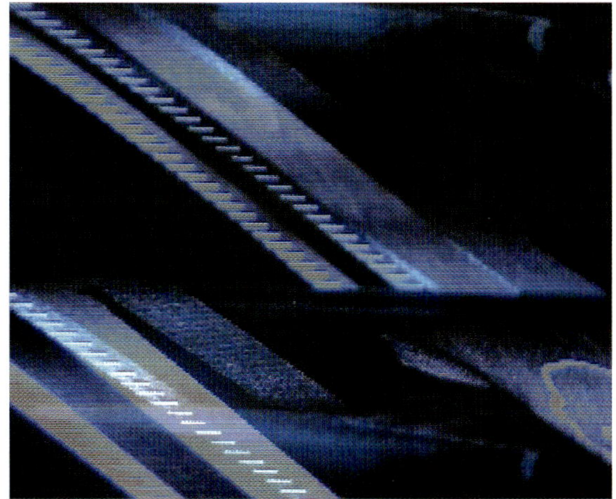

Tim Fox
Untitled
Video Still
2005

025.002

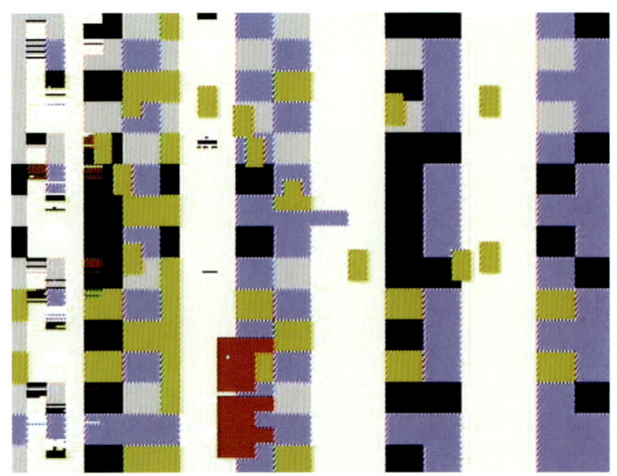

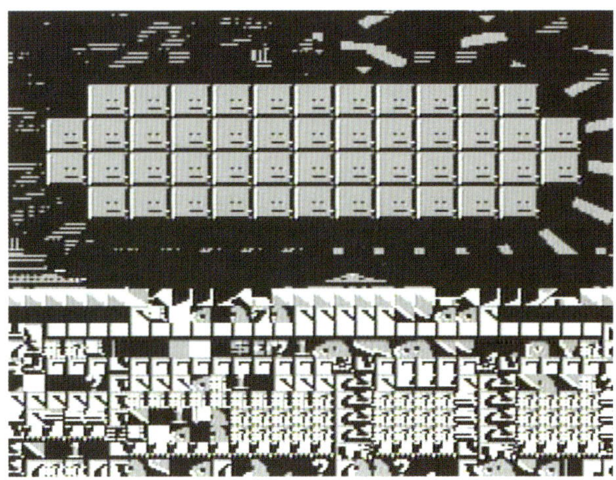

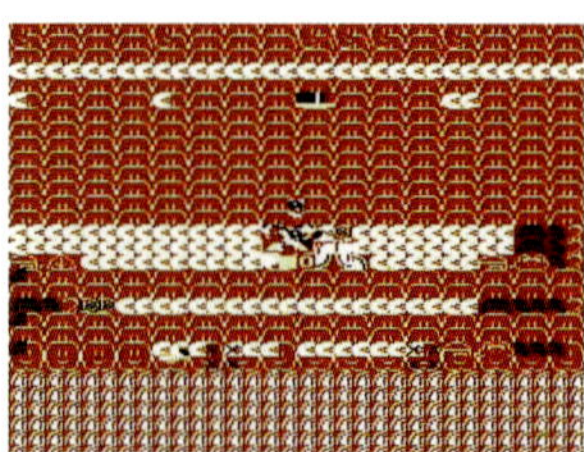

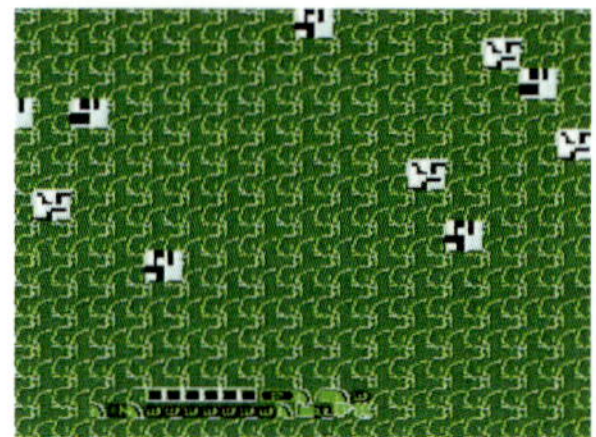

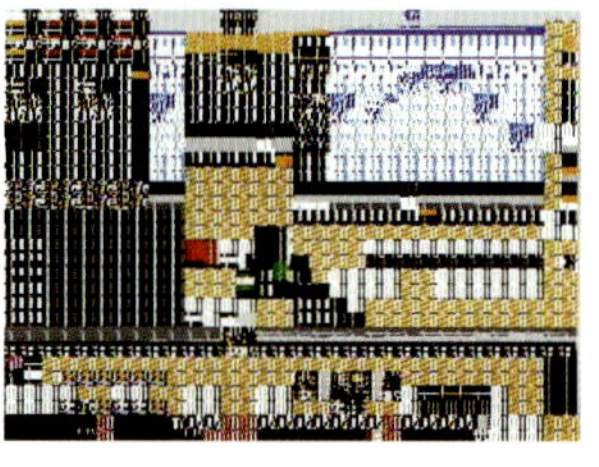

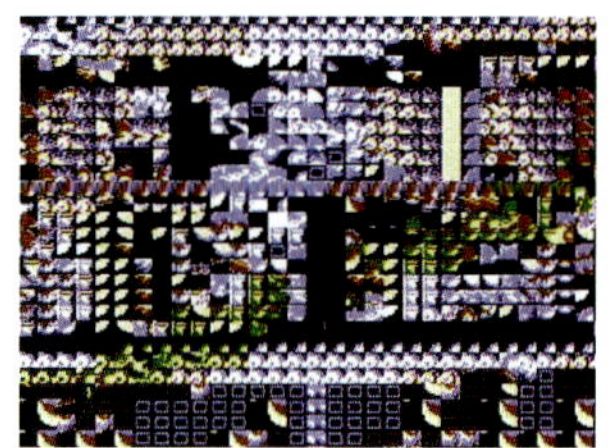

Johnny Rogers
Zelda
Video Still
2001-04

064.001

Johnny Rogers
Lolo 2 Wheel Off
Video Still
2001-04

064.002

Johnny Rogers
Mario 3
Mario 3
Wood Water Rage
Lolo 2 Wheel Off
Video Stills
2001-04

064.003
064.004
064.005
064.006

Nicky Proniewicz
Cascade
Screenshot
2005

058.001

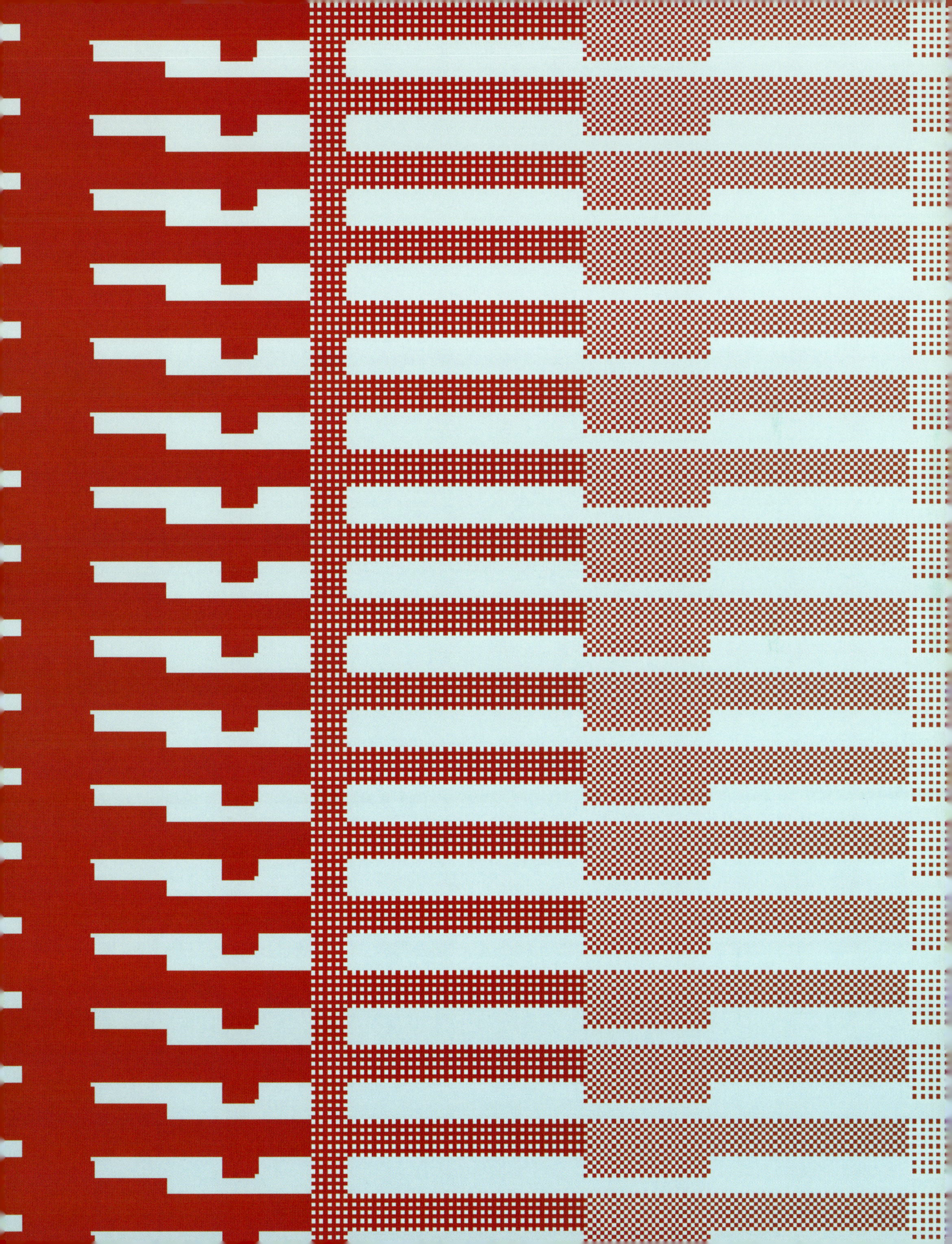

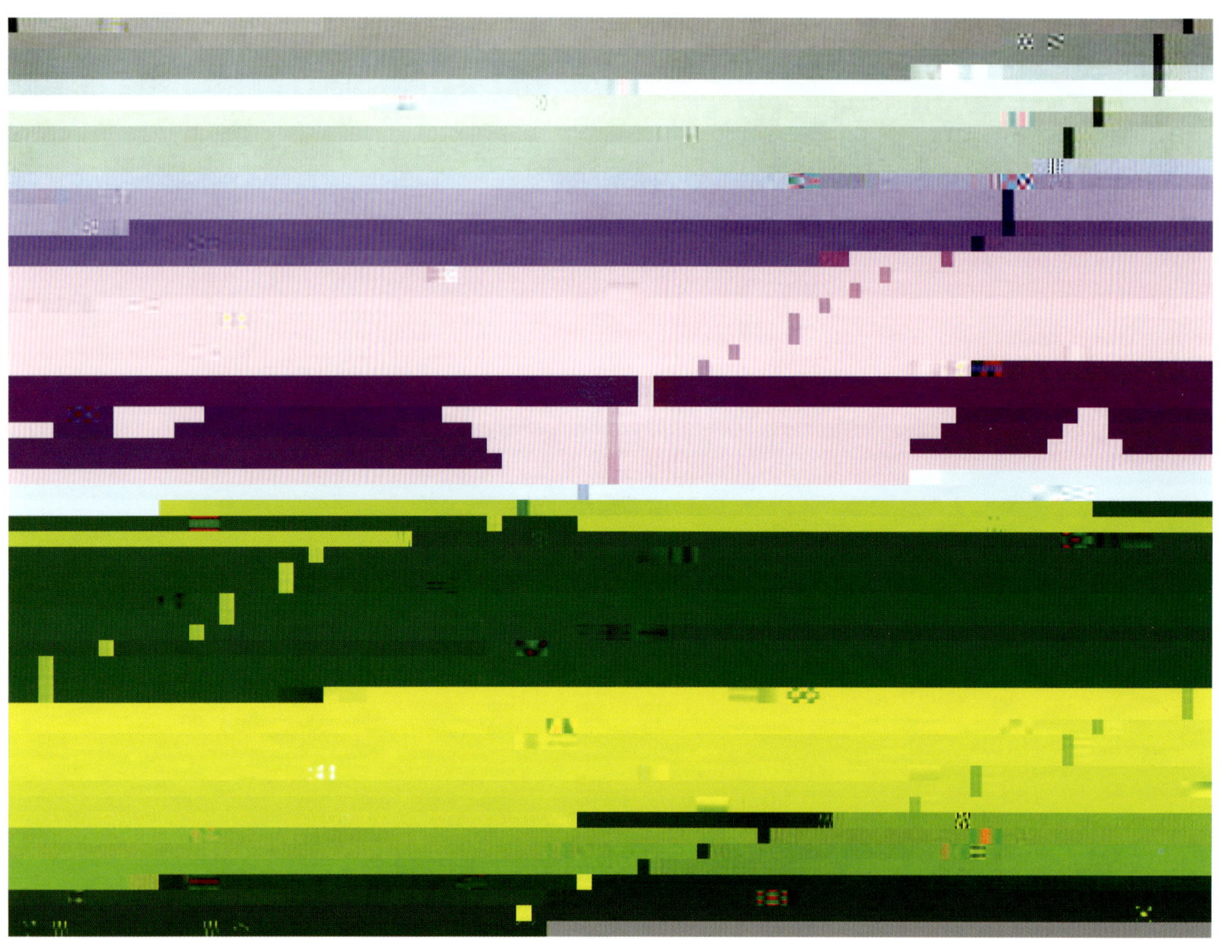

Daniel Julià
Untitled
Webcam Still
–

036.001

Cory Arcangel
January 11th Saturday
Video Still
–

003.001

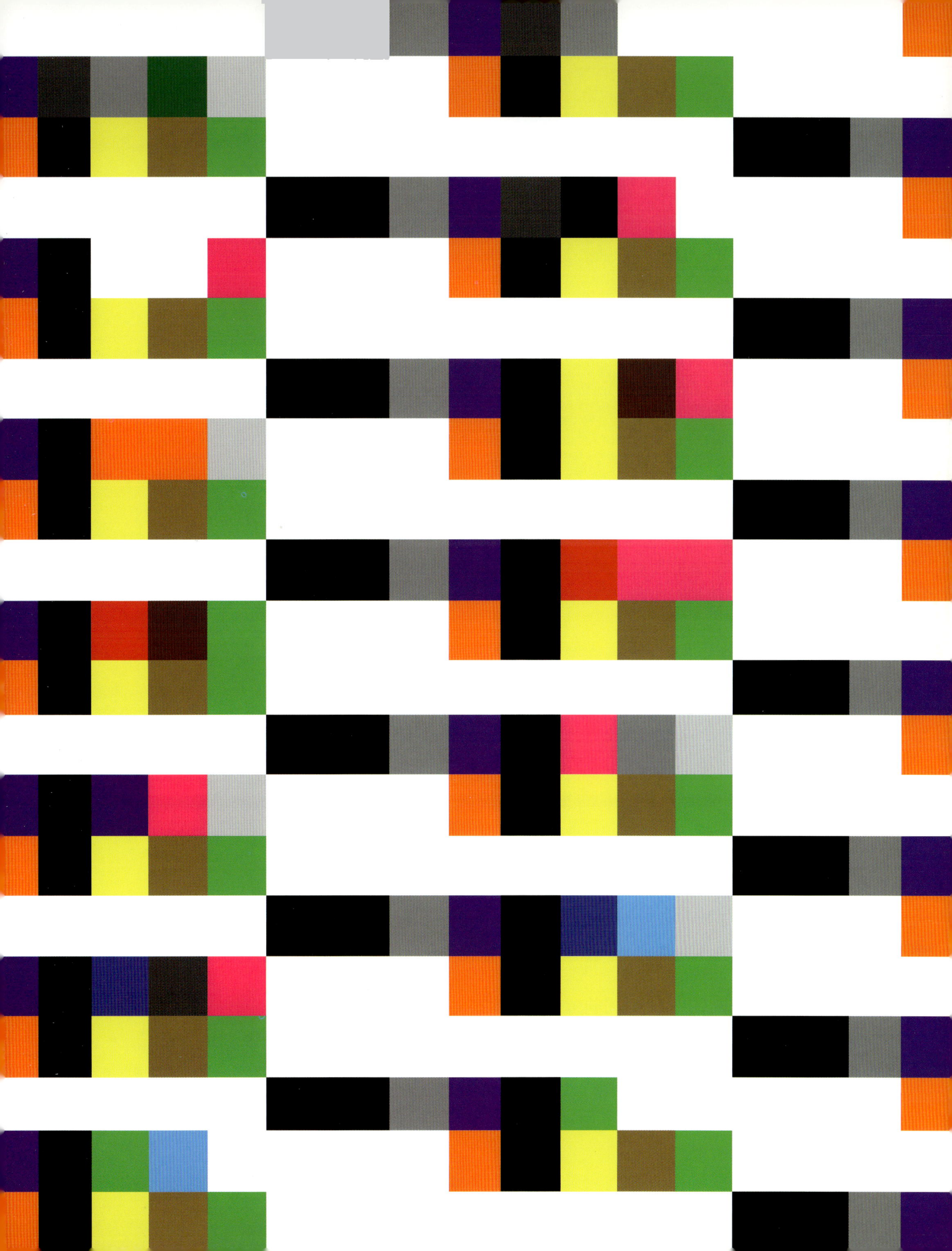

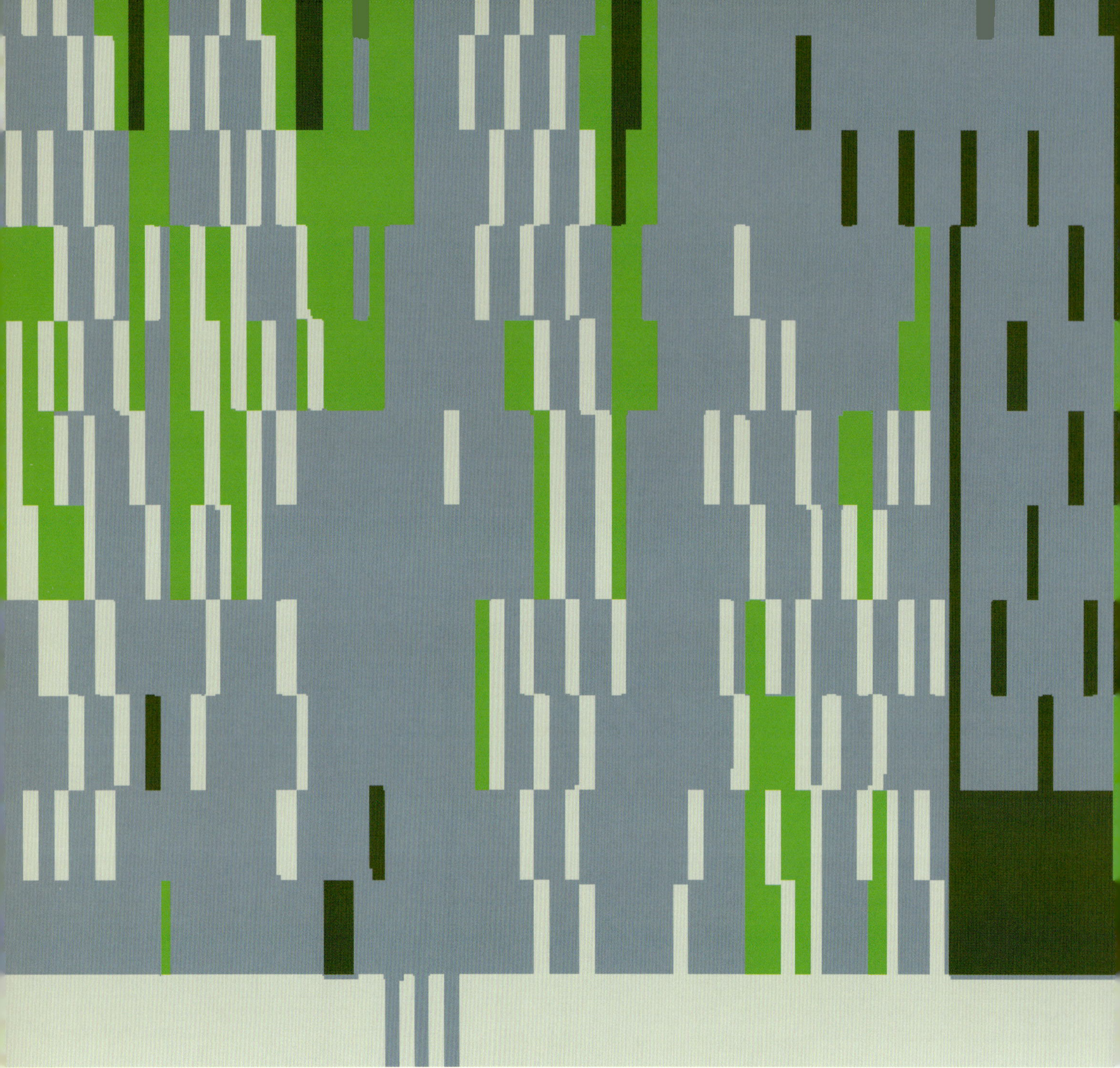

Manuel Dilly
Untitled
Screenshot
2004

016.001

Jason Kahn
For the Time Being
CD Cover
2003

037.001

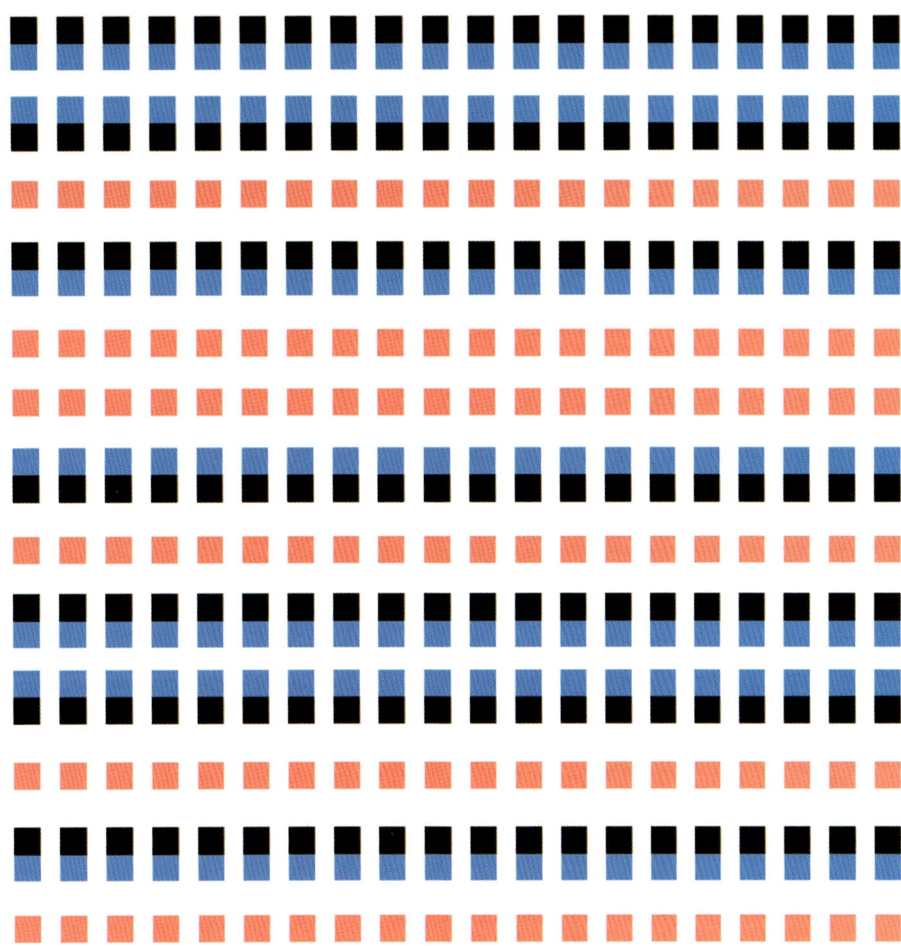

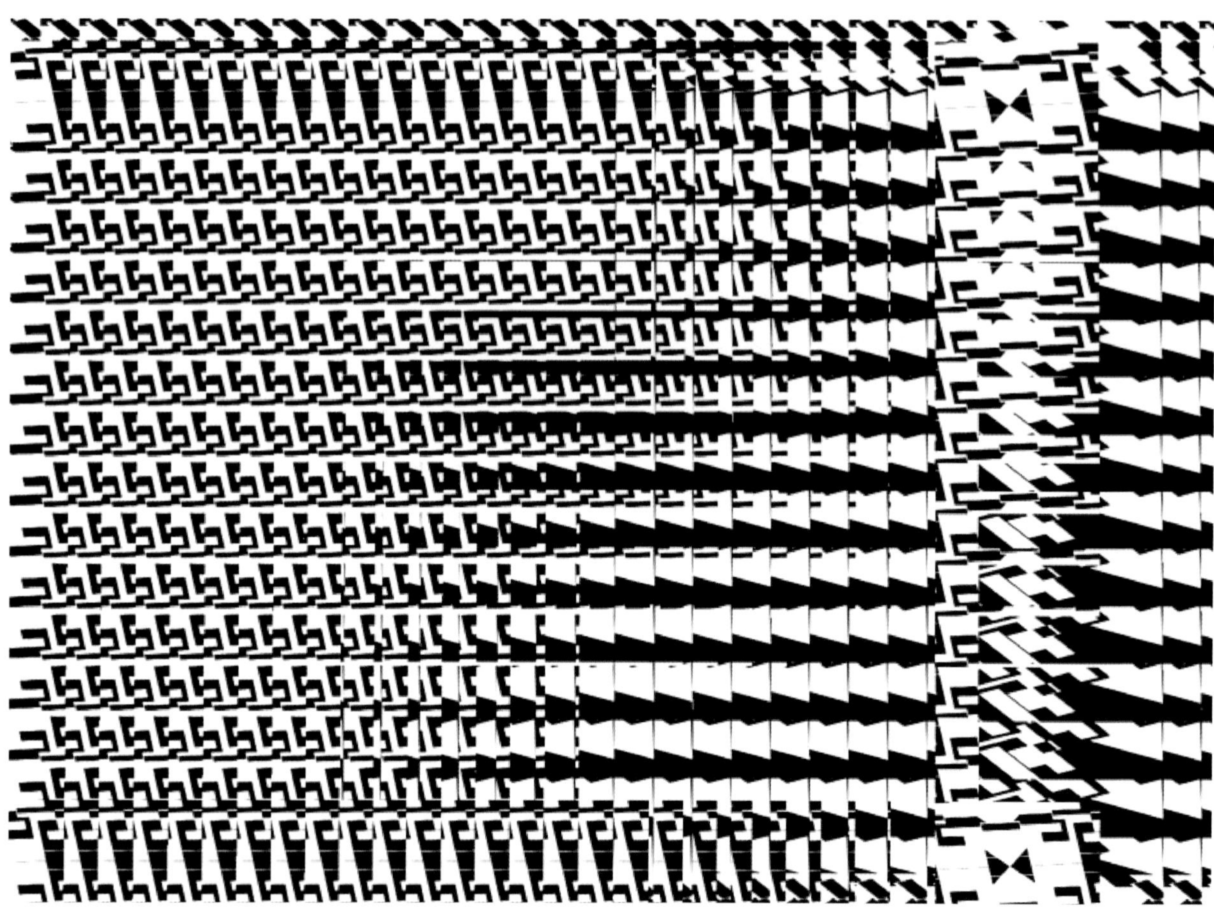

Paul Emery
Iterative Function
vvvv
2007

018.001

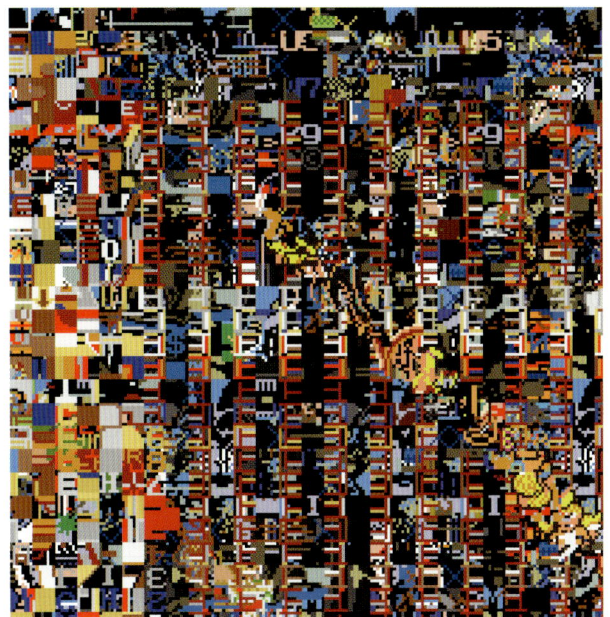

Brent Gustafson
AX|BX (Detail)
HTML / GIF
–

030.001

Daniel Stanciu
Composition
Print
–

074.001

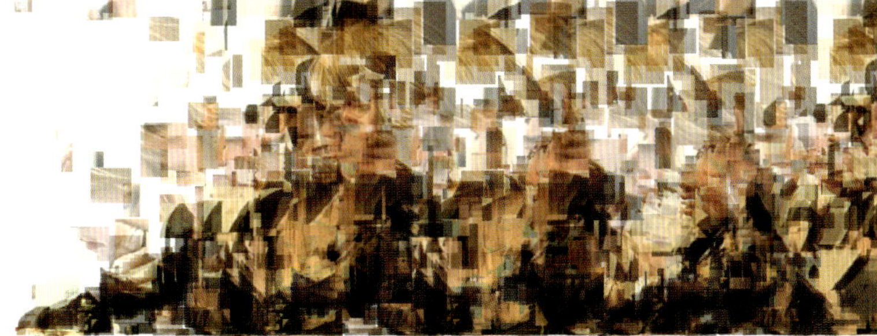

Andrea Polli
The Fly's Eye
Video Still
2002

057.001

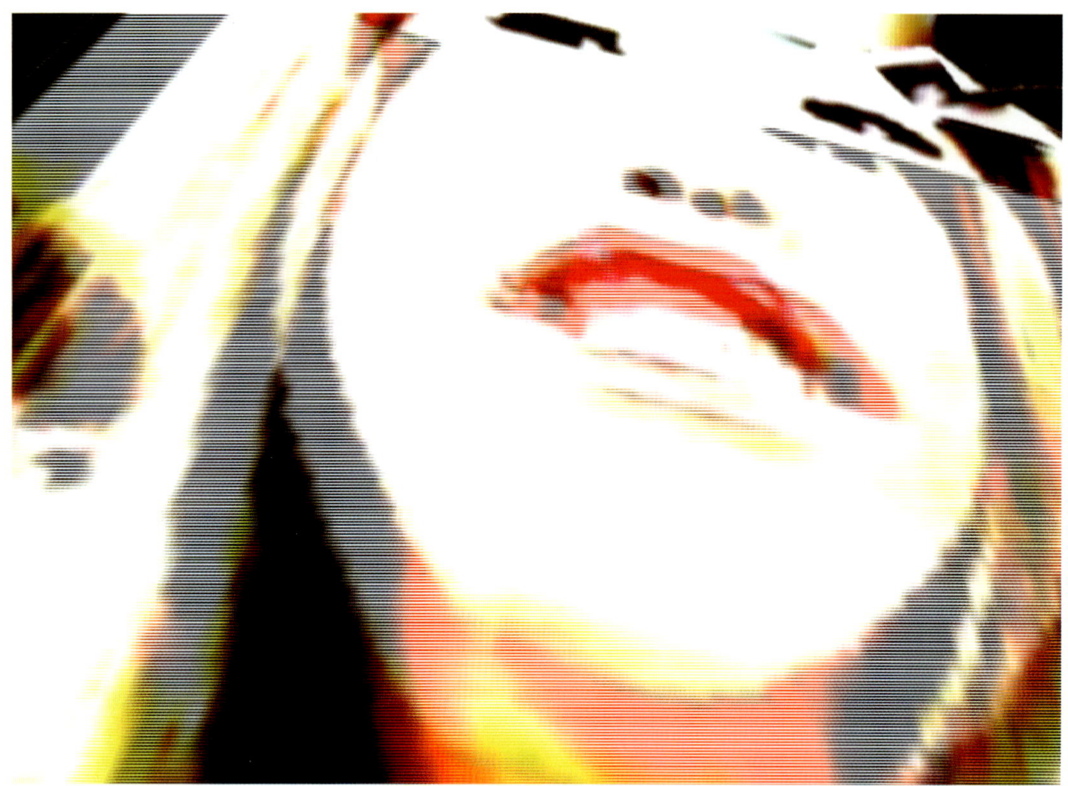

eNo
Untitled
Video Still
2002

019.001

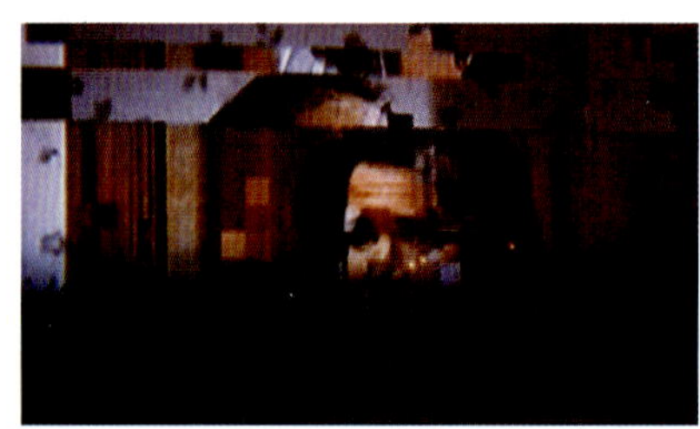

Adam Farcus
Scream
Photograph / TV Still
2005

020.001

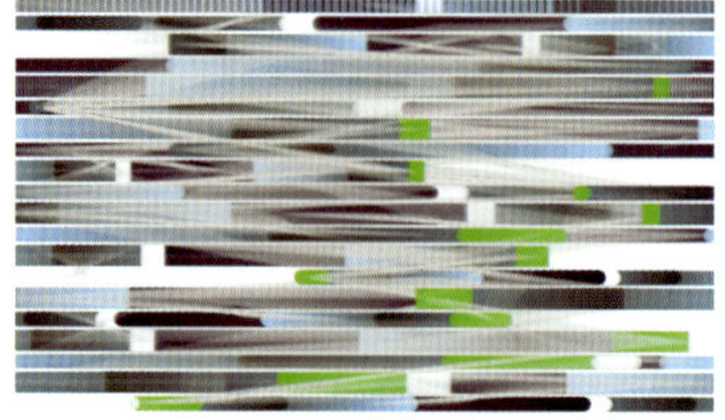

Marius Watz
amoebaAbstract_03
Processing
2003

084.001

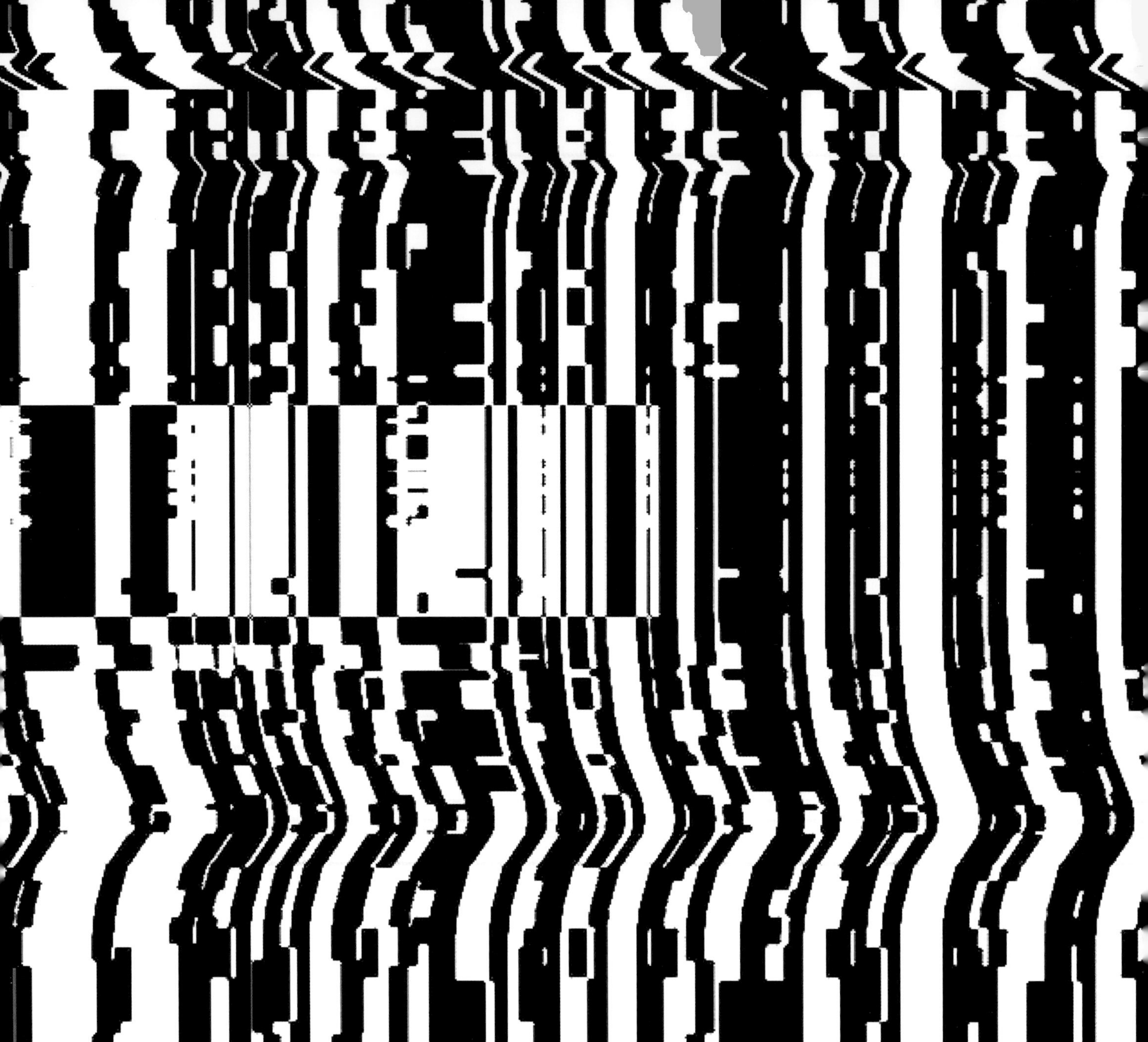

Stephan Maich
Frame 4
Animation Still
2001

048.001

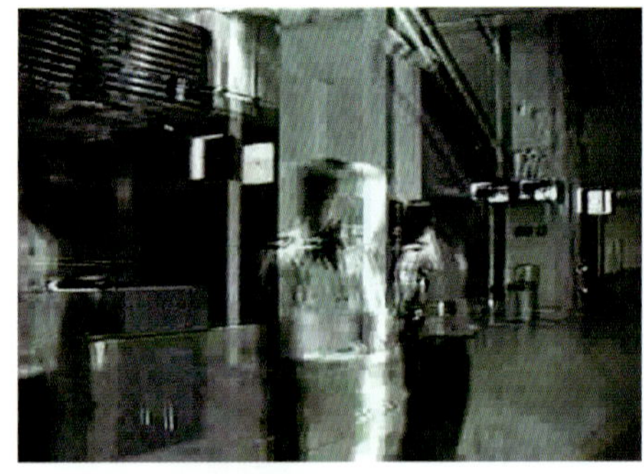
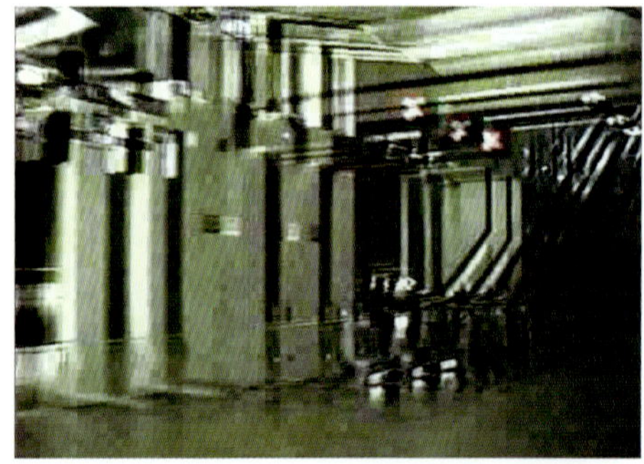
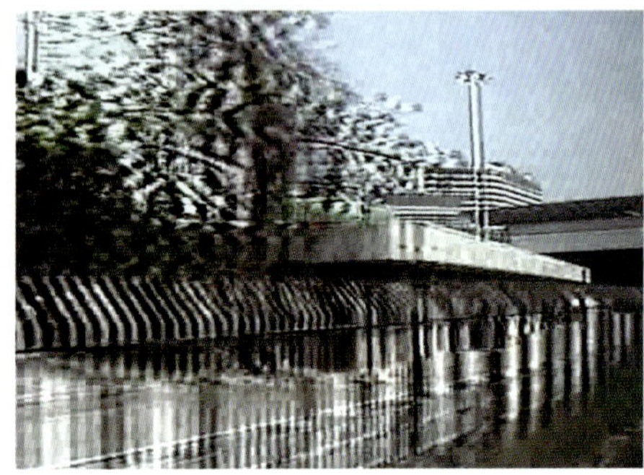
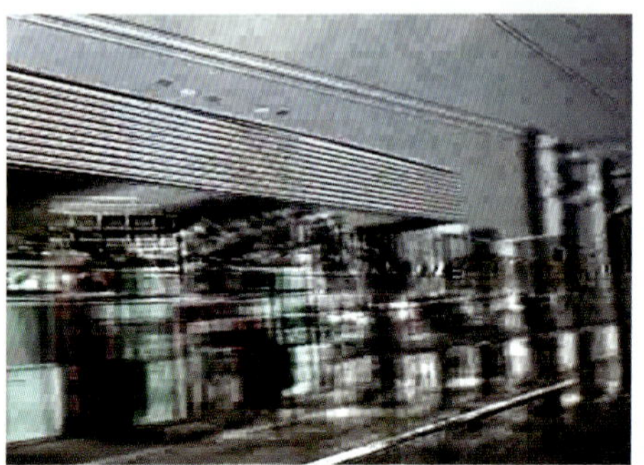

Michael R. Salmond
Excerpts from Travelschisms (divx Redux)
Video Stills
2004

066.001
066.002
066.003
066.004
066.005
066.006
066.007

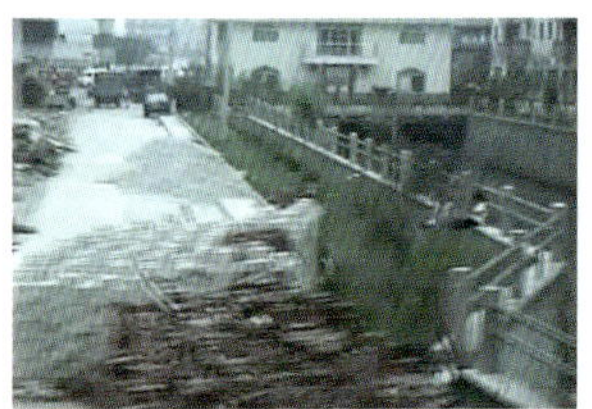
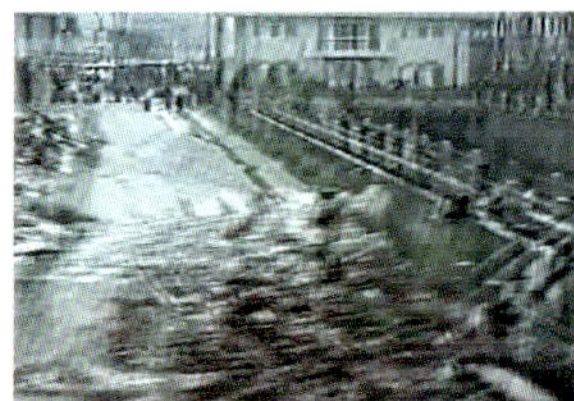
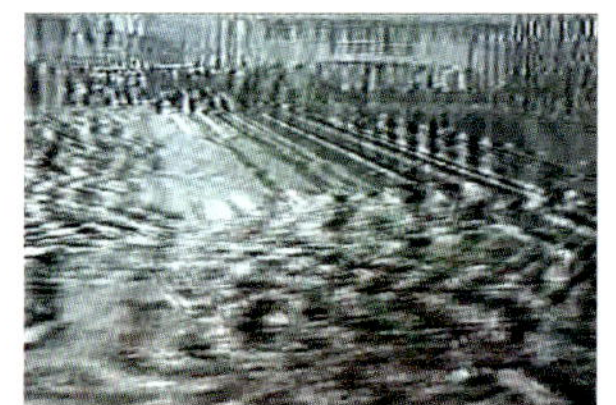

Kentaro Tsuji
Novacity
Digital Images
–

080.001
080.002

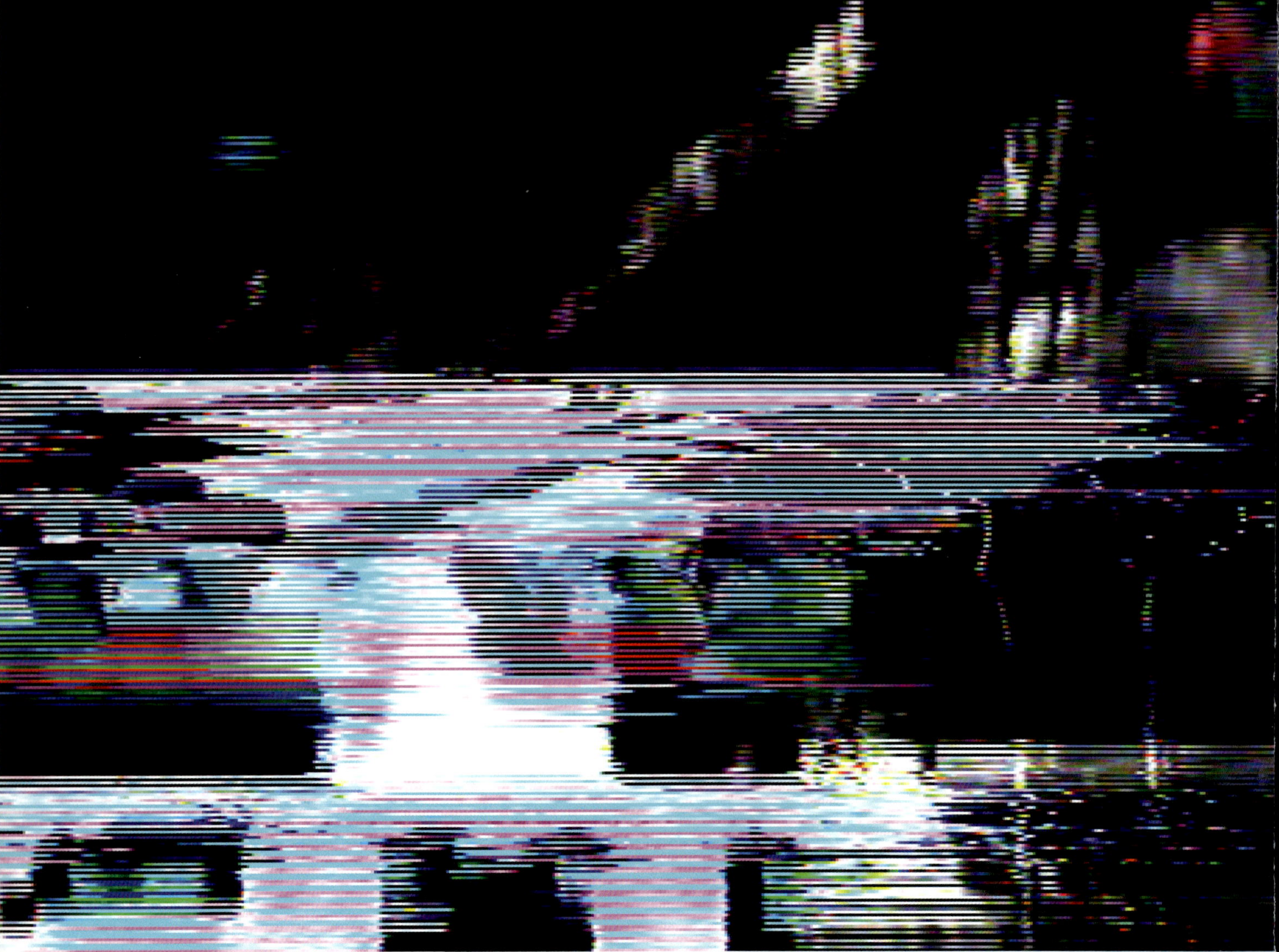

Will Hurt
Untitled
Screenshot
2005

032.001

Will Hurt
Untitled
Screenshot
2005

032.002
032.003
032.004

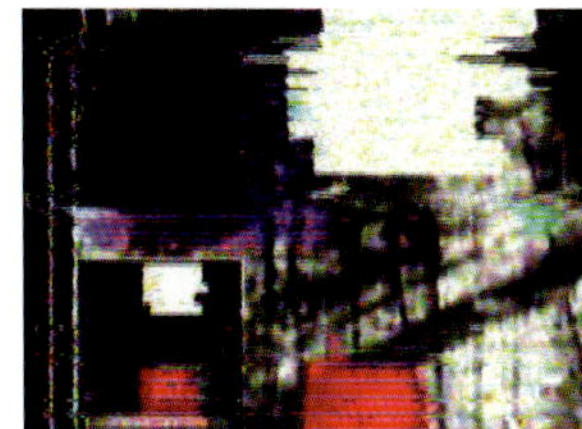

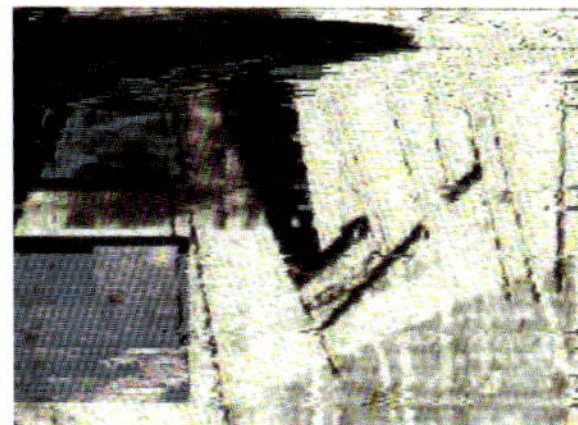

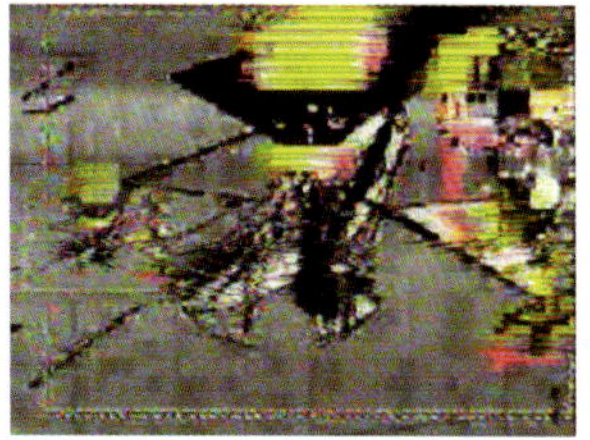

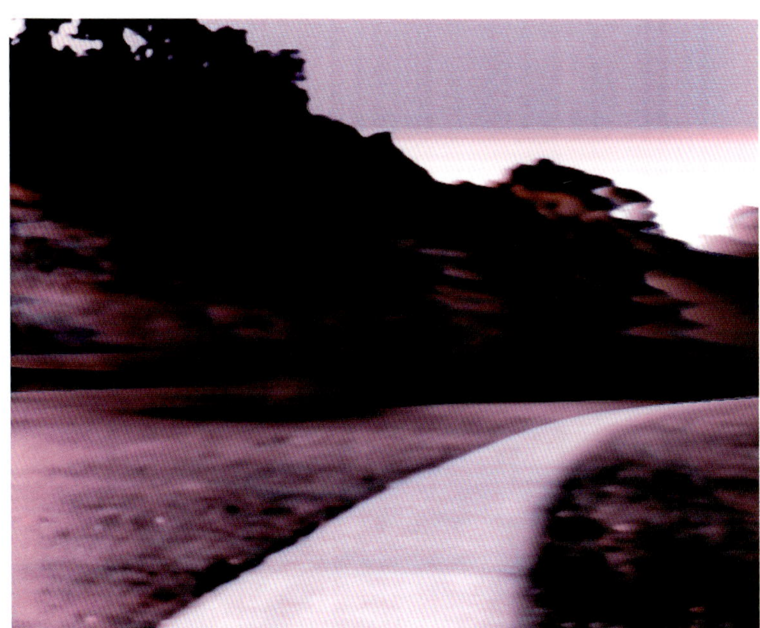

Michael Norris
Central Park, Plymouth 1
Digital Photograph
2007

053.001

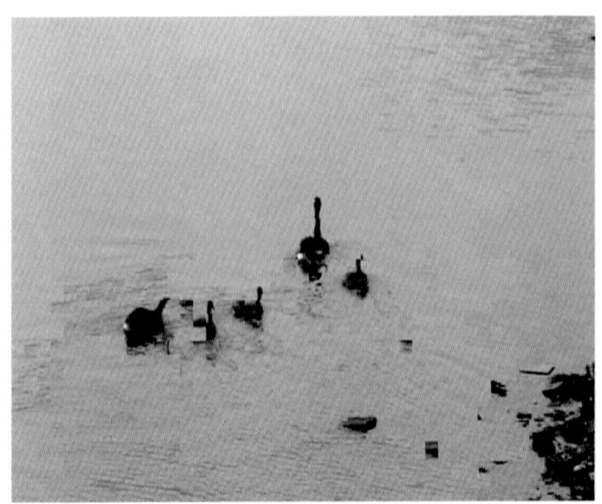

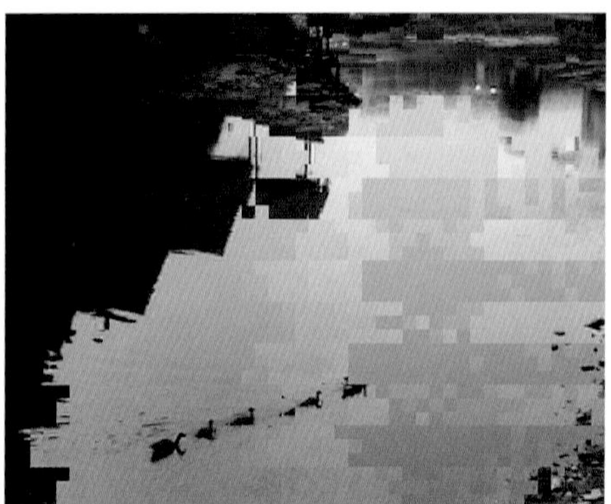

Iris Garrelfs
Dumplinks
Photographs
–

027.001
027.002

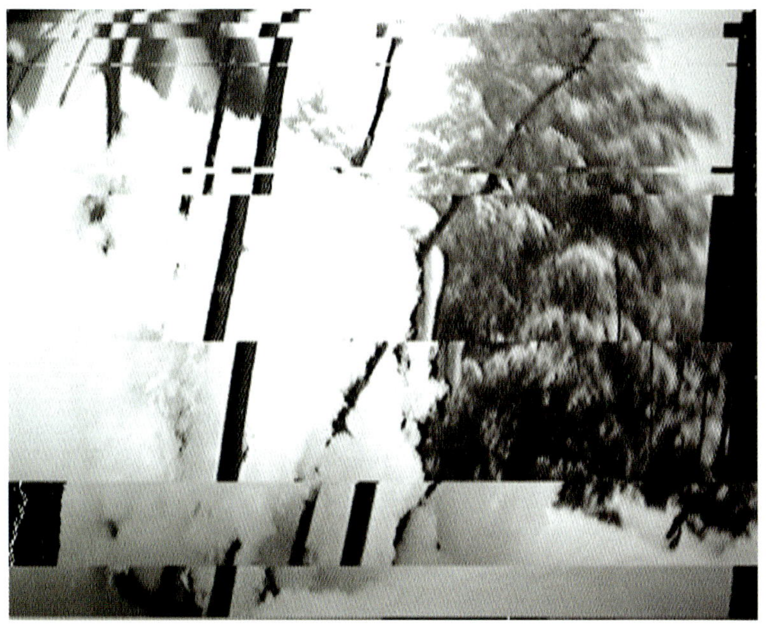

Megan Sproats
Neige 1
Video Still
2005

073.003

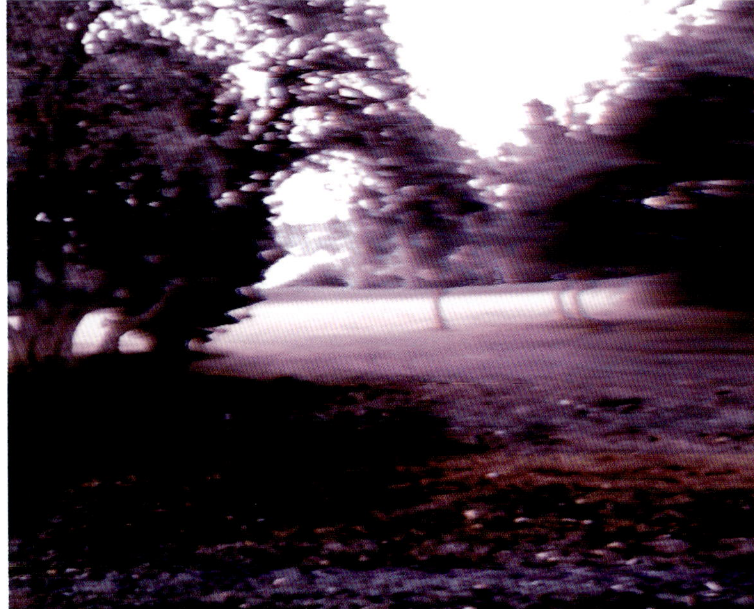

Michael Norris
Central Park, Plymouth 2
Digital Photograph
2007

053.002

2

001.001
001.002
001.003
001.004
002.001
002.002
002.003
002.004
003.001
004.001
004.002
005.001
005.002
005.003
006.001
007.001
007.002
007.003
008.001
008.002
008.003
008.004
008.005
008.006
008.007
009.001
009.002
009.003
009.004
009.005
009.006
009.007
010.001
010.002
011.001
012.001
013.001
013.002
013.003
013.004
014.001
015.001
015.002
015.003

016.001
017.001
017.002
017.003
017.004
018.001
019.001
019.002
019.003
020.001
020.002
021.001
021.002
022.001
023.001
023.002
023.003
024.001
024.002
024.003
025.001
025.002
026.001
026.002
026.003
027.001
027.002
028.001
028.002
028.003
029.001
030.001
031.001
032.001
032.002
032.003
032.004
033.001
033.002
034.001
035.001
035.002
035.003
035.004

036.001
037.001
038.001
039.001
039.002
039.003
039.004
040.001
041.001
042.001
043.001
044.001
045.001
045.002
046.001
047.001
048.001
049.001
049.002
050.001
050.002
051.001
051.002
052.001
052.002
052.003
053.001
053.002
054.001
054.002
054.003
055.001
055.002
056.001
056.002
056.003
056.004
057.001
058.001
059.001
060.001
060.002
060.003
060.004

061.001
061.002
061.003
062.001
062.002
062.003
062.004
062.005
062.006
062.007
062.008
062.009
062.010
062.011
062.012
062.013
062.014
062.015
062.016
062.017
062.018
062.019
062.020
063.001
063.002
063.003
064.001
064.002
064.003
064.004
064.005
064.006
065.001
066.001
066.002
066.003
066.004
066.005
066.006
066.007
067.001
067.001
067.003
067.004

067.005
067.006
067.007
068.001
069.001
070.001
070.002
070.003
070.004
071.001
072.001
073.001
073.002
073.003
074.001
074.002
075.001
076.001
077.001
077.002
078.001
079.001
079.002
080.001
080.002
081.001
082.001
082.002
083.001
083.002
084.001
085.001
086.001
086.002
086.003

Jan Robert Leegte
untitled[hotmail]
HTML
2000

043.001

Meta
Vermille 0000
Adobe Illustrator
2004

051.001

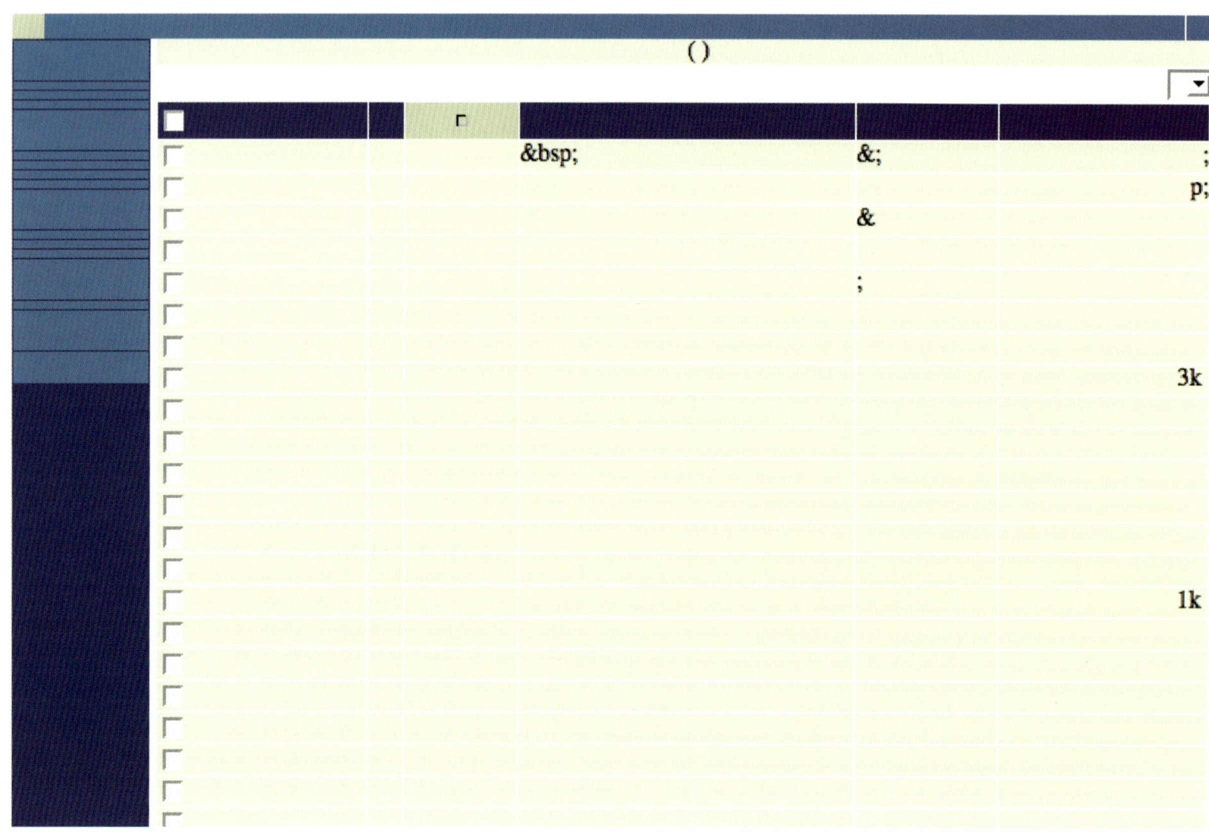

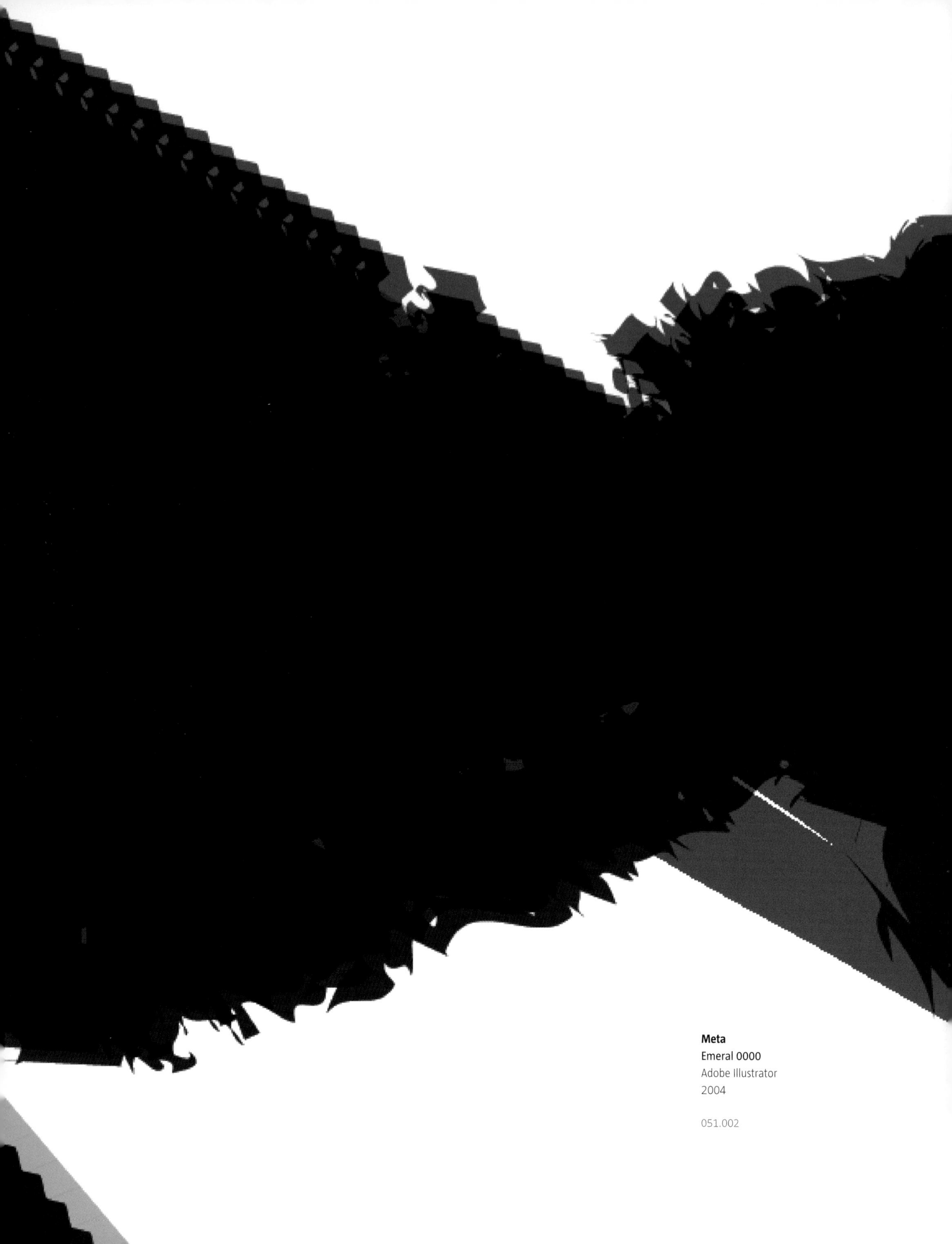

Meta
Emeral 0000
Adobe Illustrator
2004

051.002

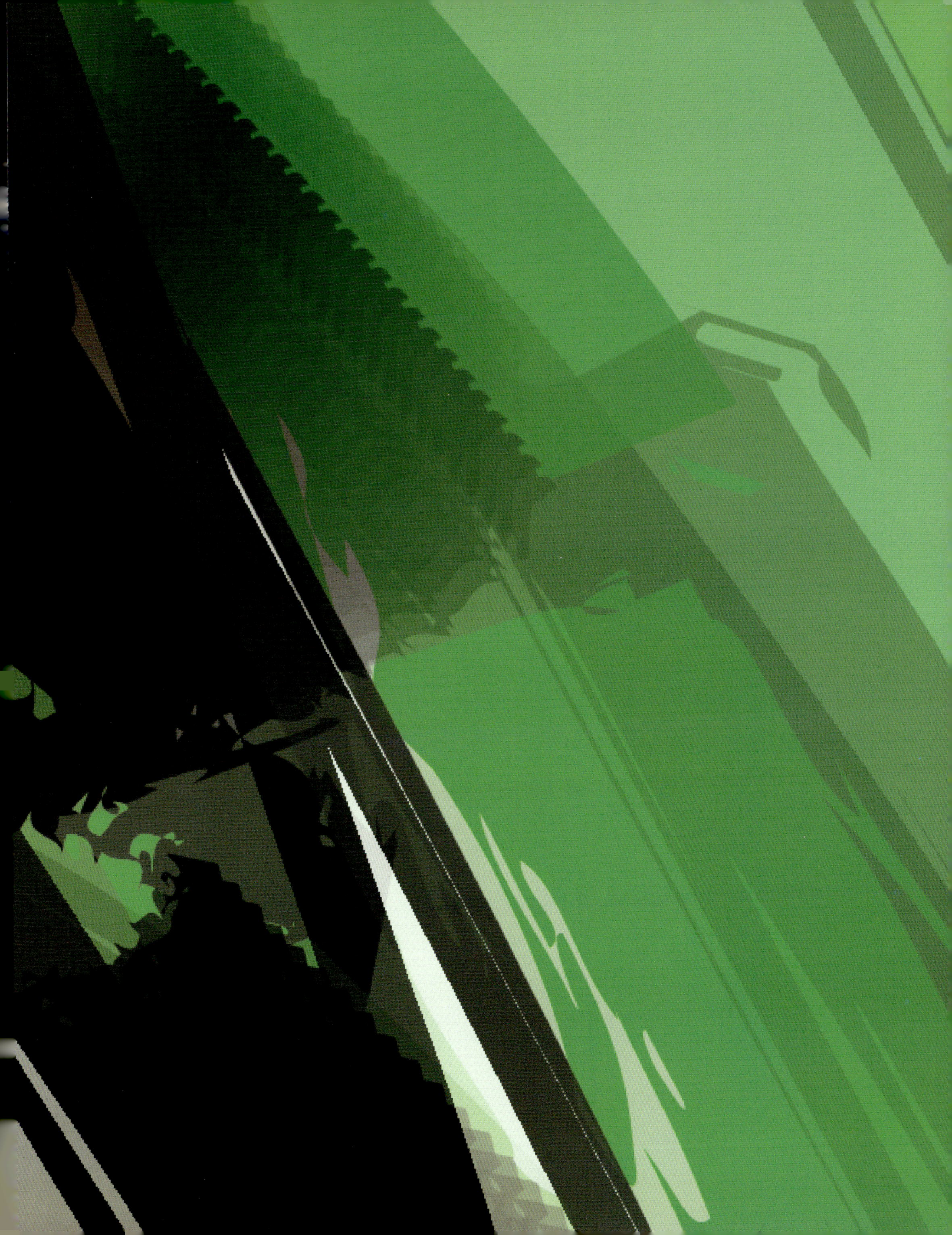

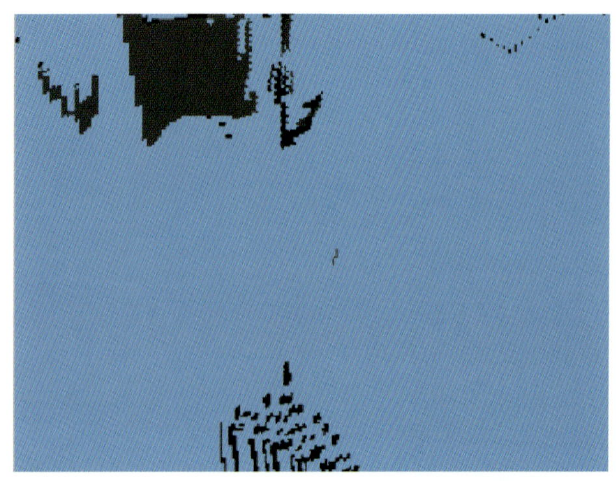

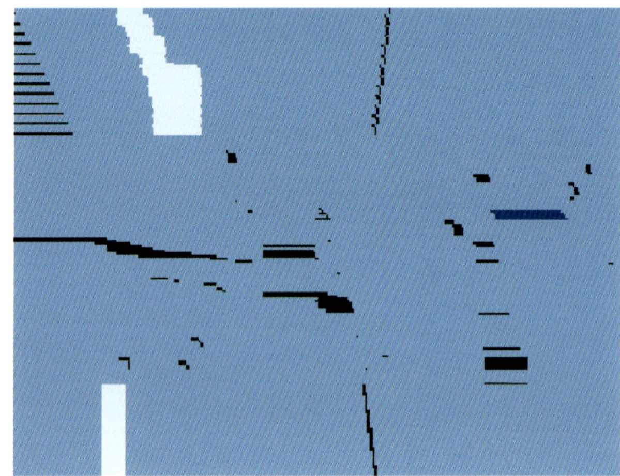

Joe Gilmore
Gelk 3
Video Stills
2004

028.001
028.002
028.003

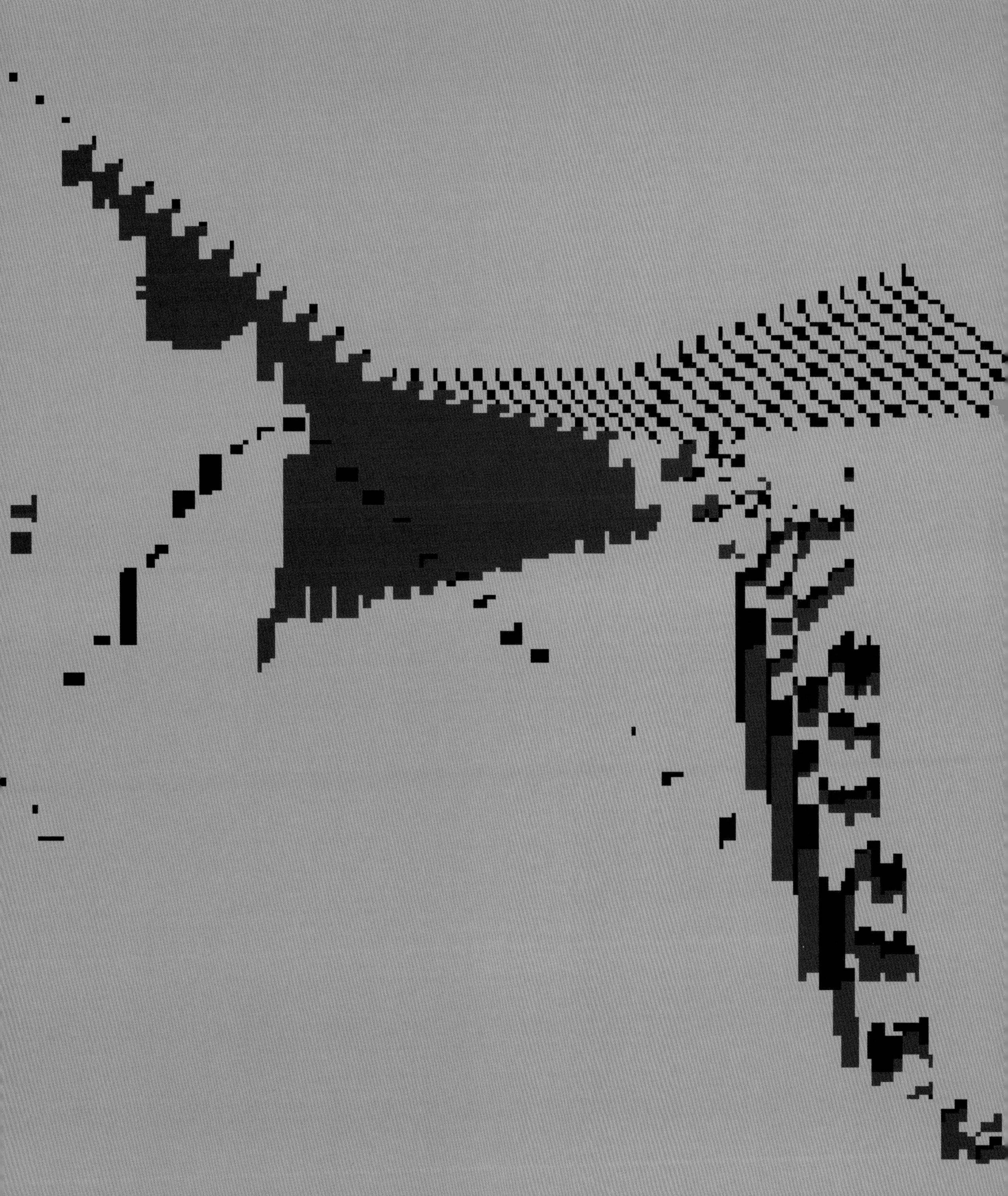

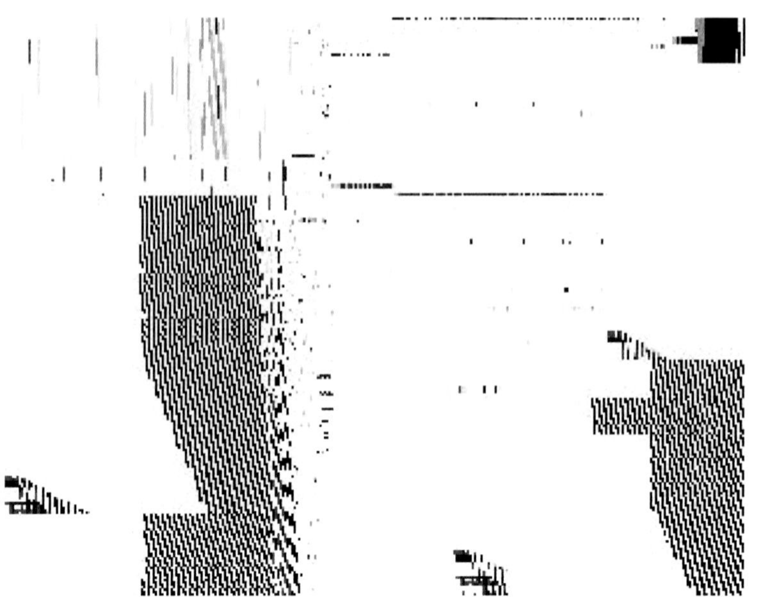

Telcosystems
Reconstructions 02102002
Video Still
2002

076.001

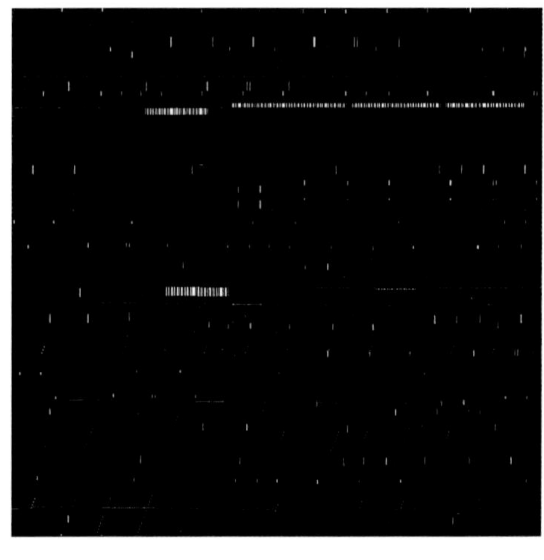

Tim Redfern
Incognito
Screenshot
2004

061.001

Tim Redfern
Incognito
Screenshot
2004

061.002

Tim Redfern
Incognito (overleaf)
Screenshot
2004

061.003

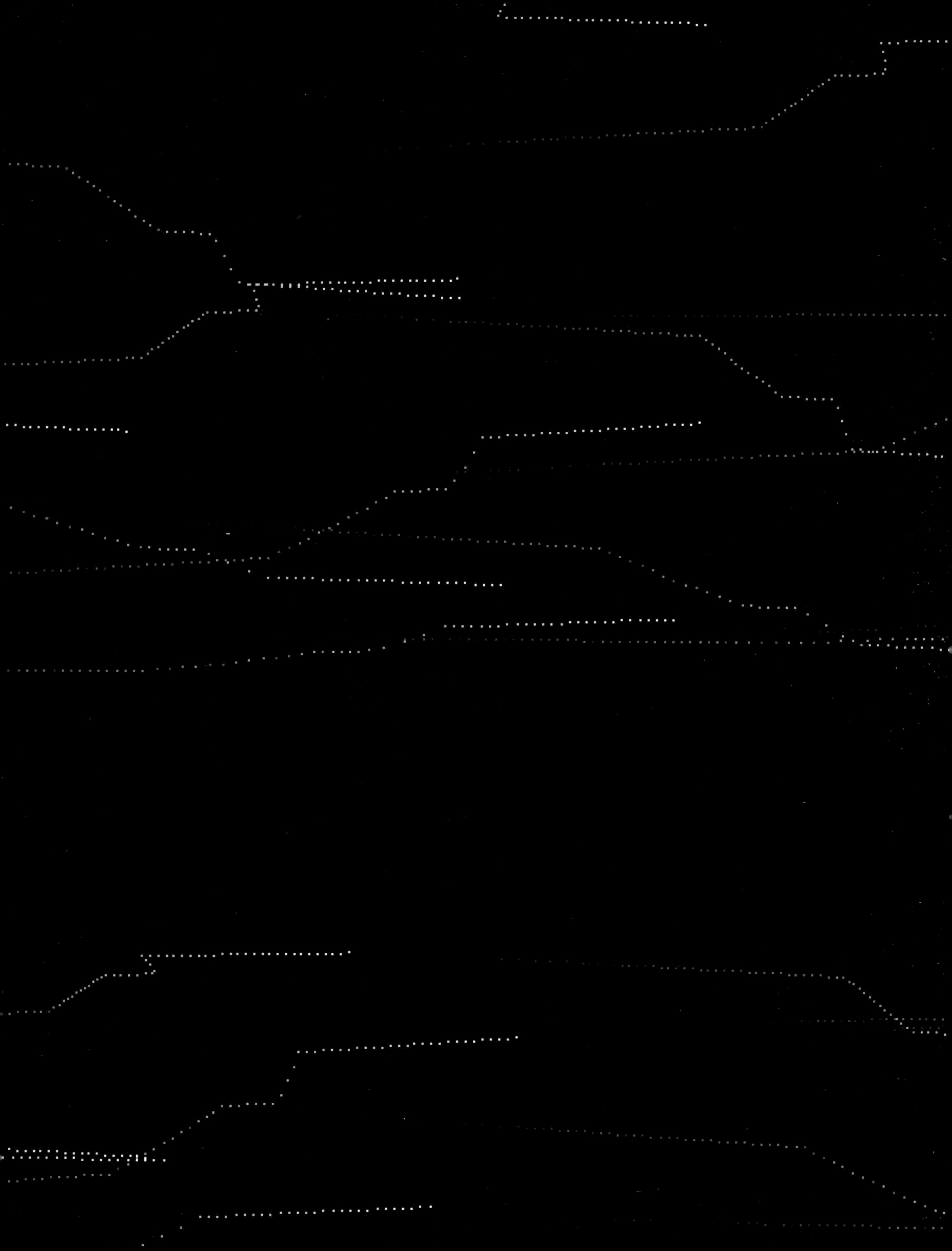

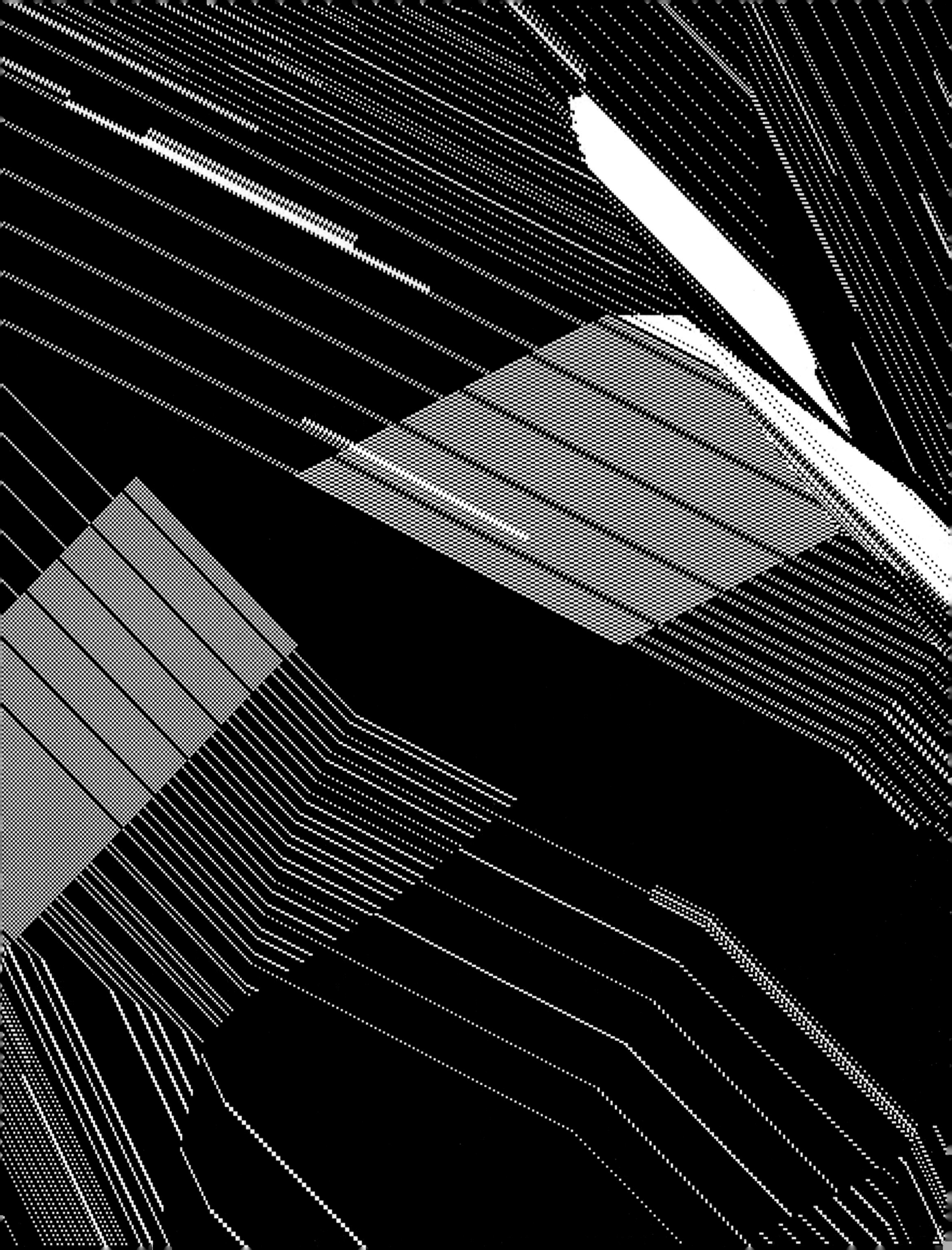

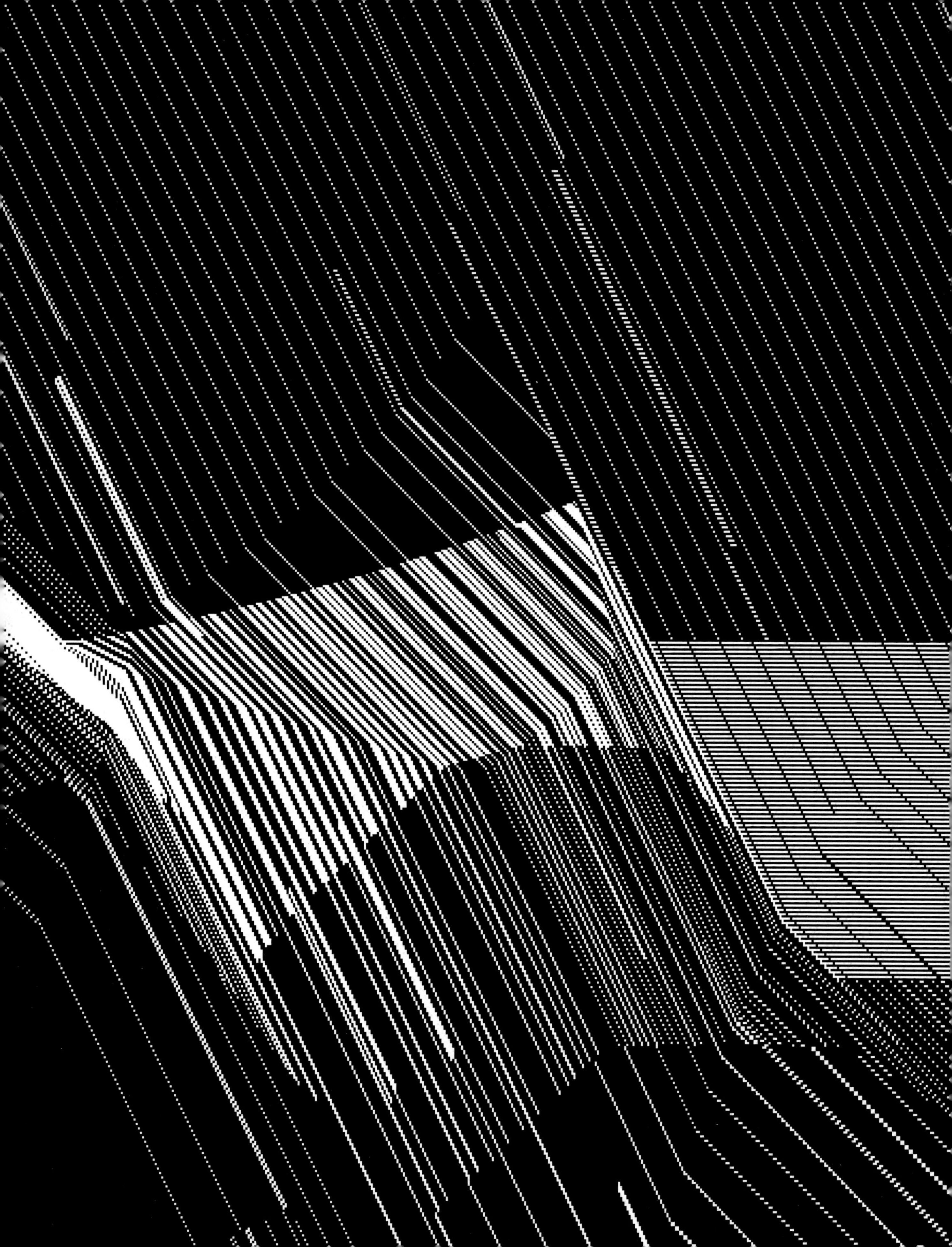

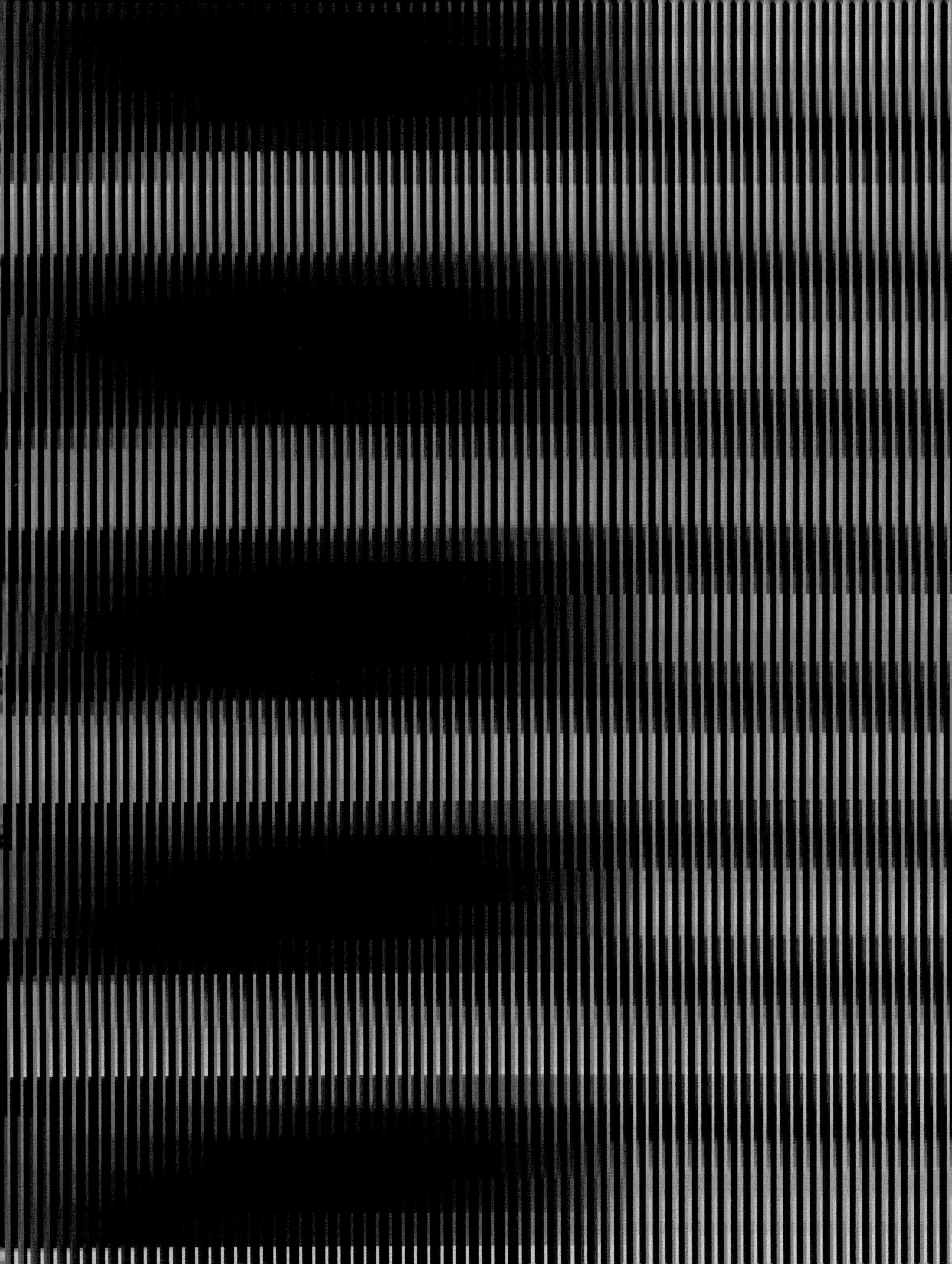

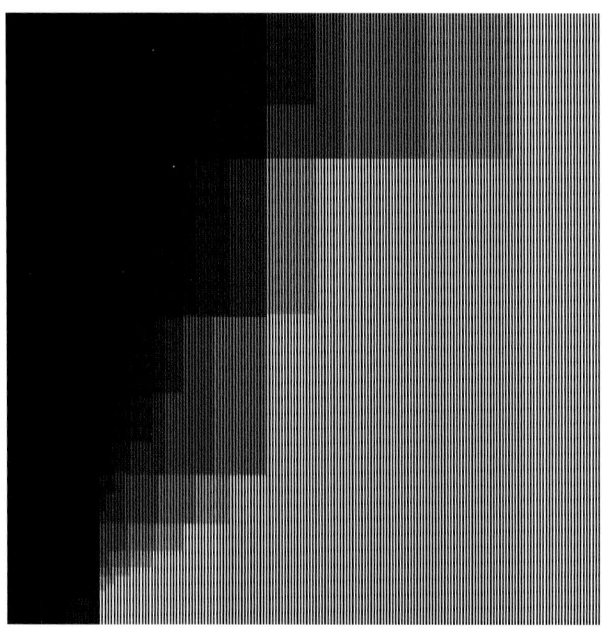

Enrico Bravi
Graphica Programmata
Shockwave
2002

007.001

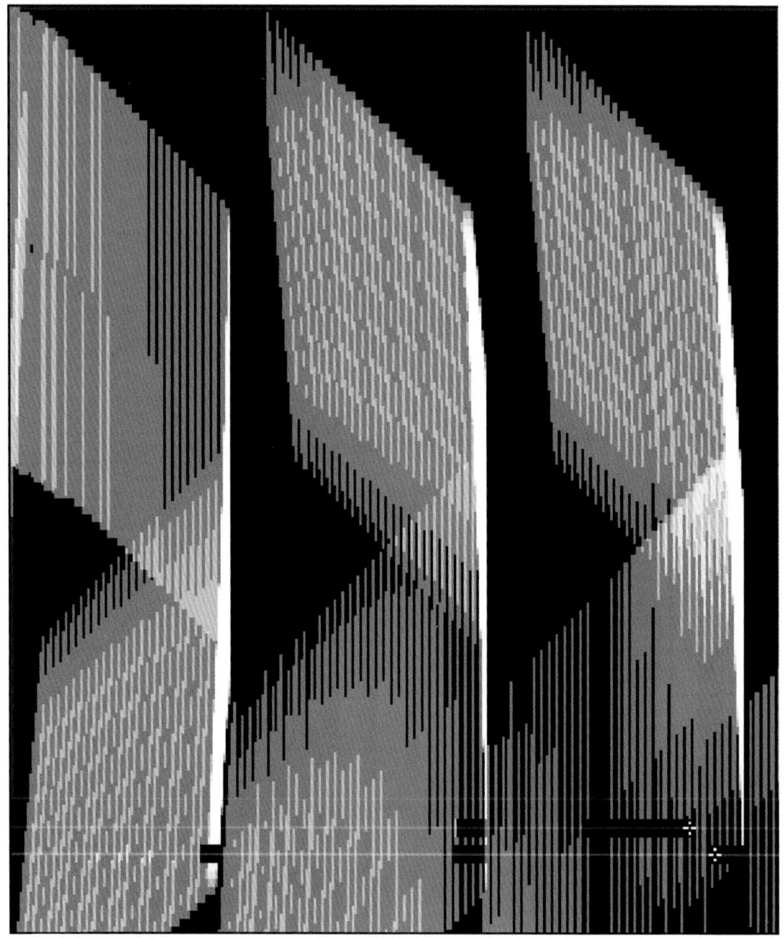

Enrico Bravi
Graphica Programmata
Shockwave
2002

007.002

Enrico Bravi
Graphica Programmata
Shockwave
2002

007.003

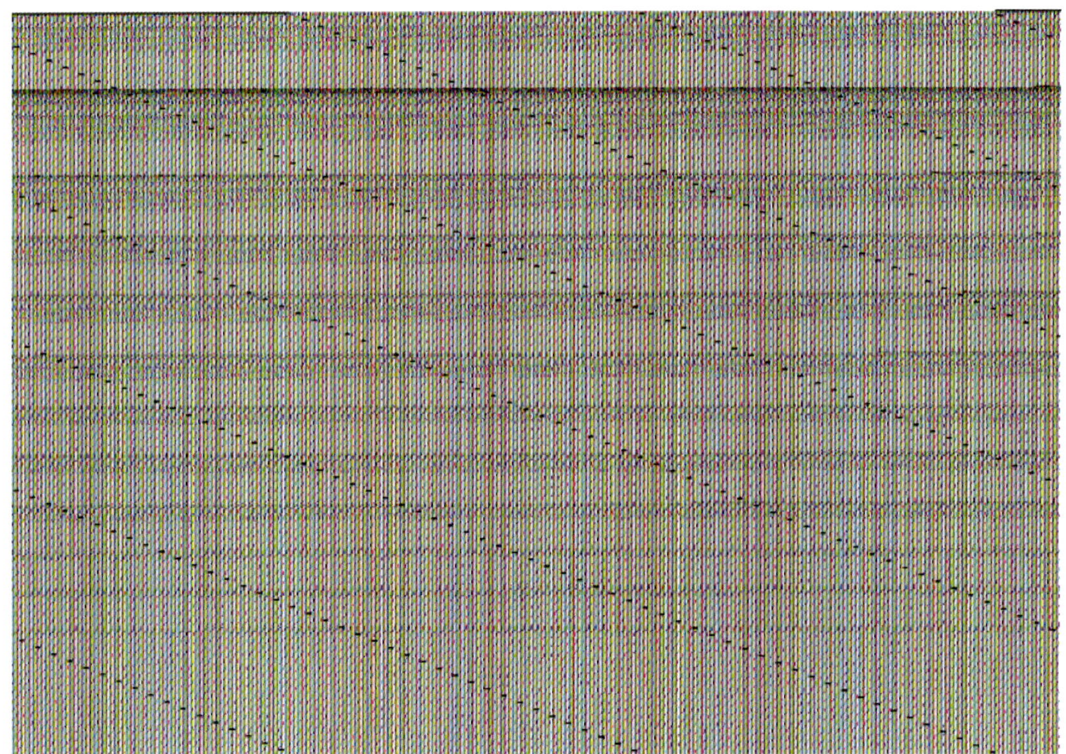

Benjamin Fischer
Neuordnung
Digital Images
2003

023.001
023.002
023.003

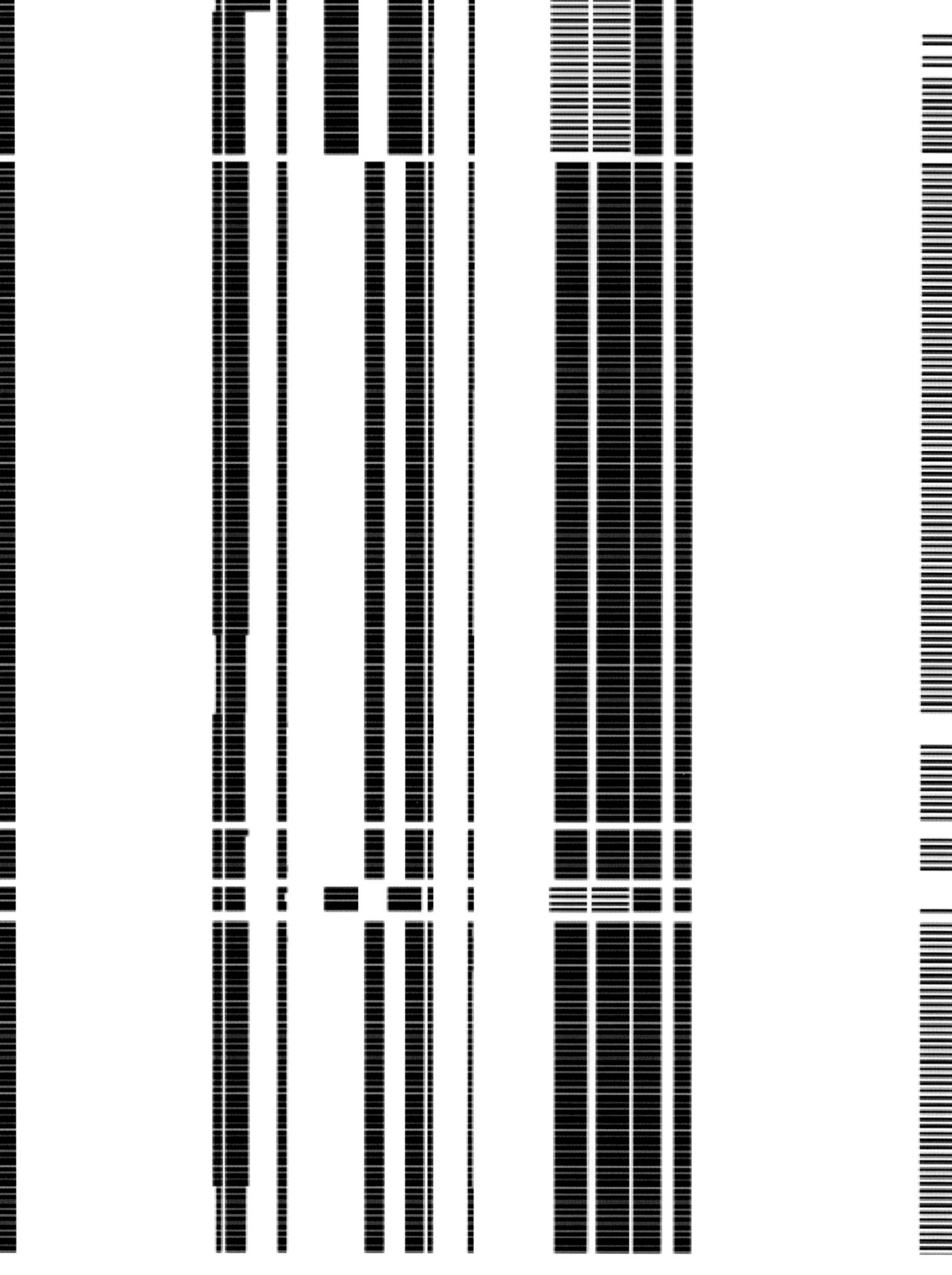

Taylor Deupree
Piana Royalties - PDF Error
PDF
2007

014.001

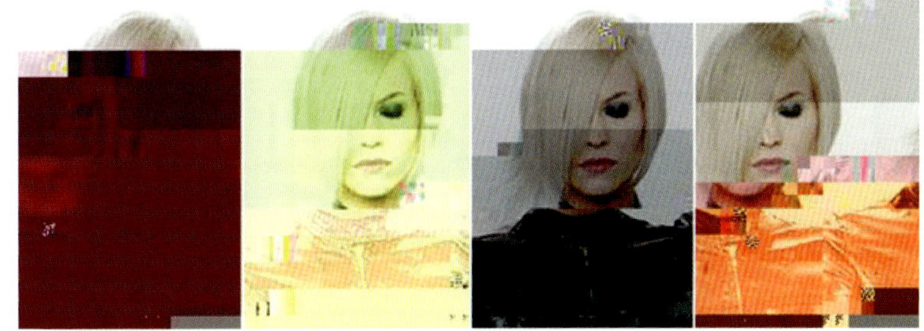

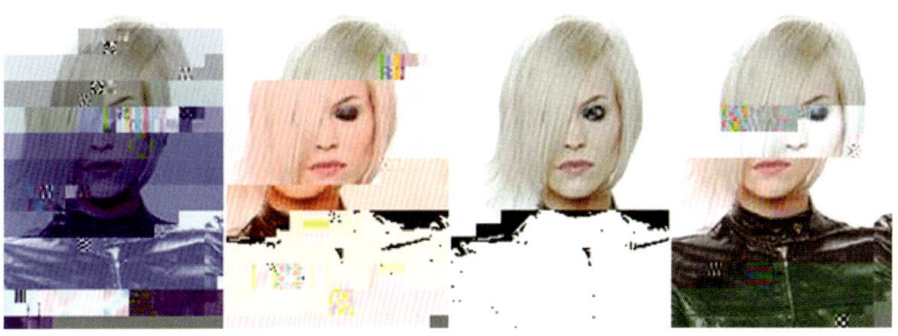

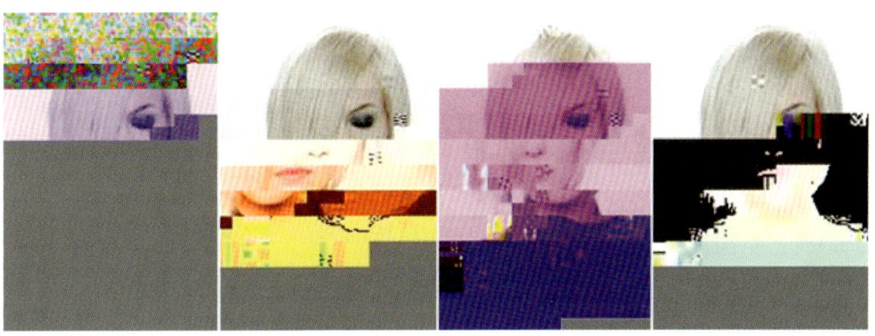

Kate Wintjes
Contact Sheet
Video Stills
–

085.001

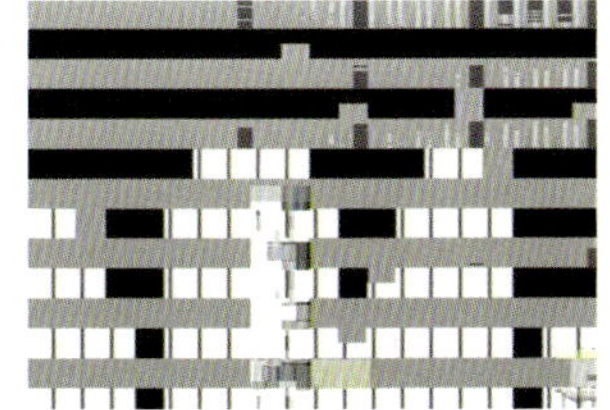

Dan Tombs
Grey Cityscape
Game Modification / Video Still
2004

078.001

Jerome Faria
Burn Baby Burn
Digital Image
–

021.001

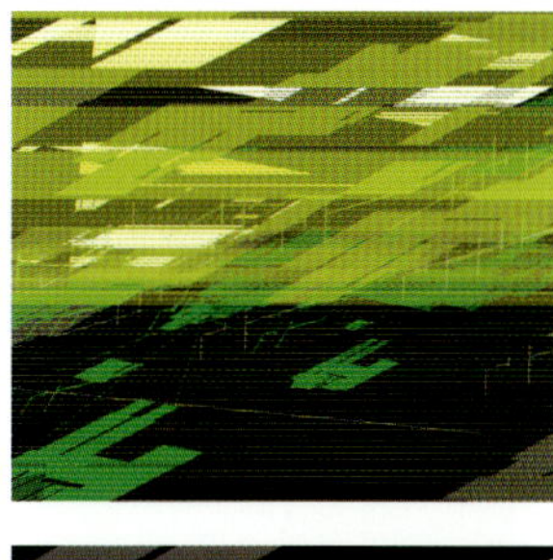
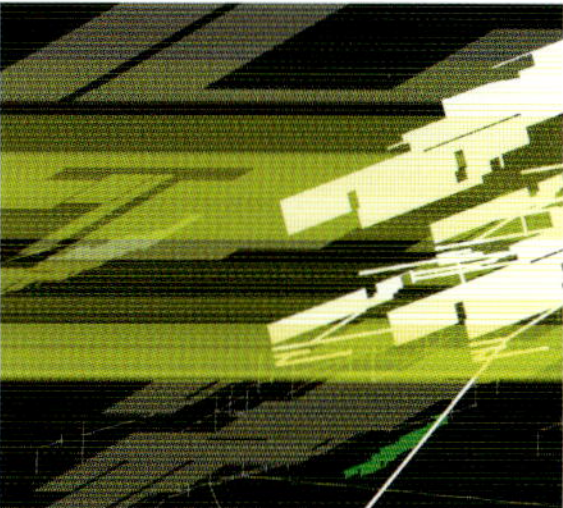
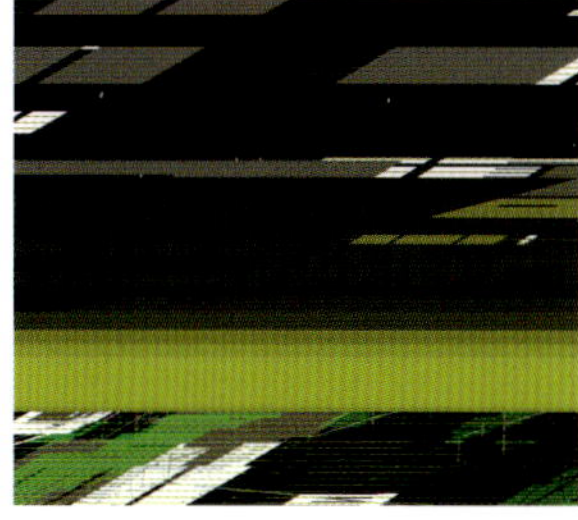
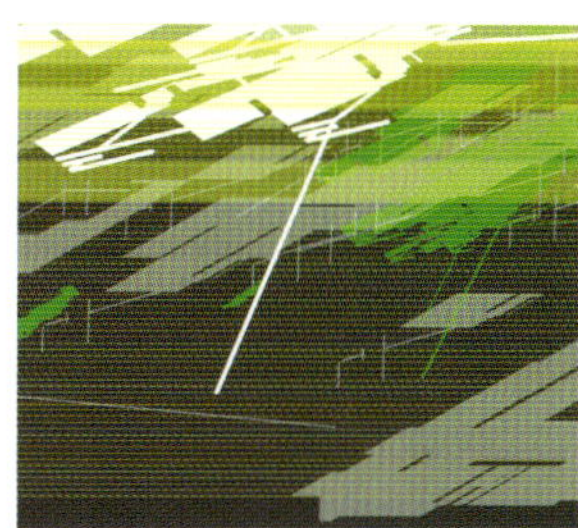

Paul Prudence
Struktur Masheens
Flash
2004

060.001
060.002
060.003
060.004

Jerome Faria
The Song Remains The Same
Digital Image
–

021.002

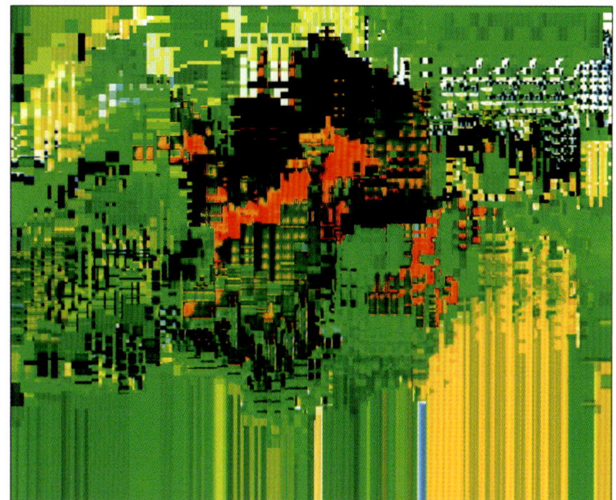

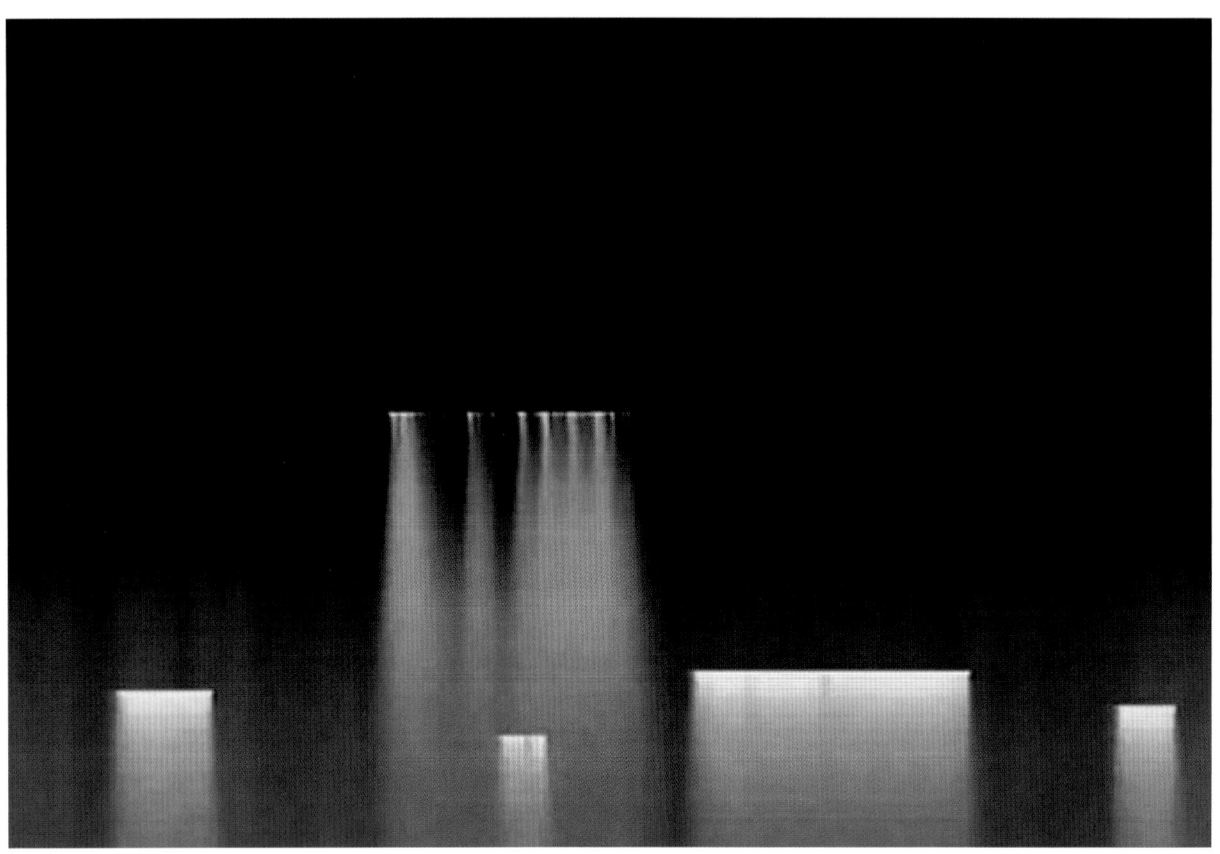

Scott Arford
Static Room
Video Still
2002

004.001

Dextro
xmx/idea_mag:02.002_hell_rot
xmx/idea_mag:07.022
xmx/idea_mag:12.025
3D Render
2003

015.001
015.002
015.003

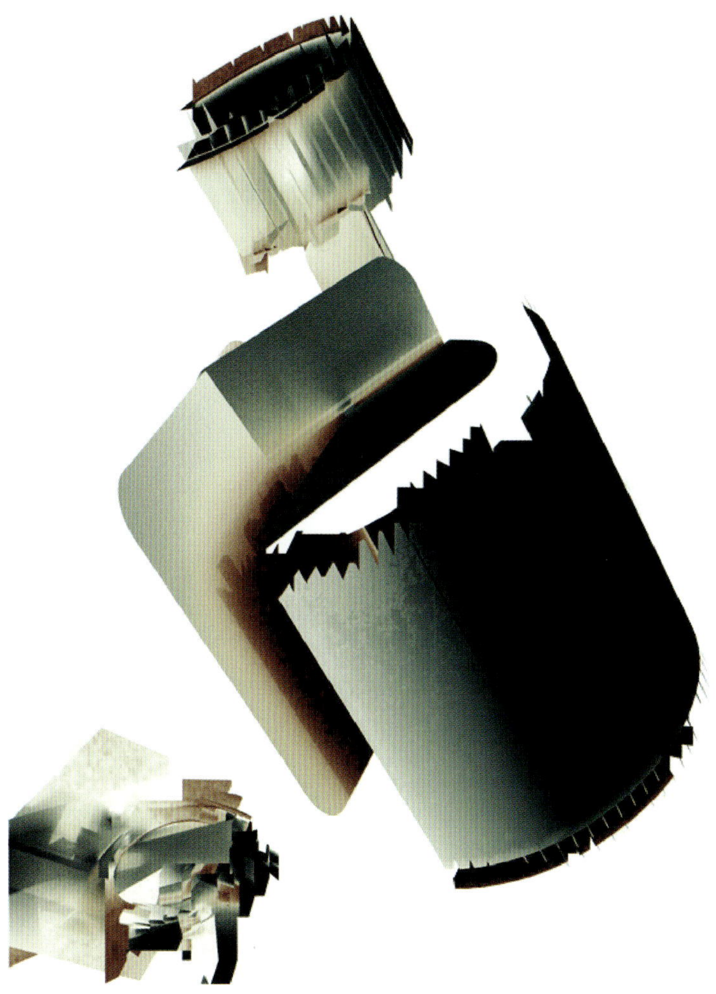

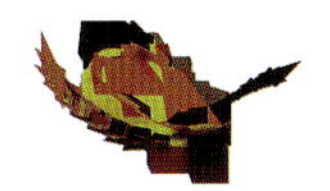

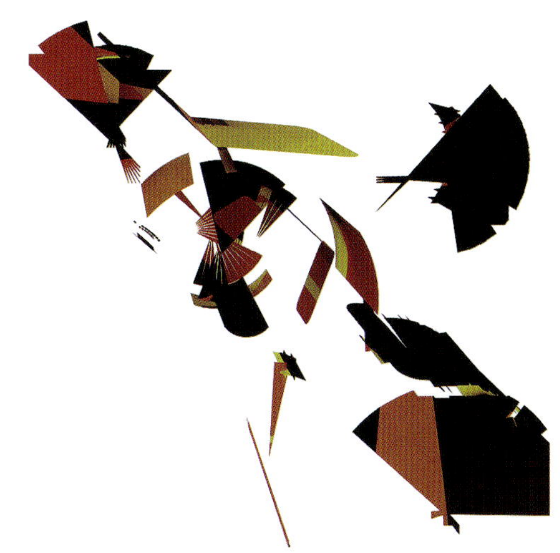

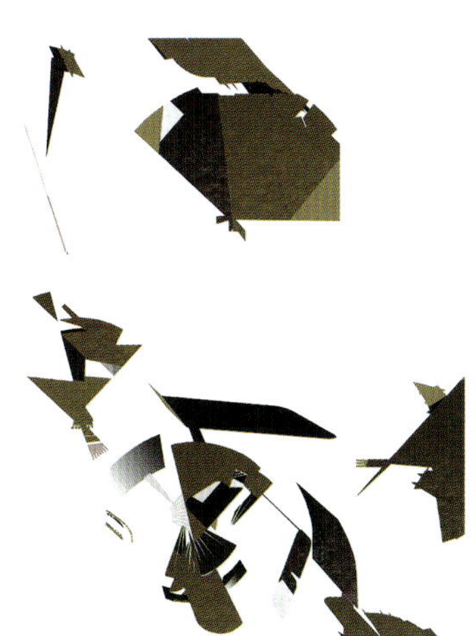

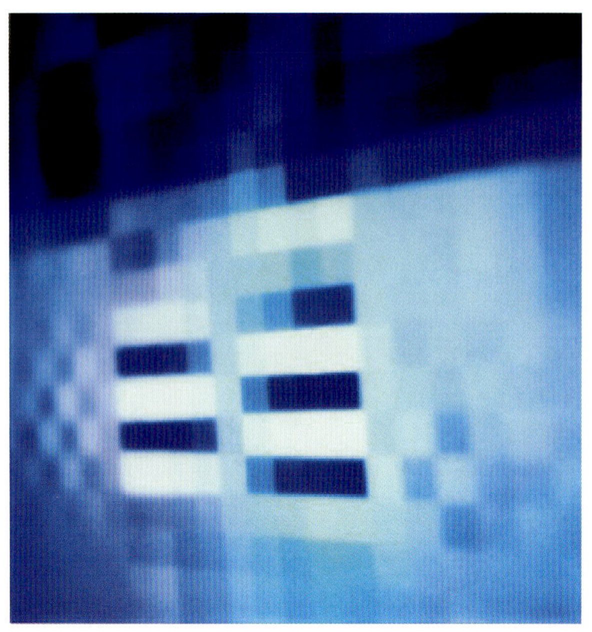

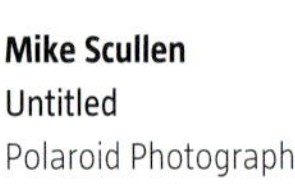

Mike Scullen
Untitled
Polaroid Photograph
–

068.001

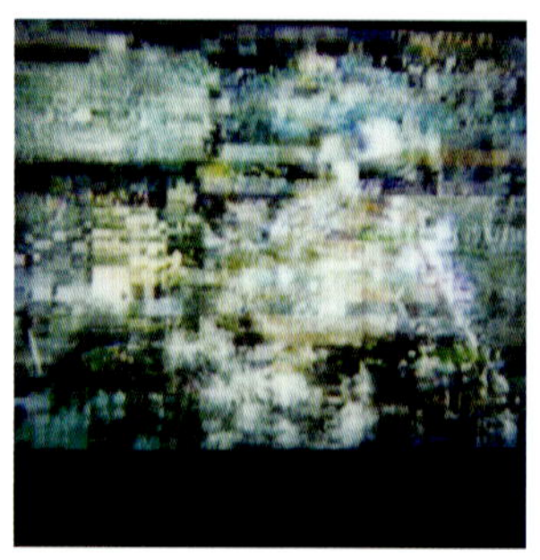

Adam Farcus
Disrupted Cable
Polaroid Photograph / TV Still
2005

020.002

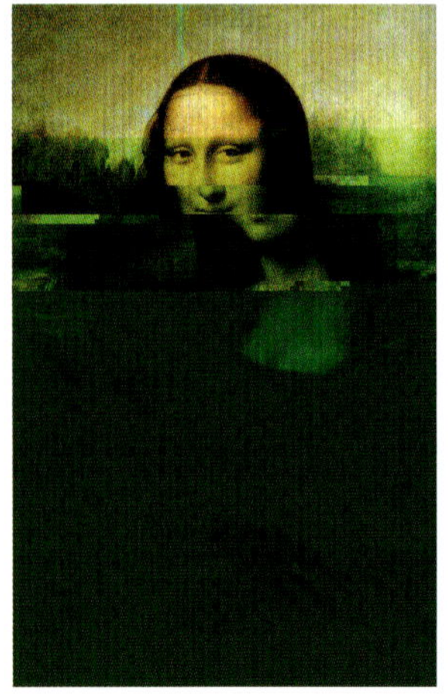

Luciano Testi Paul
JPEGED Mona Lisa
Digital Image
2002

077.001

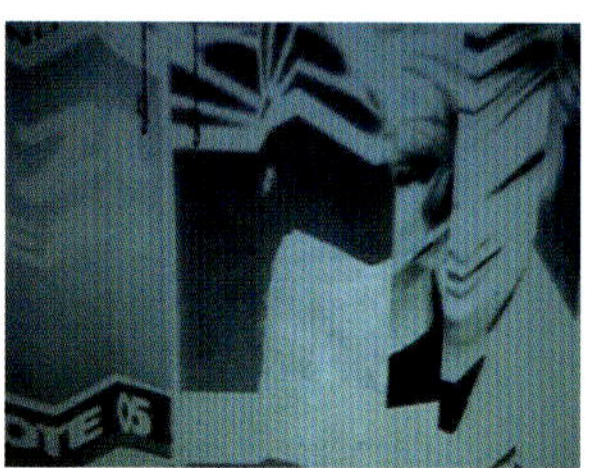

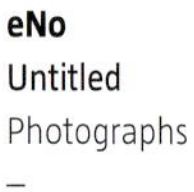

eNo
Untitled
Photographs
–

019.002
019.003

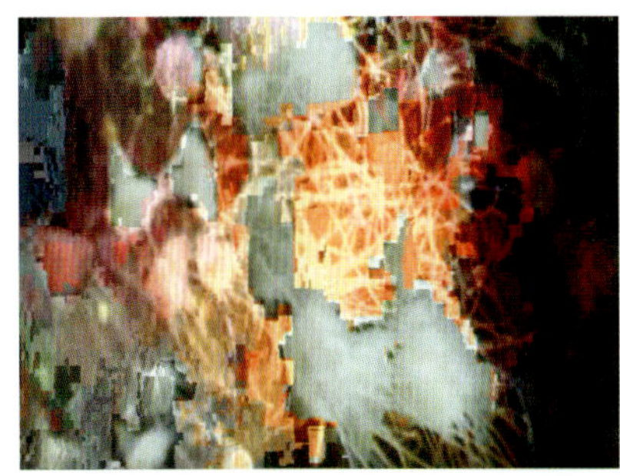

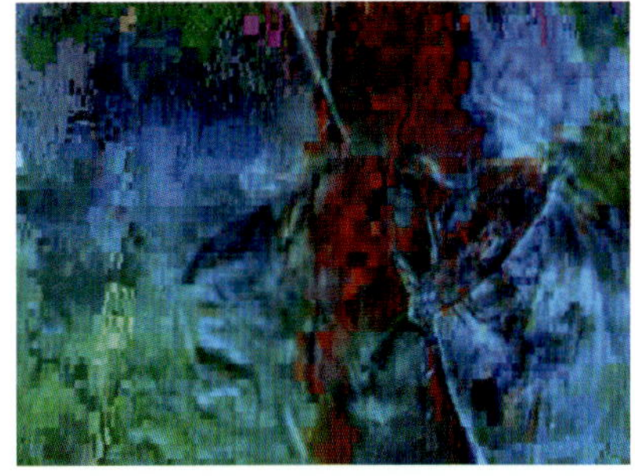

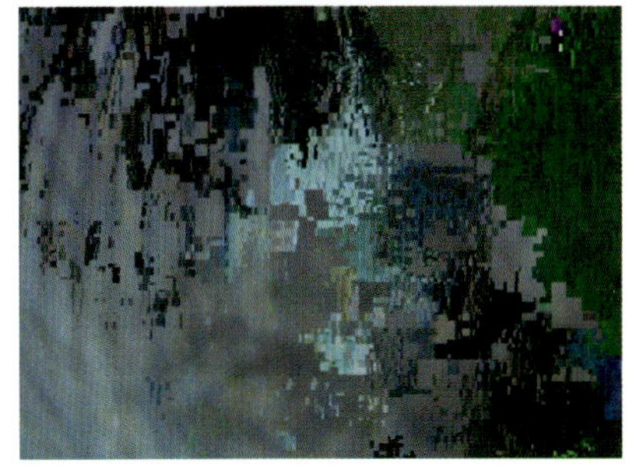

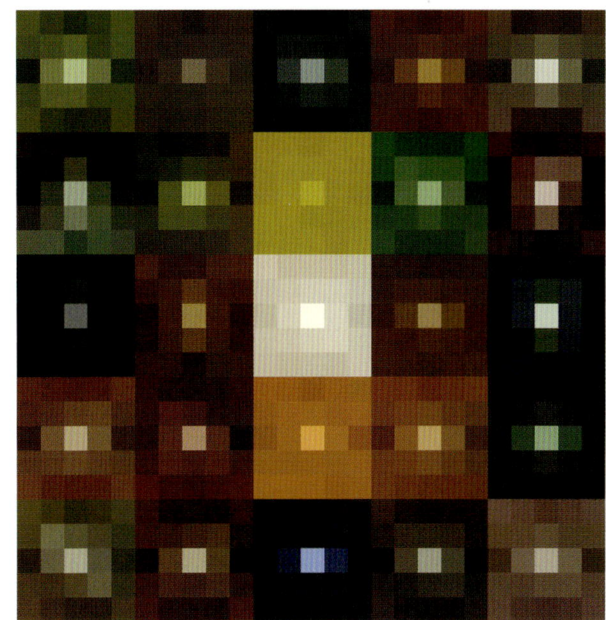

Nik Gaffney
x
xxxx
yyyy
JPEG

026.001
026.002
026.003

Derek Collie
Perished Pixels
Giclée Print
2004

012.001

Alex Horber
Bad4000
Print
2005

031.001

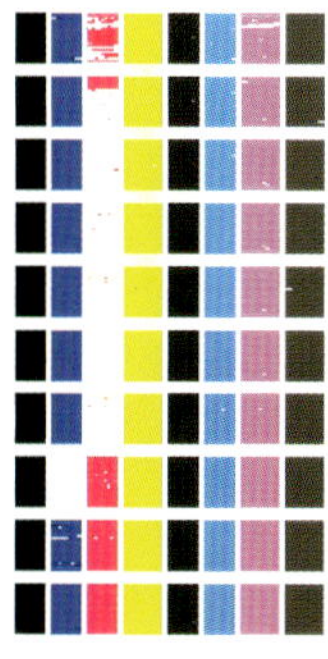

Christophe Behrens
Compression Series
JPEGs
1996

005.001
005.002
005.003

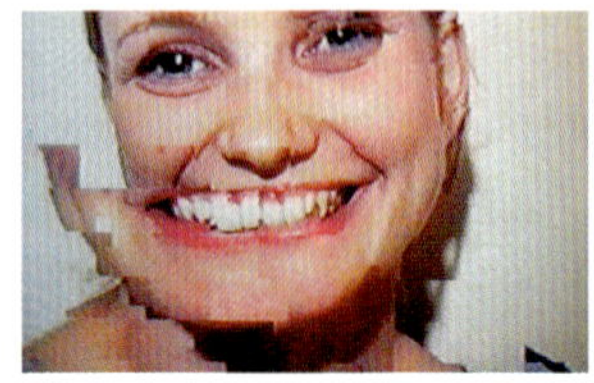
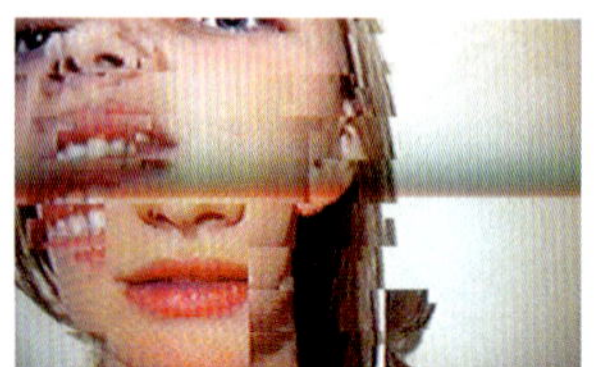

Andrew Townsend / Wig-01
Blenk3
Blenk2
TV Stills
2004

079.001
079.002

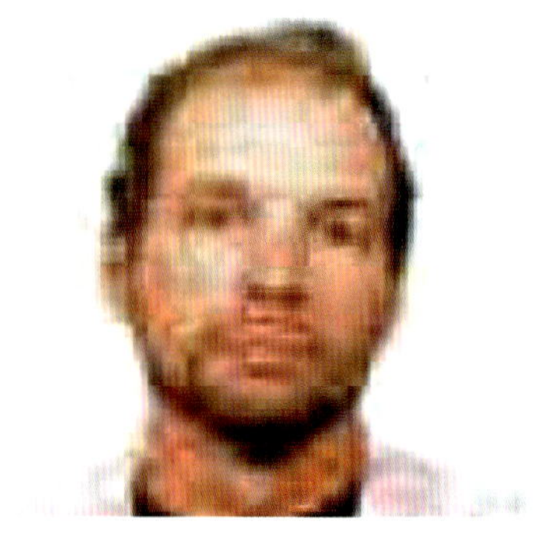

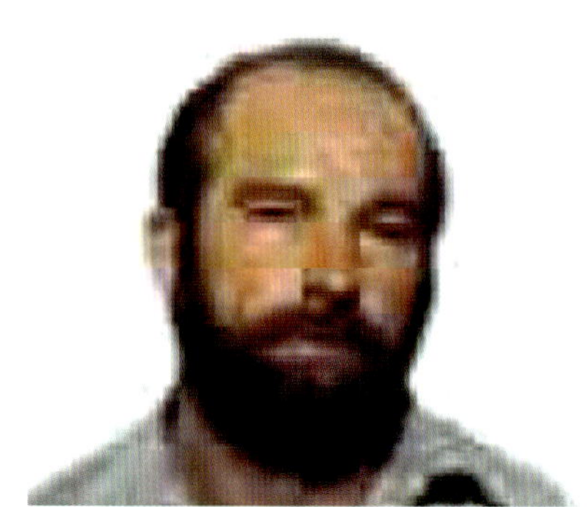

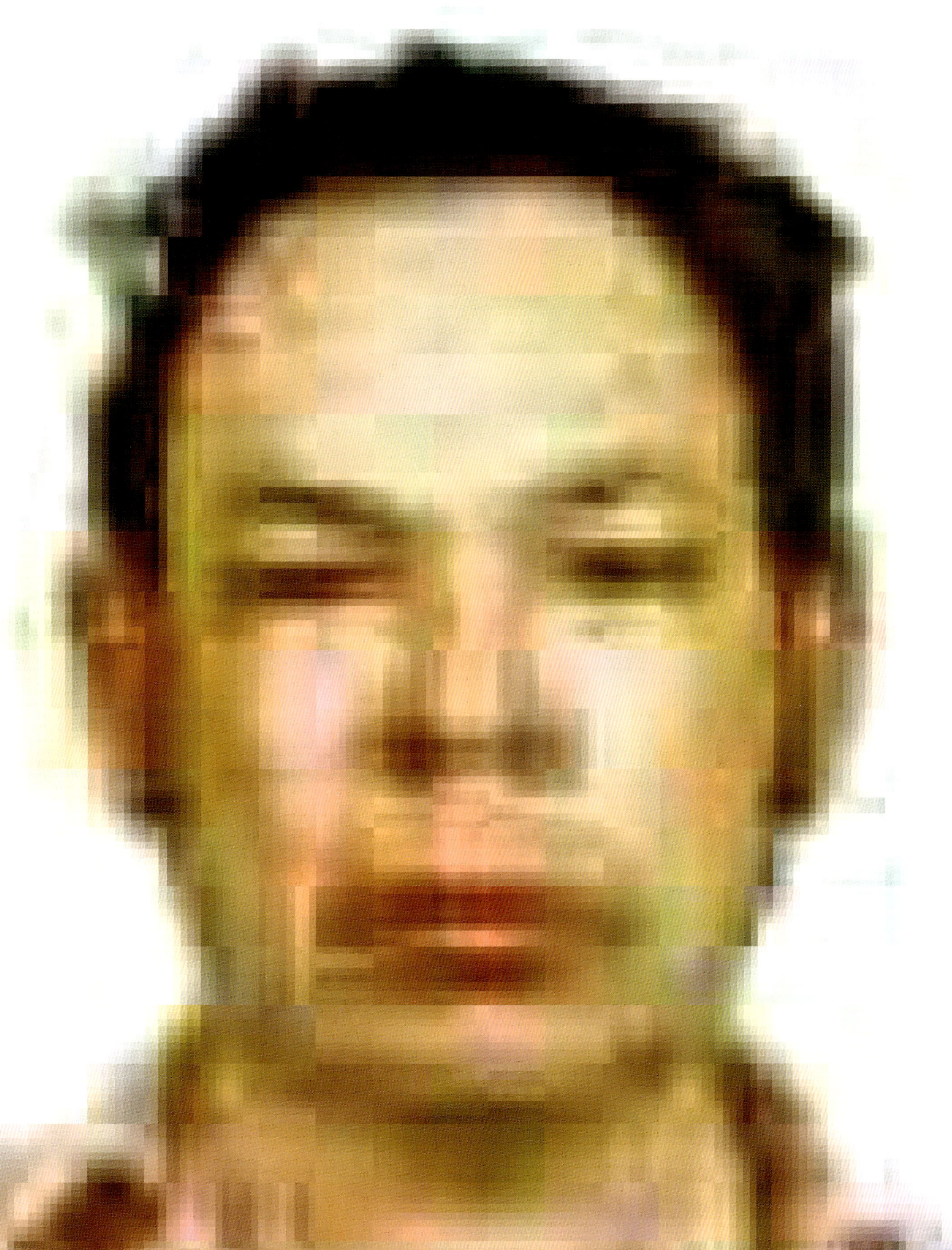

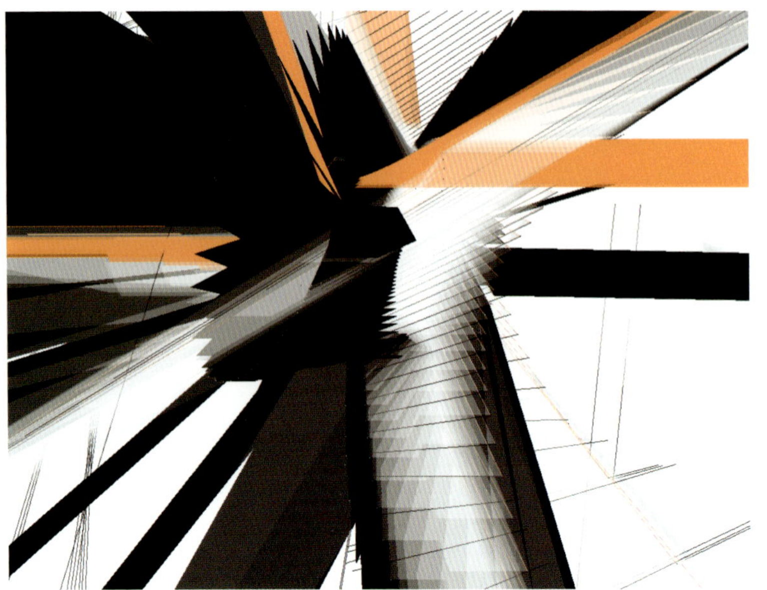

Lia
Re-move 09
Director
2002

041.001

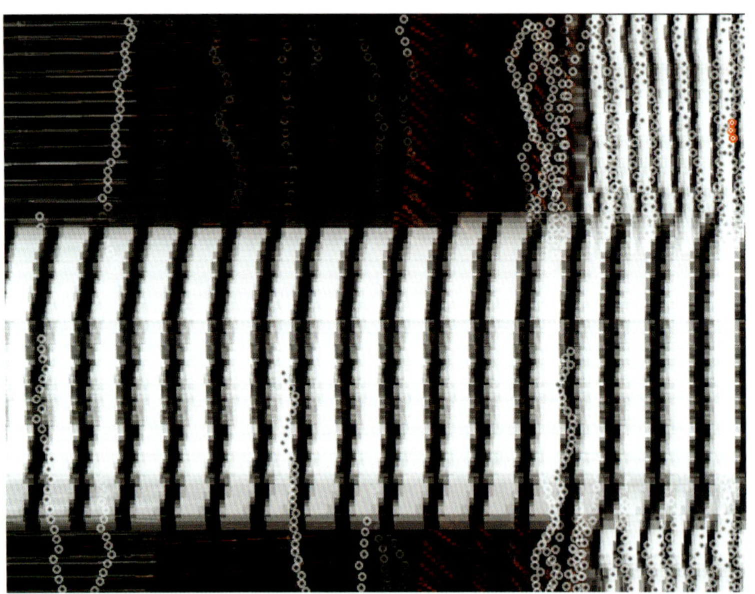

Lia + Miguel Carvalhais
LMLB03
Director
2003

042.001

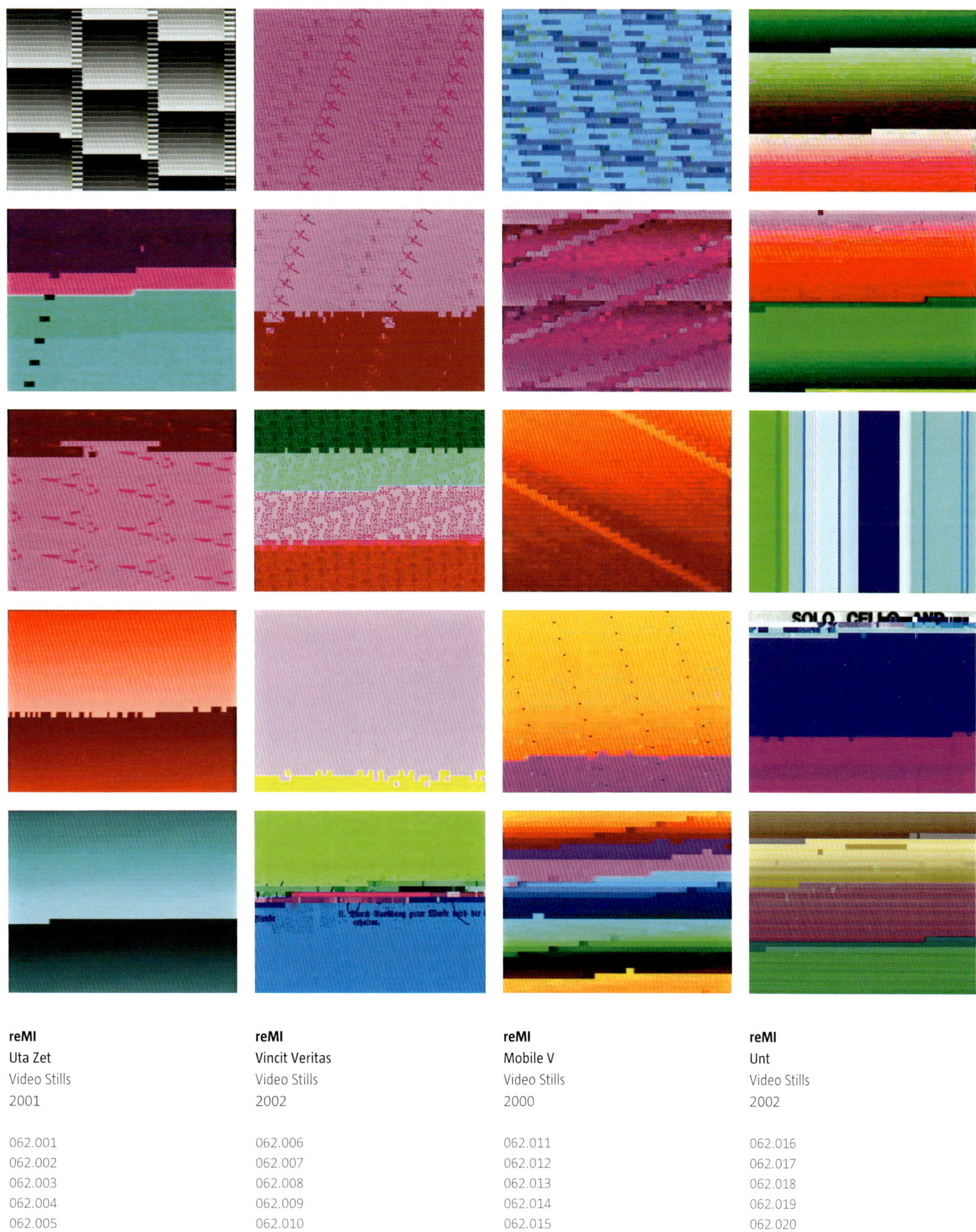

reMI
Uta Zet
Video Stills
2001

062.001
062.002
062.003
062.004
062.005

reMI
Vincit Veritas
Video Stills
2002

062.006
062.007
062.008
062.009
062.010

reMI
Mobile V
Video Stills
2000

062.011
062.012
062.013
062.014
062.015

reMI
Unt
Video Stills
2002

062.016
062.017
062.018
062.019
062.020

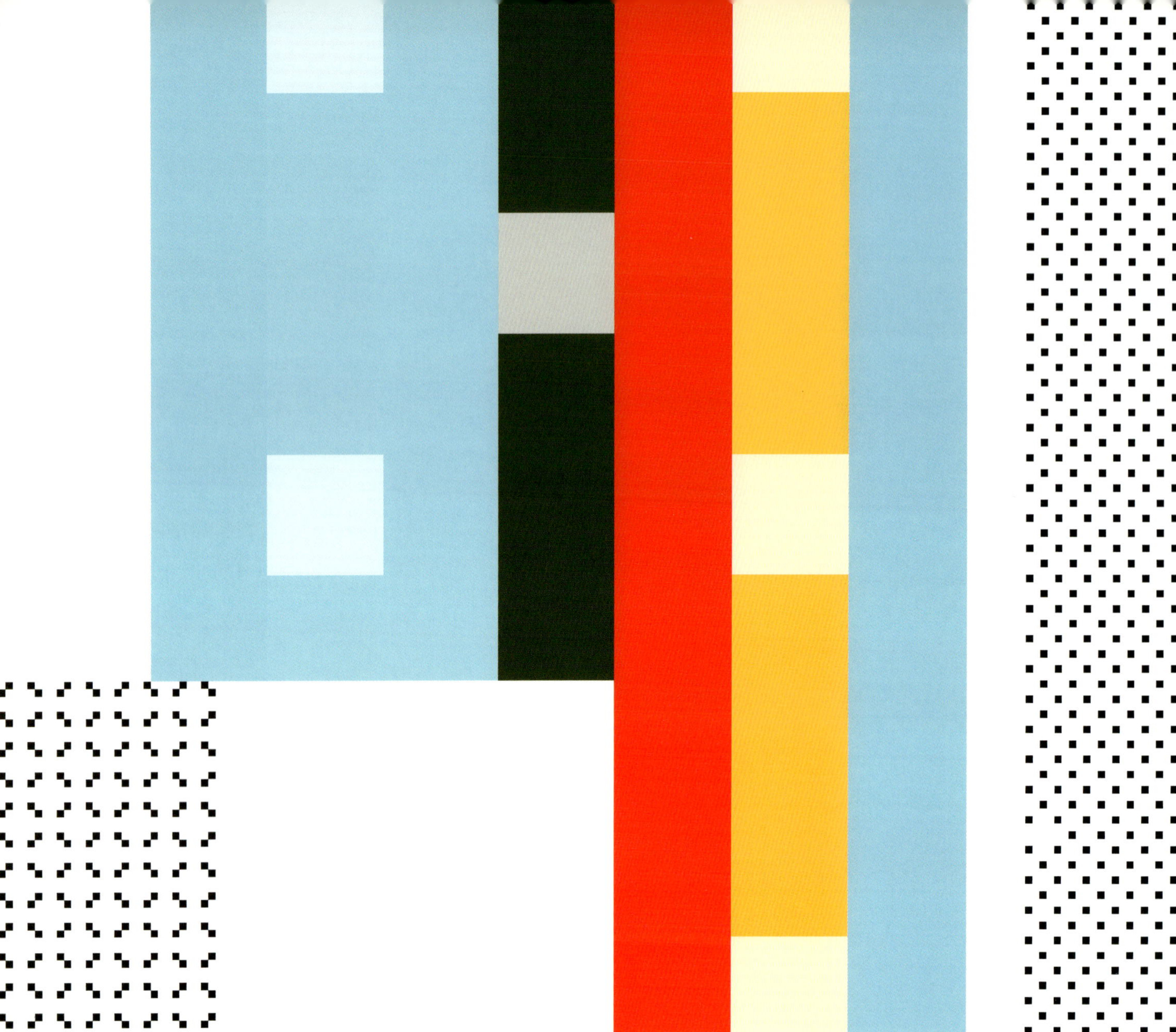

James Warfield / Wig-01
Glitch Pattern 8
Digital Image
2004

083.001

James Warfield / Wig-01
Glitch Pattern 2
Digital Image
2004

083.002

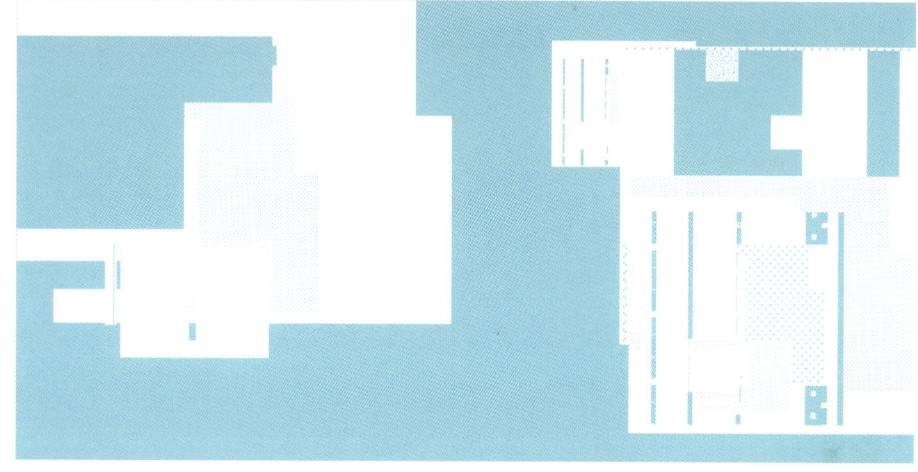

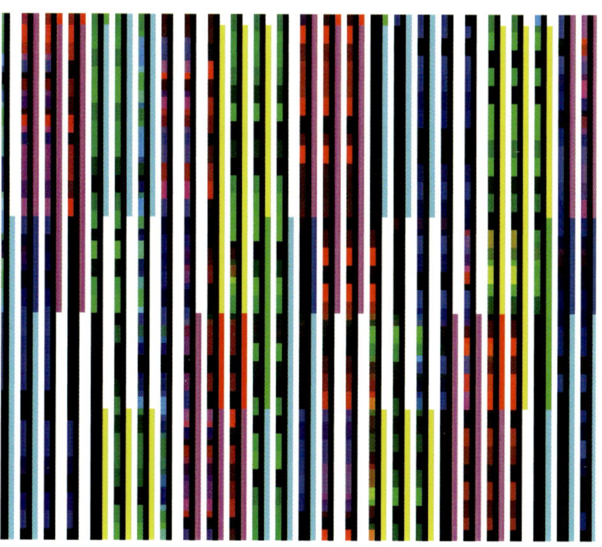

Ben Ullman
Technicolor
JPEG
–

081.001

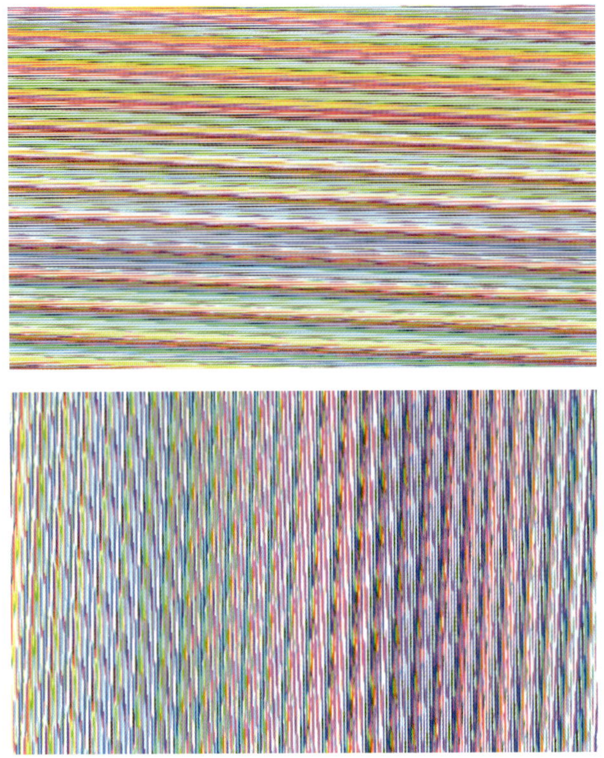

Yve Choquard
.raw-art #1
.raw-art #2
Digital Images
2004

010.001
010.002

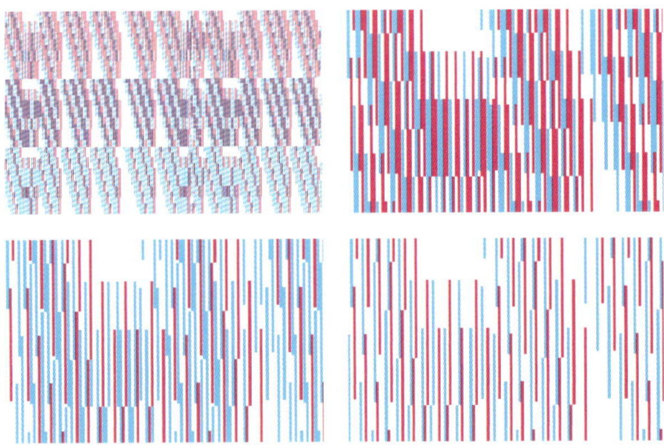

Daniel Althausen
RedBlue 1 - 4
Digital Images
–

002.001
002.002
002.003
002.004

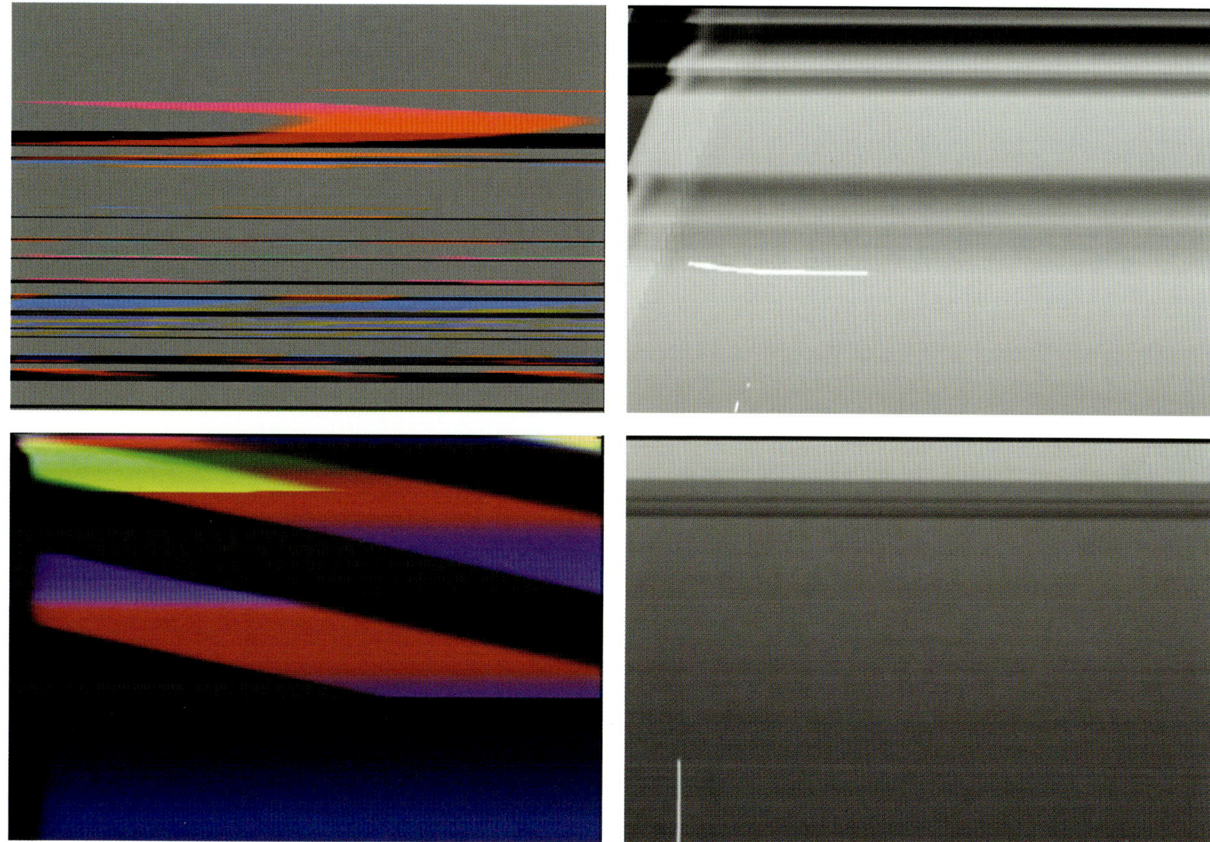

LoVid
Sync Armonica
Video Stills
2005

045.001
045.002

Karl Klomp
Family Glitch 1
Family Glitch 4
Video Stills
2006

039.001
039.002

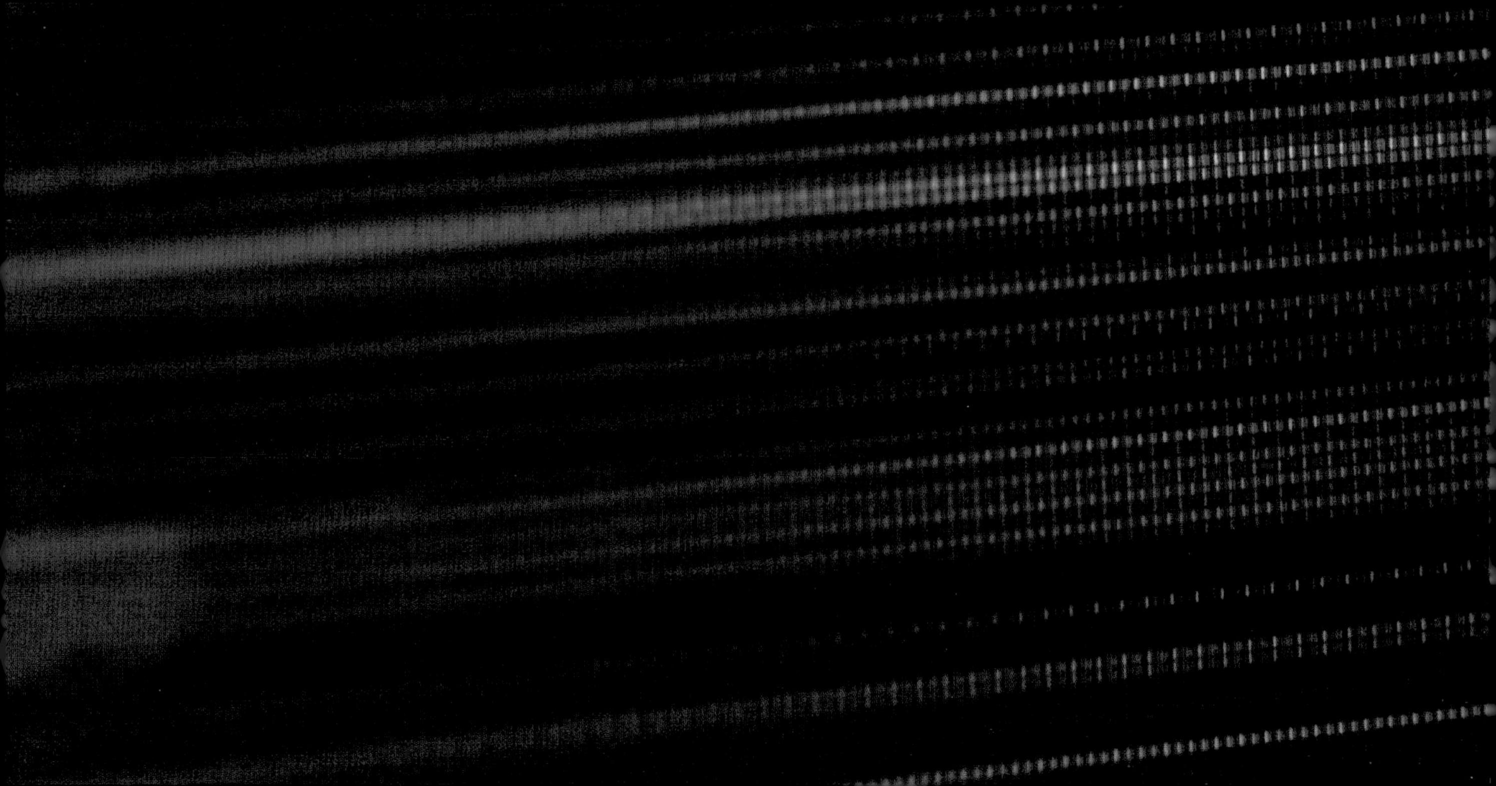

Iman Moradi
Expensive Paperweight
Digital Photograph
2007

052.001

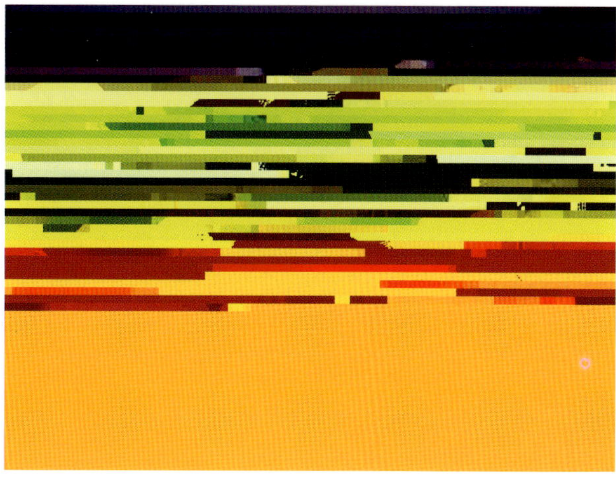

Iman Moradi
Examiner's Delight
Digital Image
2004

052.002

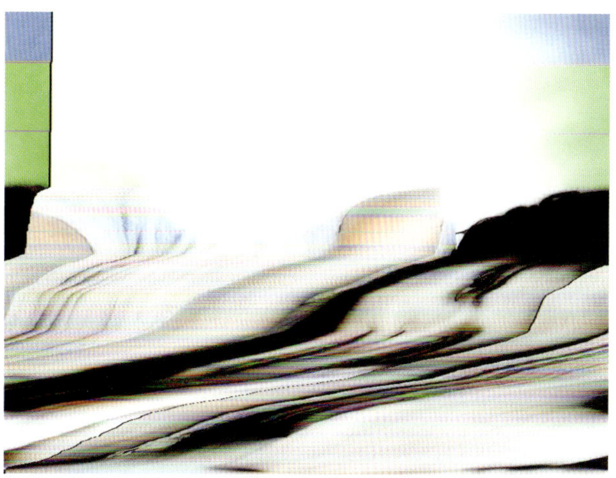

Iman Moradi
Hayek
Digital Image
2003

052.003

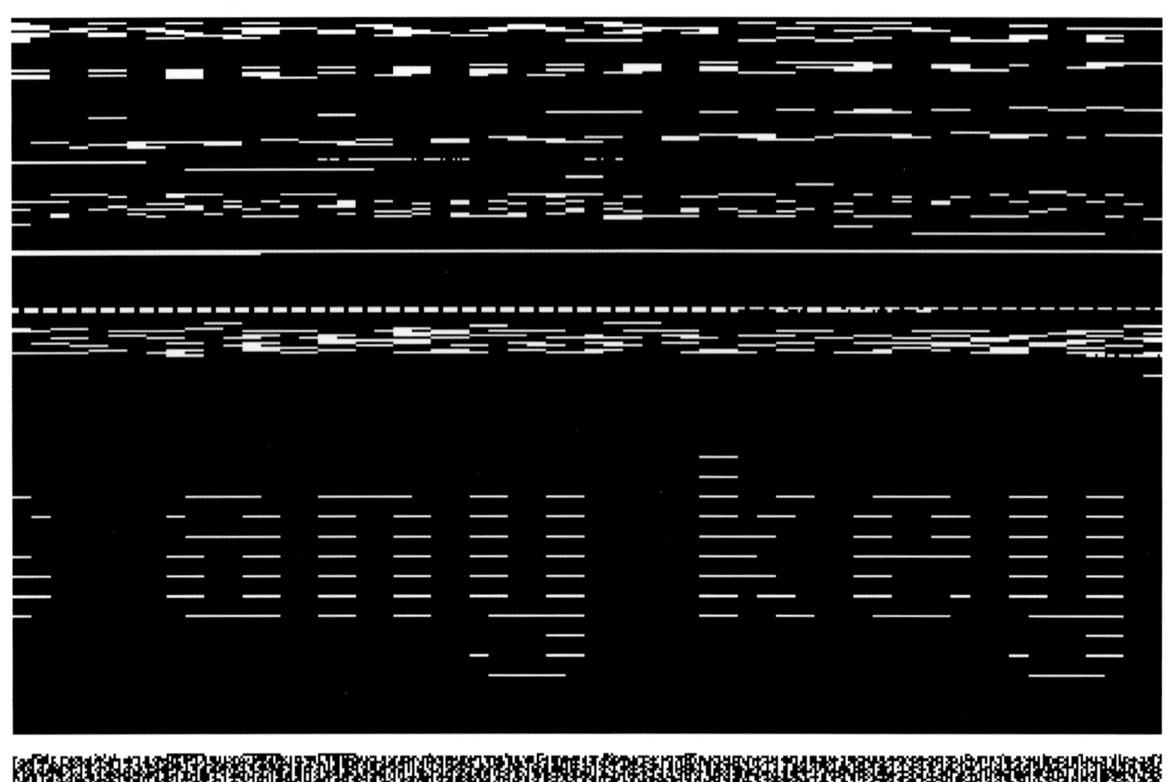

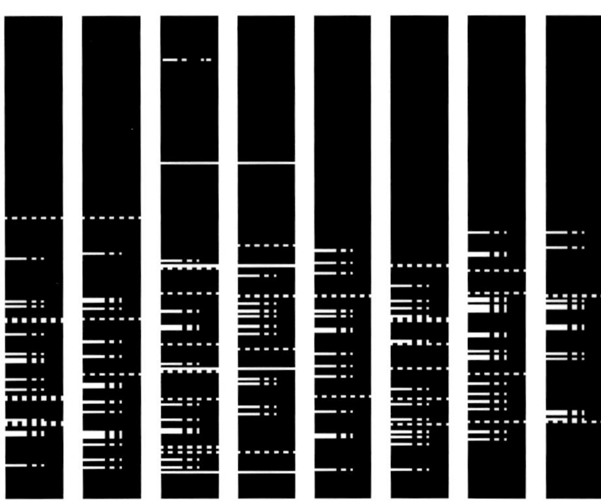

alorenz
procedure #09
Application
2001

001.001
001.002

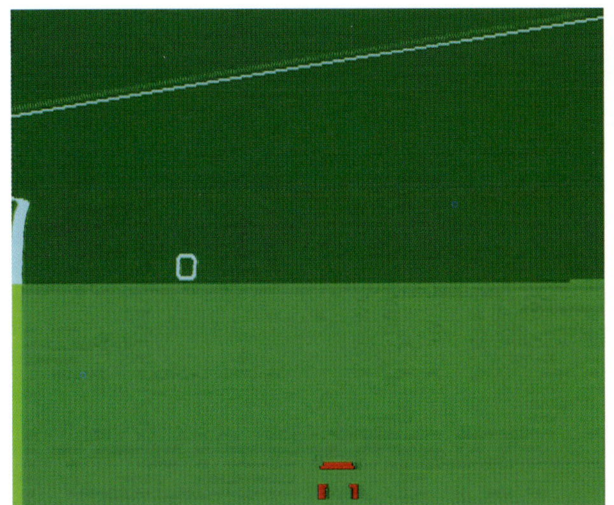

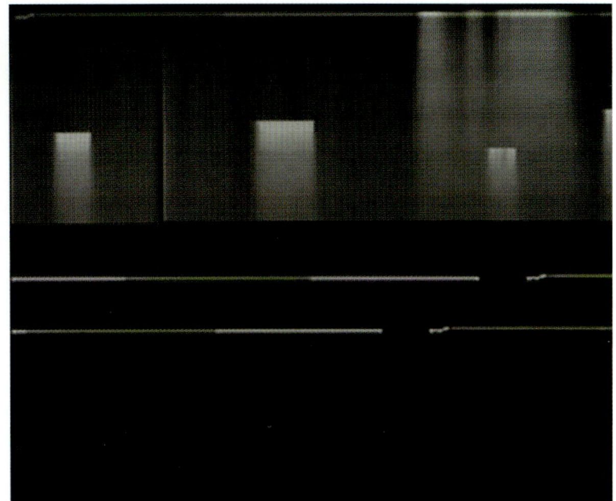

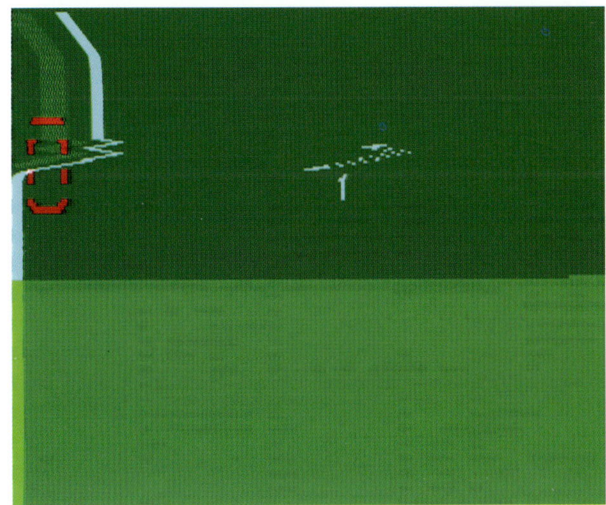

Karl Klomp
gr03
gr10
Video Stills
2006

039.003
039.004

Scott Arford
Static Room
JPEG
–

004.002

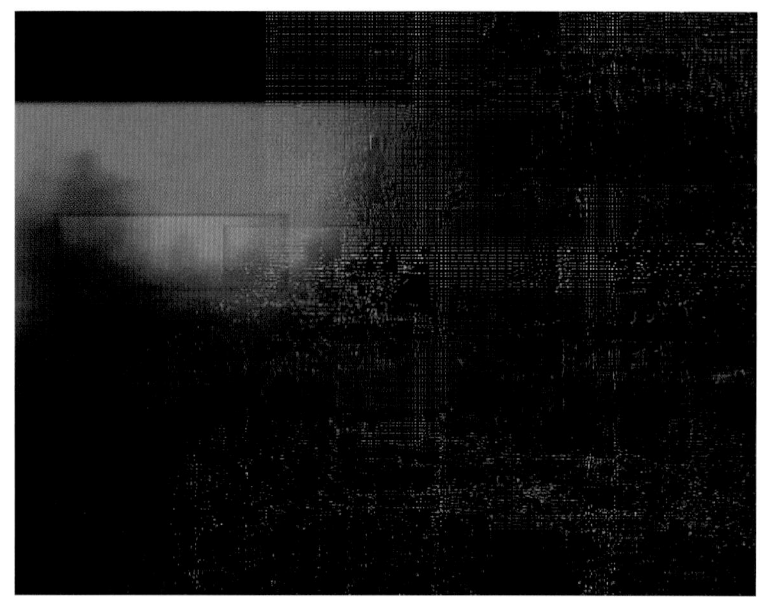

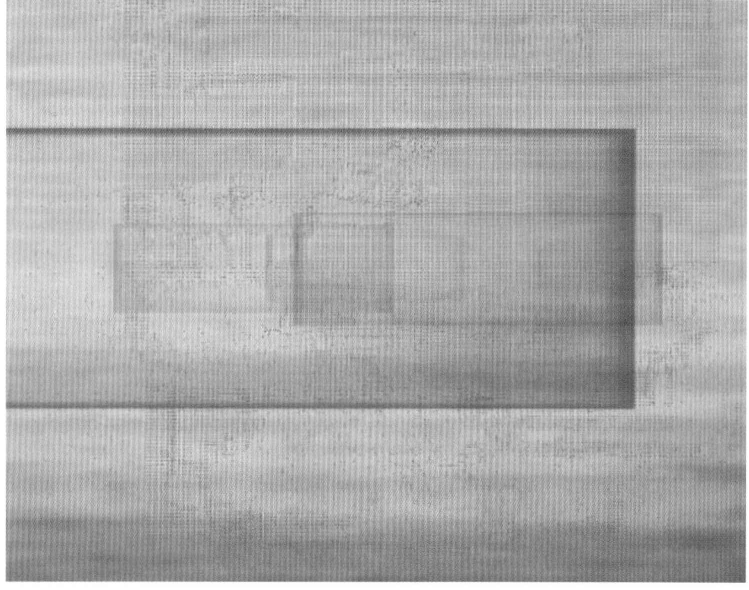

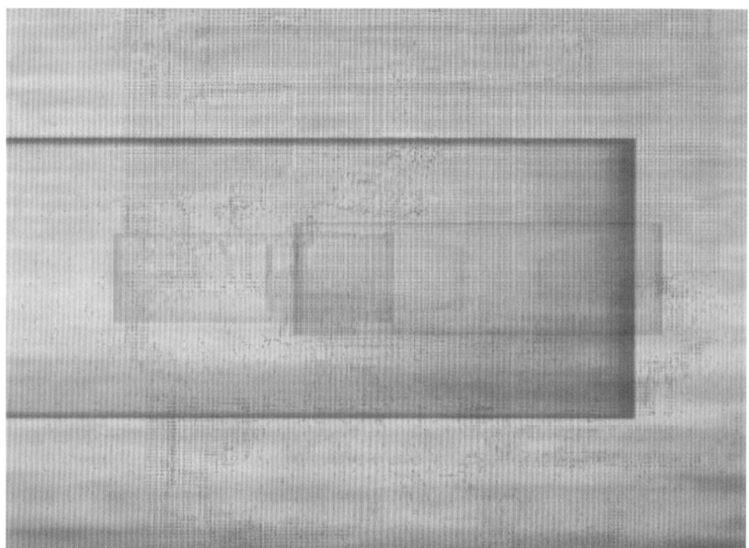

Rainer Kohlberger
What a Day!
Print
2004

040.001

U-Sun
Zeroth Stage
Digital Images
–

082.001
082.002

Luciano Testi Paul
BRNNGFRNTR Composition No108
Digital Image
2002

077.002

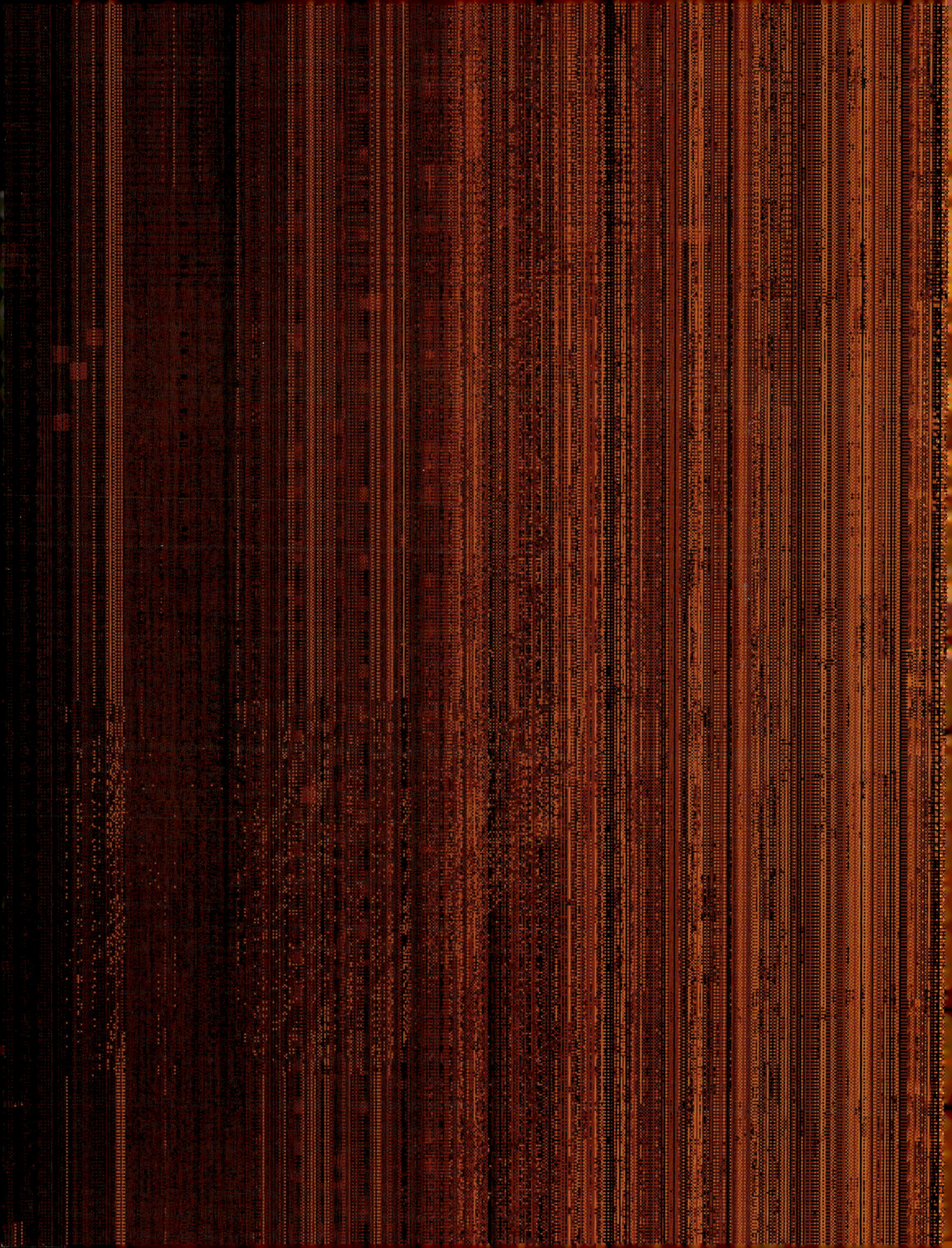

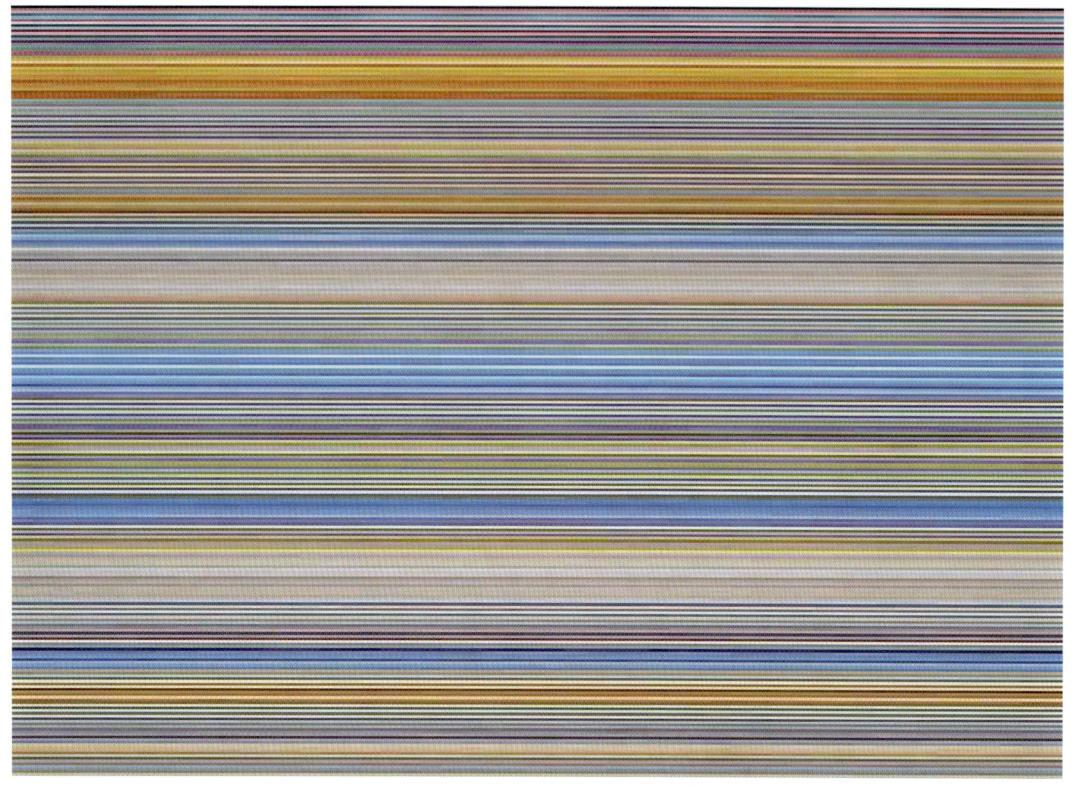

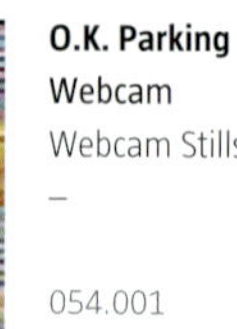

O.K. Parking
Webcam
Webcam Stills
–

054.001
054.002

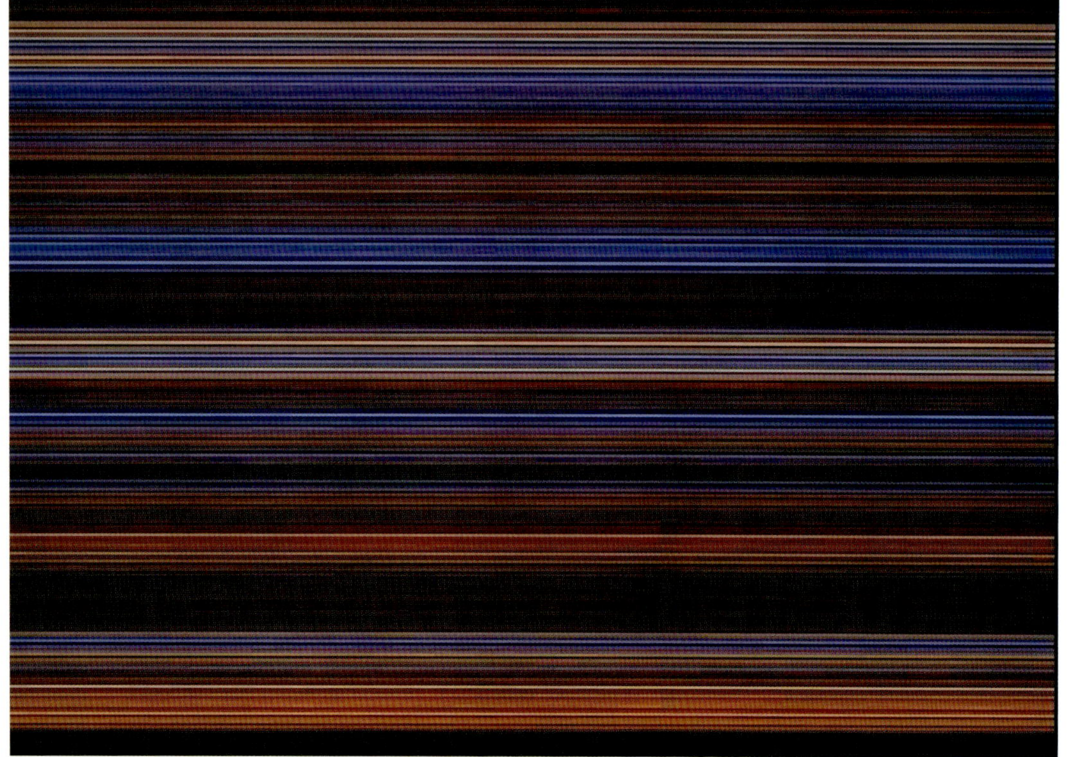

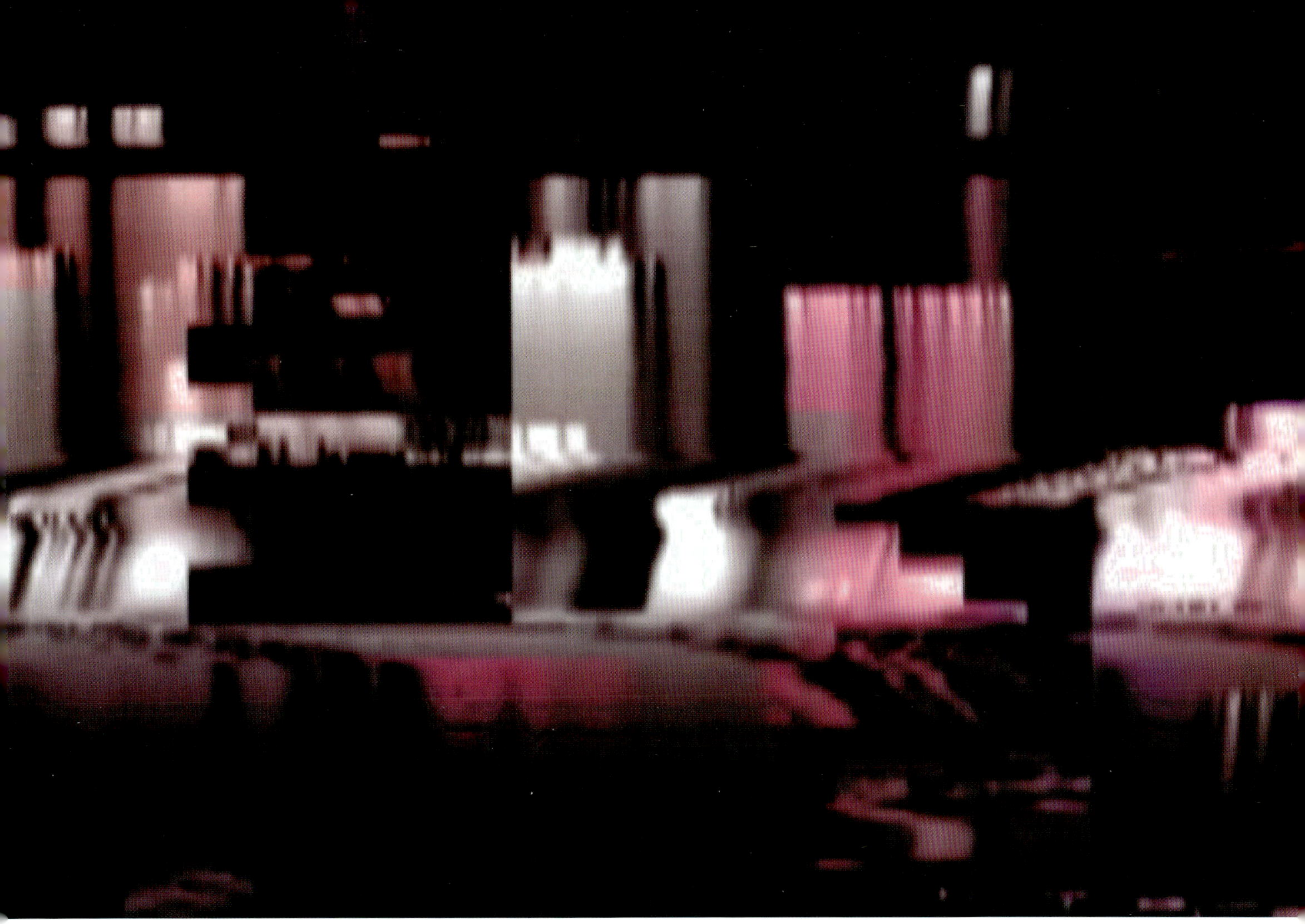

Michael Betancourt
September
Video Still
–

006.001

O.K. Parking
Monitor
Photograph
–

054.003

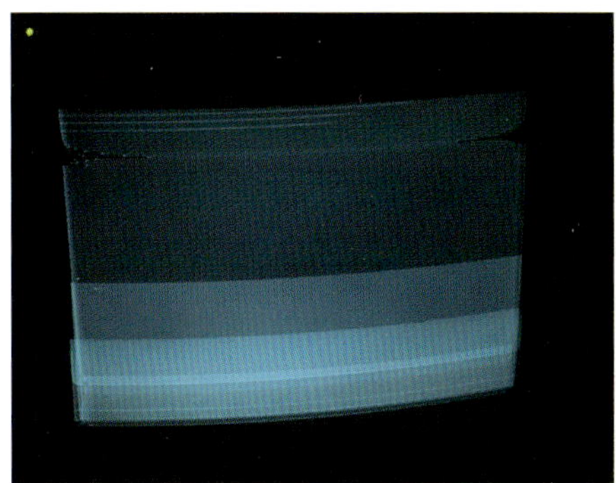

3

001.001
001.002
001.003
001.004
002.001
002.002
002.003
002.004
003.001
004.001
004.002
005.001
005.002
005.003
006.001
007.001
007.002
007.003
008.001
008.002
008.003
008.004
008.005
008.006
008.007
009.001
009.002
009.003
009.004
009.005
009.006
009.007
010.001
010.002
011.001
012.001
013.001
013.002
013.003
013.004
014.001
015.001
015.002
015.003

016.001
017.001
017.002
017.003
017.004
018.001
019.001
019.002
019.003
020.001
020.002
021.001
021.002
022.001
023.001
023.002
023.003
024.001
024.002
024.003
025.001
025.002
026.001
026.002
026.003
027.001
027.002
028.001
028.002
028.003
029.001
030.001
031.001
032.001
032.002
032.003
032.004
033.001
033.002
034.001
035.001
035.002
035.003
035.004

036.001
037.001
038.001
039.001
039.002
039.003
039.004
040.001
041.001
042.001
043.001
044.001
045.001
045.002
046.001
047.001
048.001
049.001
049.002
050.001
050.002
051.001
051.002
052.001
052.002
052.003
053.001
053.002
054.001
054.002
054.003
055.001
055.002
056.001
056.002
056.003
056.004
057.001
058.001
059.001
060.001
060.002
060.003
060.004

061.001
061.002
061.003
062.001
062.002
062.003
062.004
062.005
062.006
062.007
062.008
062.009
062.010
062.011
062.012
062.013
062.014
062.015
062.016
062.017
062.018
062.019
062.020
063.001
063.002
063.003
064.001
064.002
064.003
064.004
064.005
064.006
065.001
066.001
066.002
066.003
066.004
066.005
066.006
066.007
067.001
067.002
067.003
067.004

067.005
067.006
067.007
068.001
069.001
070.001
070.002
070.003
070.004
071.001
072.001
073.001
073.002
073.003
074.001
074.002
075.001
076.001
077.001
077.002
078.001
079.001
079.002
080.001
080.002
081.001
082.001
082.002
083.001
083.002
084.001
085.001
086.001
086.002
086.003

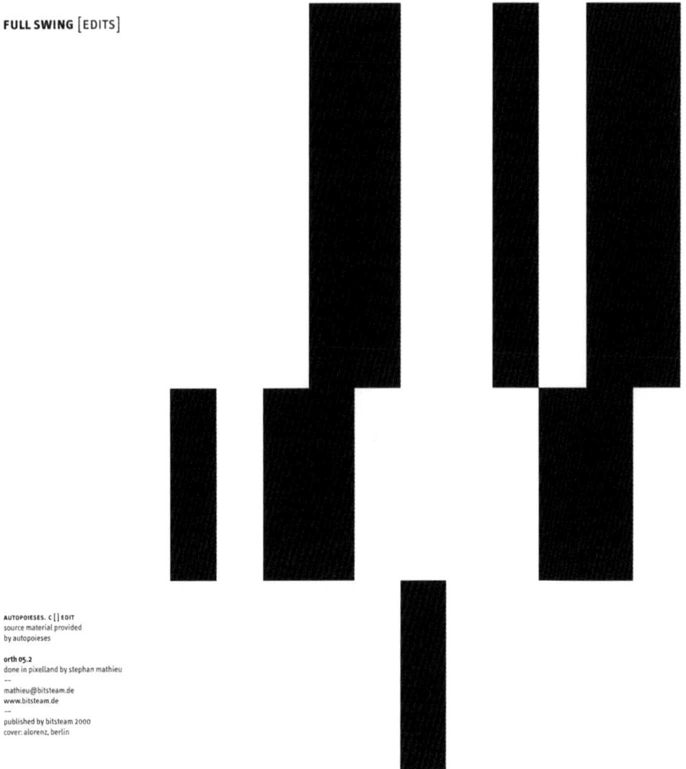

alorenz
Full Swing Edits
Record Cover
2001

001.003

alorenz
Full Swing Edits (detail)
Record Cover
2001

001.004

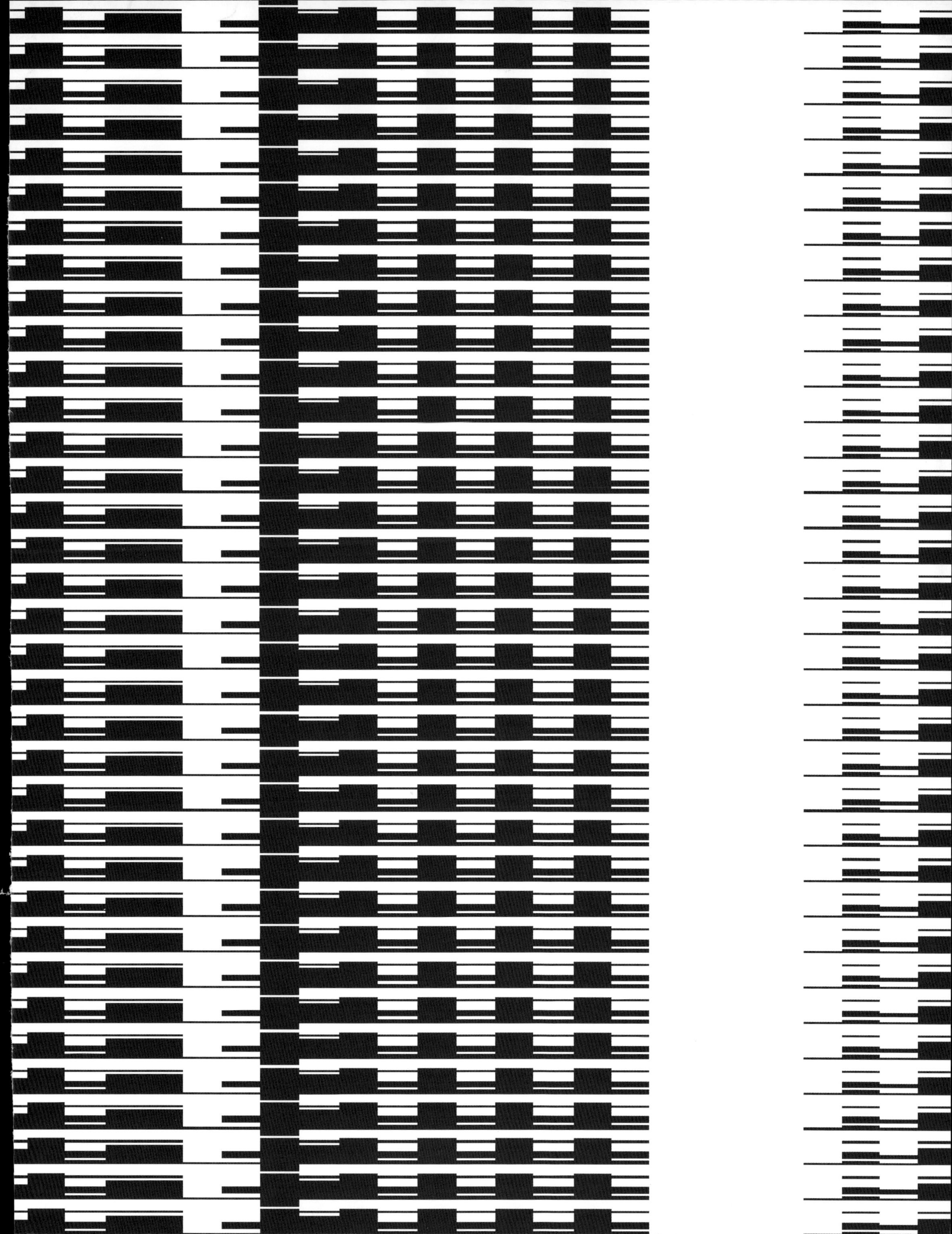

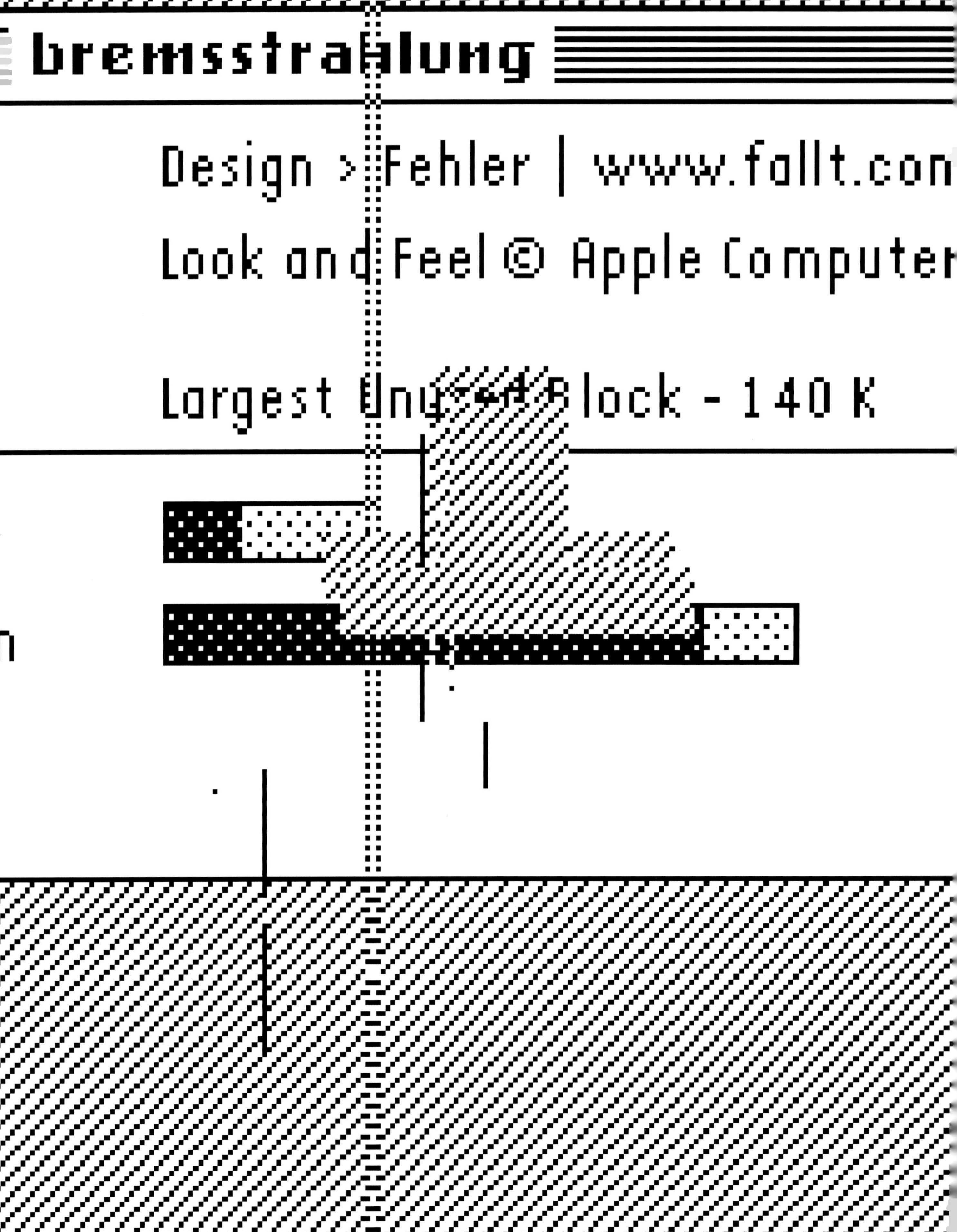
bremsstrahlung
Design > Fehler | www.fallt.co
Look and Feel © Apple Compute
Largest Unused Block - 140 K

Fehler
Bremsstrahlung Website
Website
2000

022.001

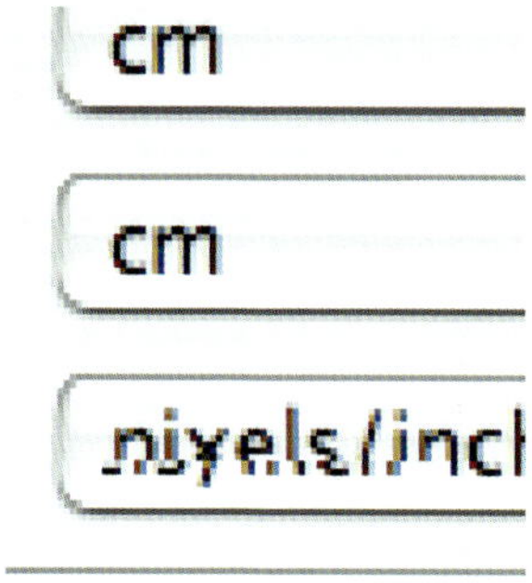

Fairchild Semiconductor
PPI (Detail)
Giclée Print
2007

069.001

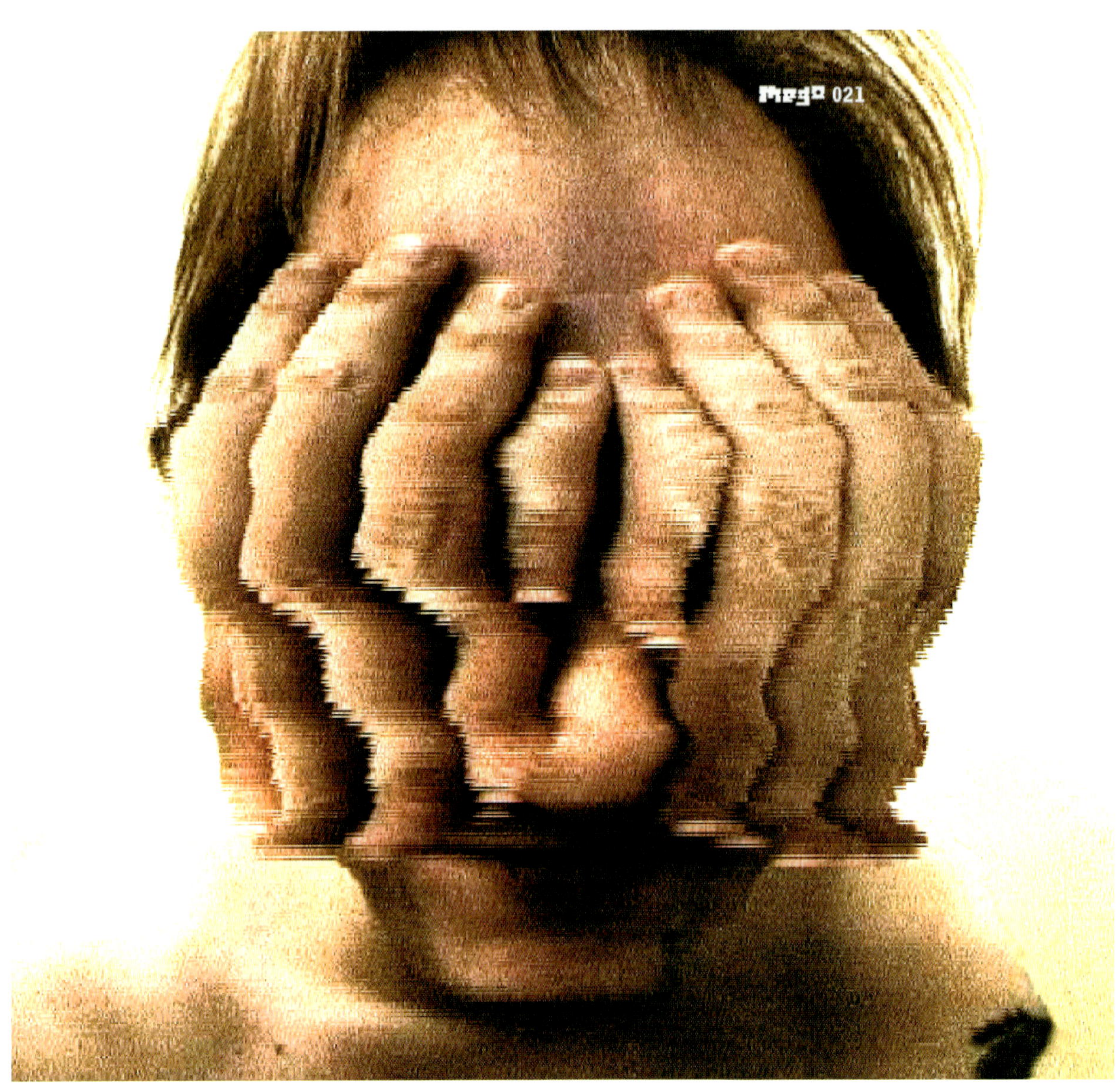

Mathias Gmachl
GCTTCATT: Amperase
CD Cover
2001

029.001

Skot (Tina Frank + Mathias Gmachl)
Aus
Video Still
1997

072.001

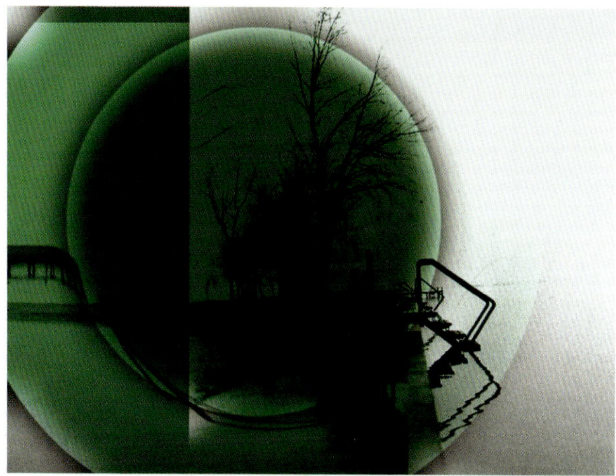

Billy Roisz
RagTag
Video Still
2006

065.001

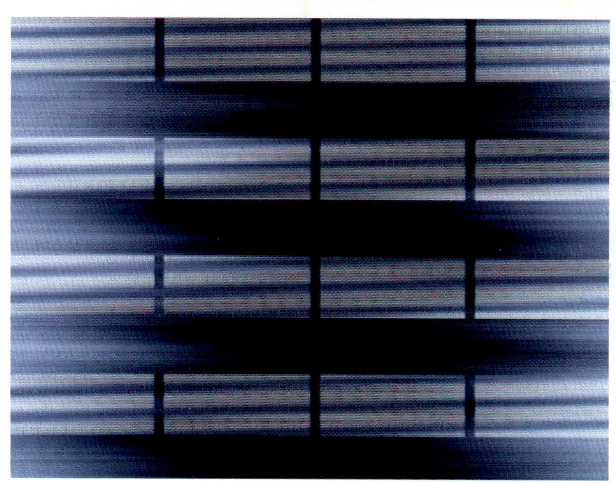

Steinbrüchel + Brusa
-00:dedaih
Mini CD-Rom Cover
2000

075.001

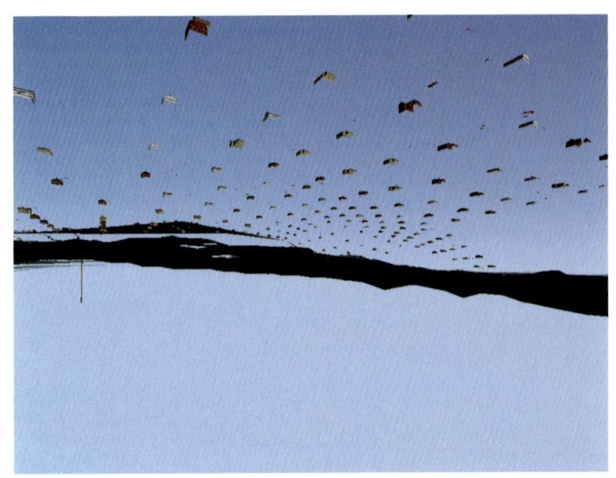

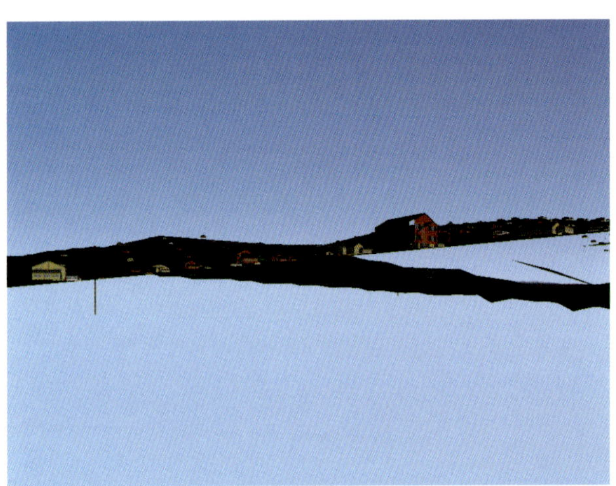

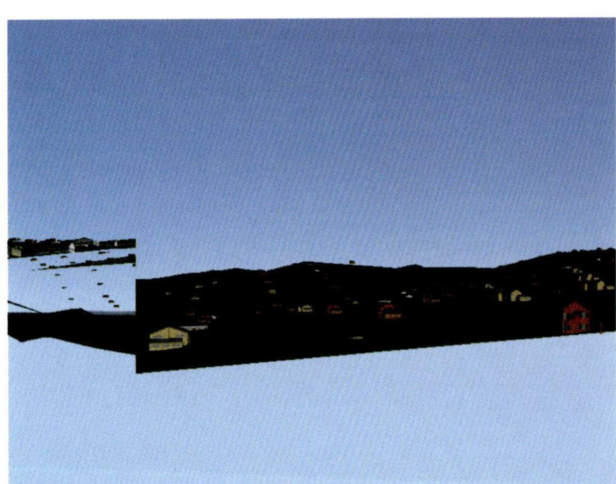

RetroYou
nostalG
Game Modification
2003

063.001
063.002
063.003

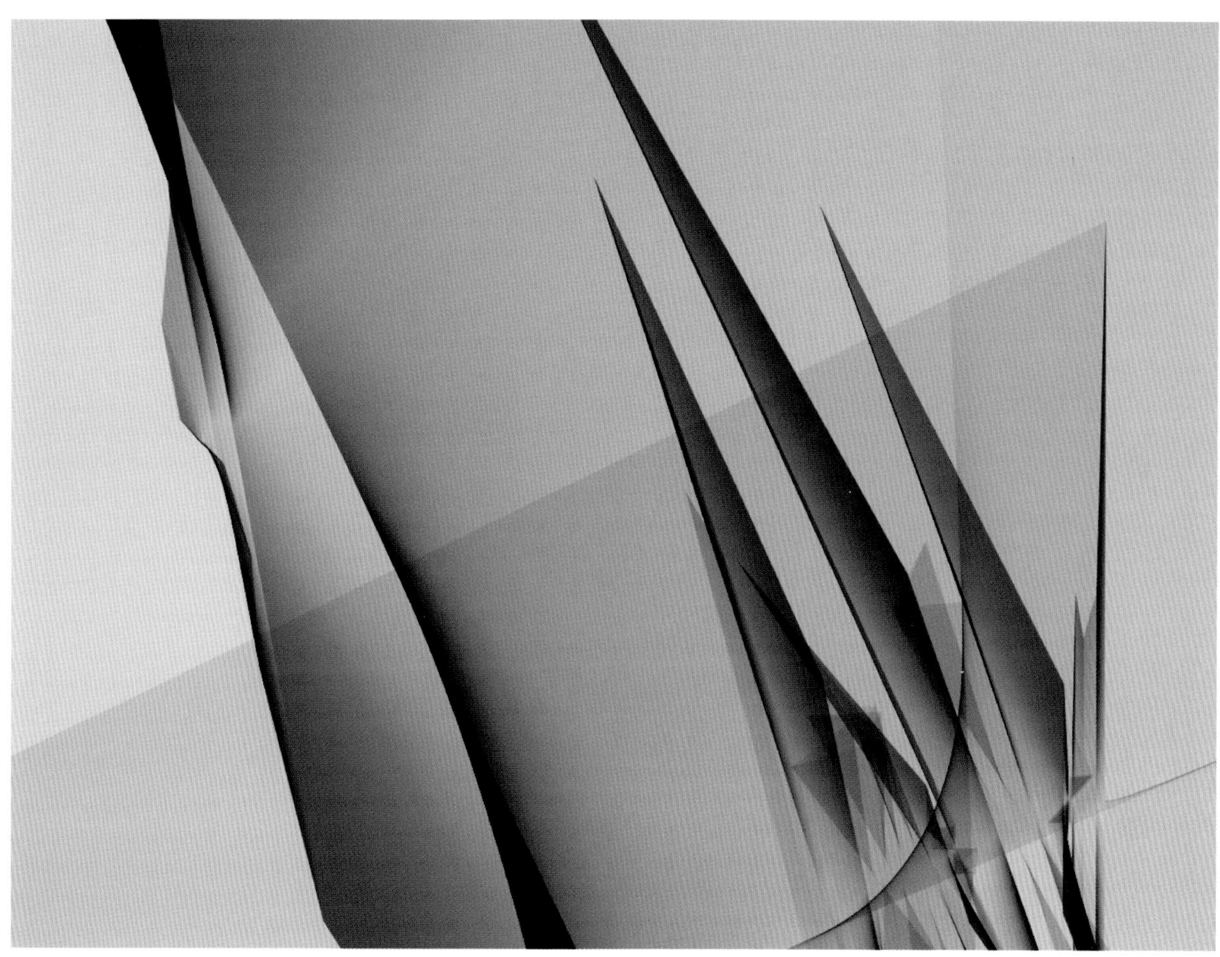

David Lu
Magnetic Fields on a Distant Trustworthy Star
Processing
2006

047.001

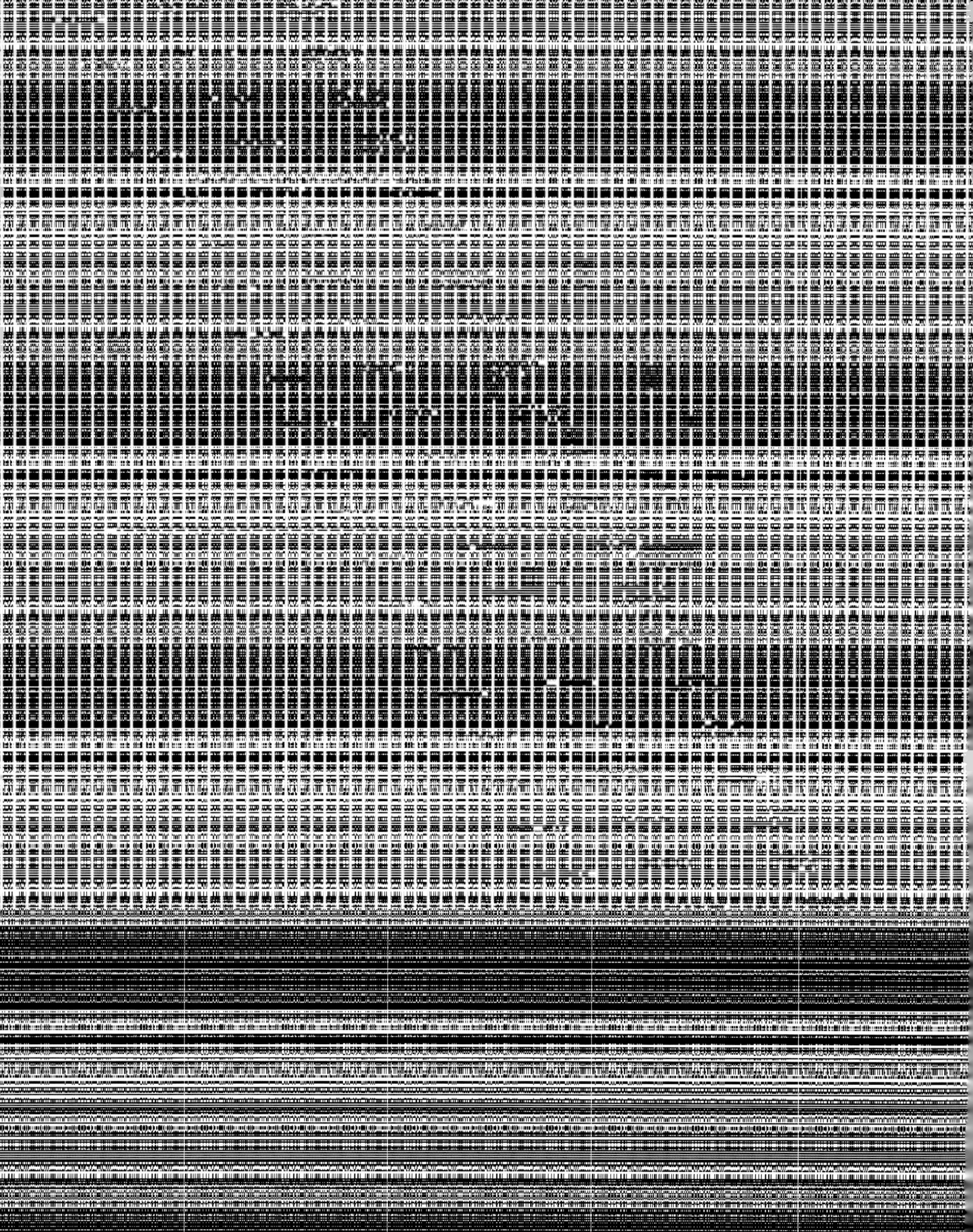

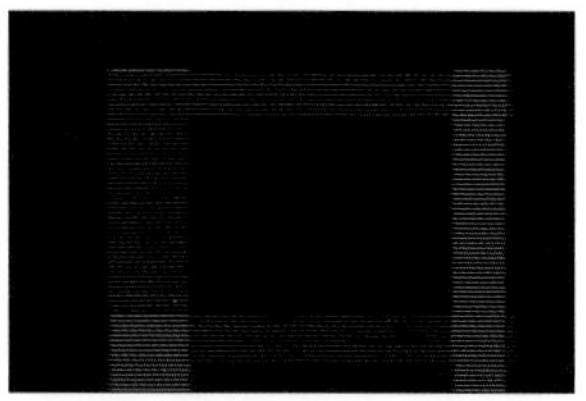
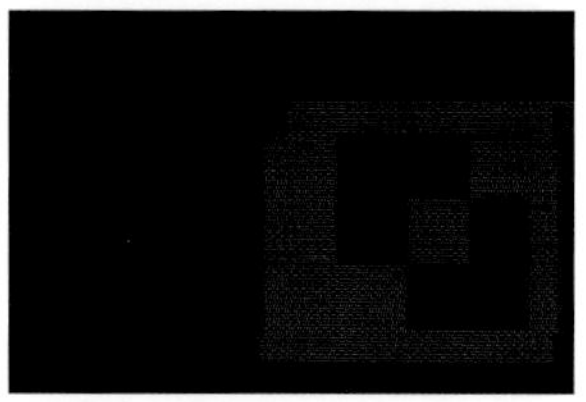
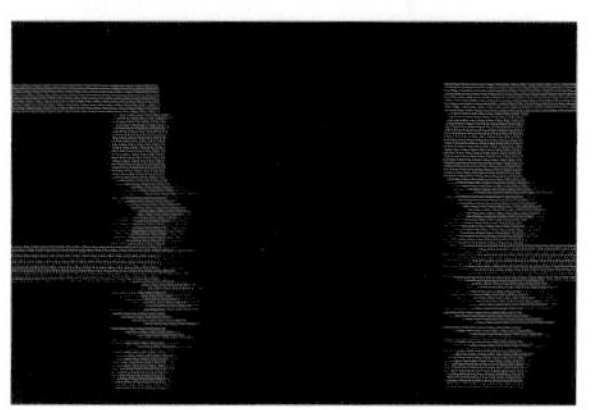

Curt Cloninger
Electronic Card (detail)
Screenshot
2003

011.001

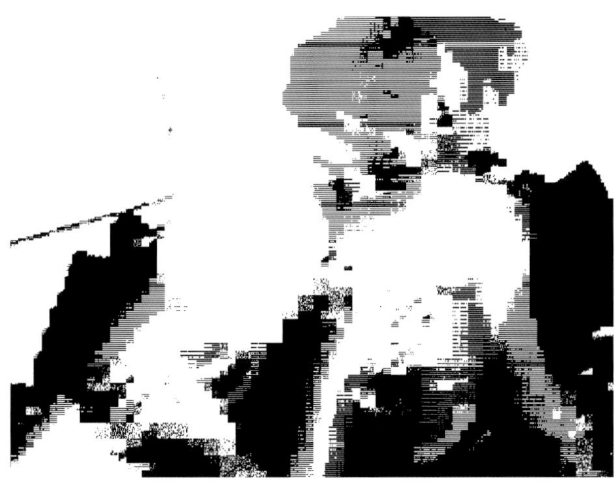

Scott Fitzgerald
PicTV
Video Stills
–

024.001
024.002
024.003

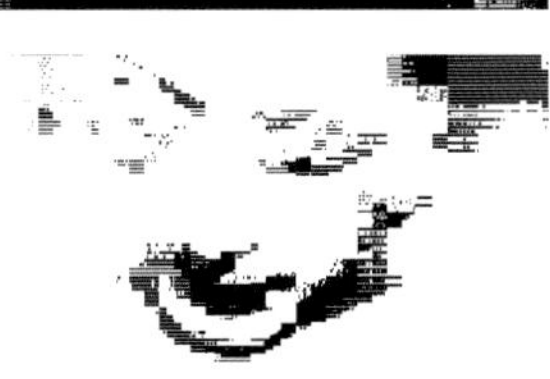
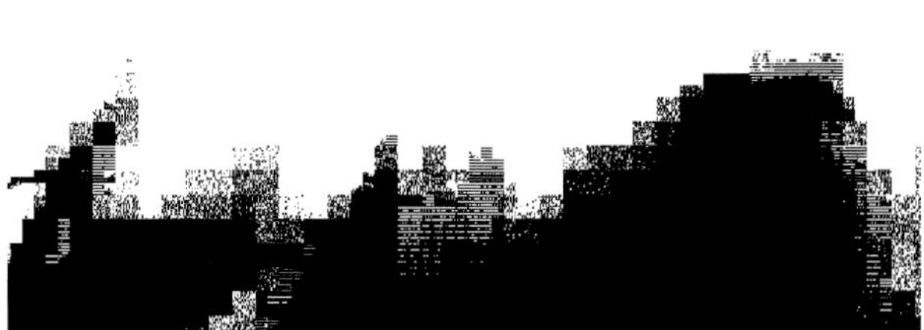

Roger Cosseboom
Waterloo
Video Stills
–

013.001
013.002

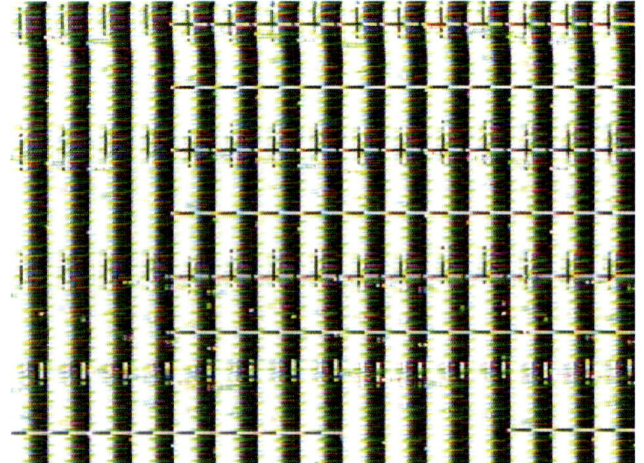

Ant Scott
Chroma 03
Screenshot
1984-2006

067.001

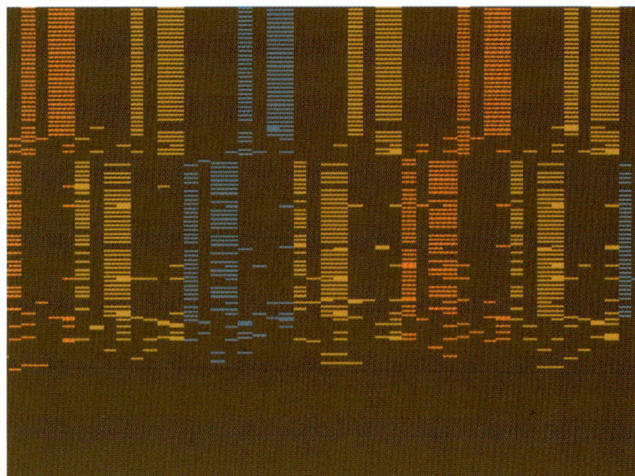

Ant Scott
Cookies
Screenshot
2001

067.002

Ant Scott
Skyscrapers
Luminogram
2005

067.003

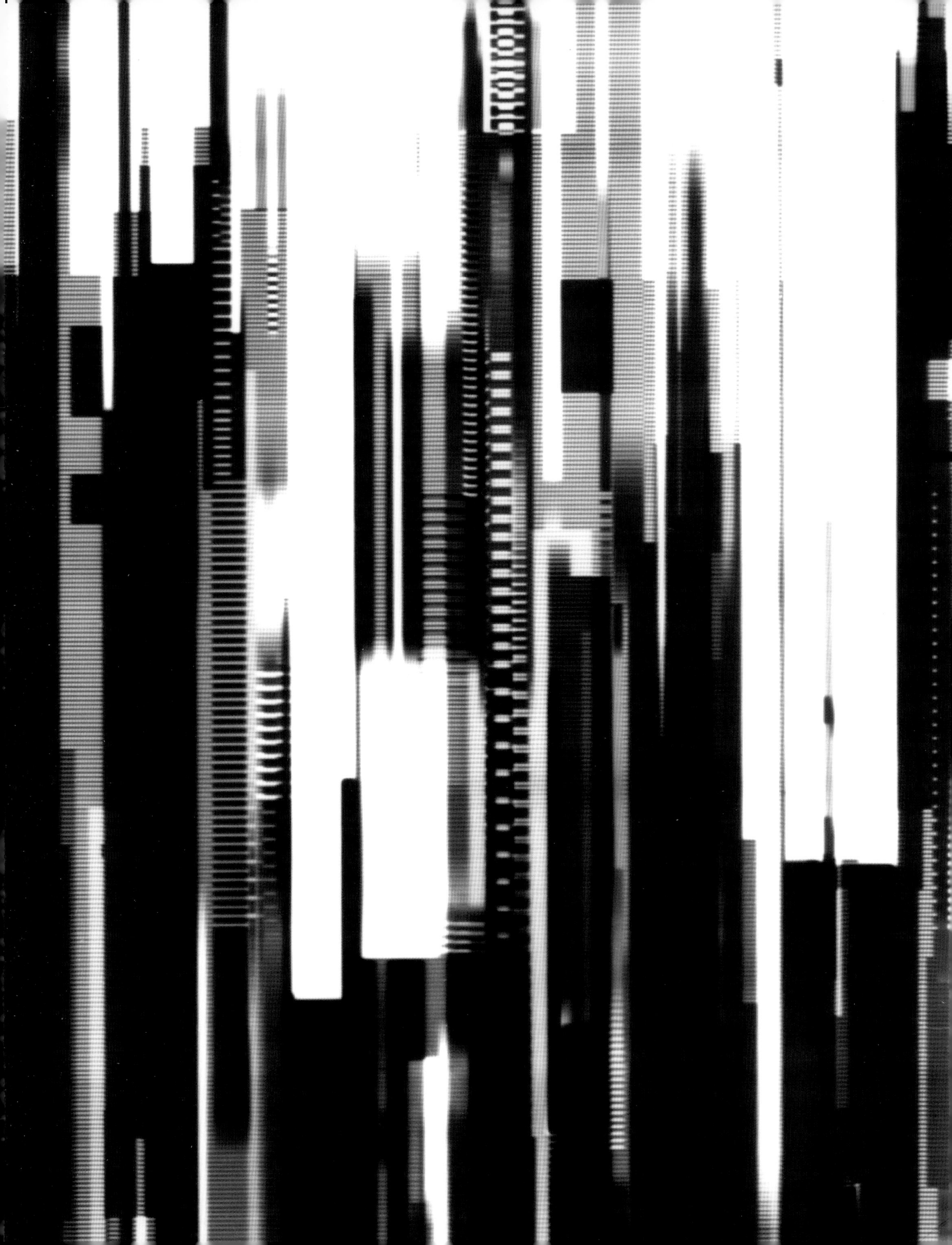

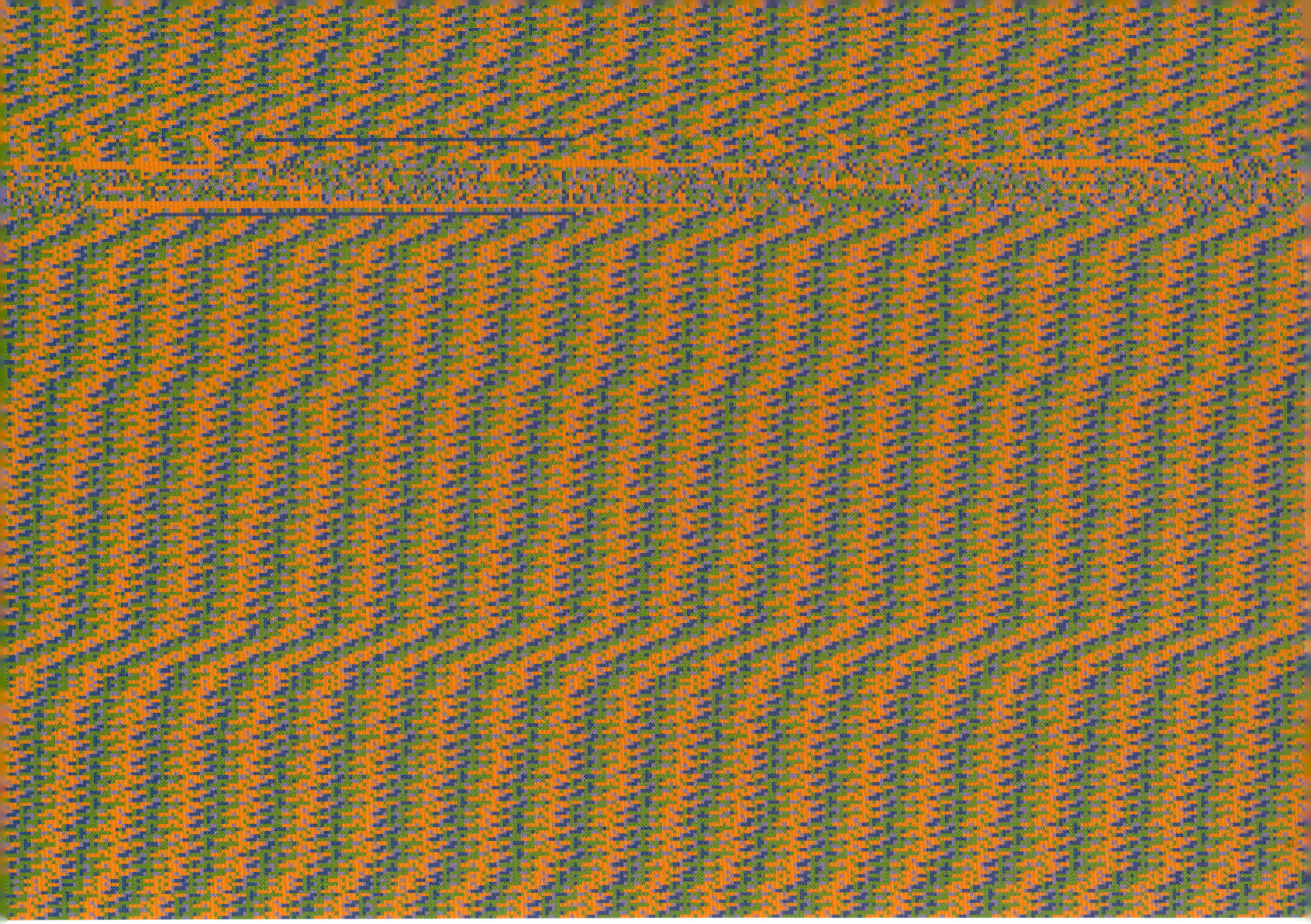

Ant Scott
Make 5 Not 4
Screenshot
2003

067.004

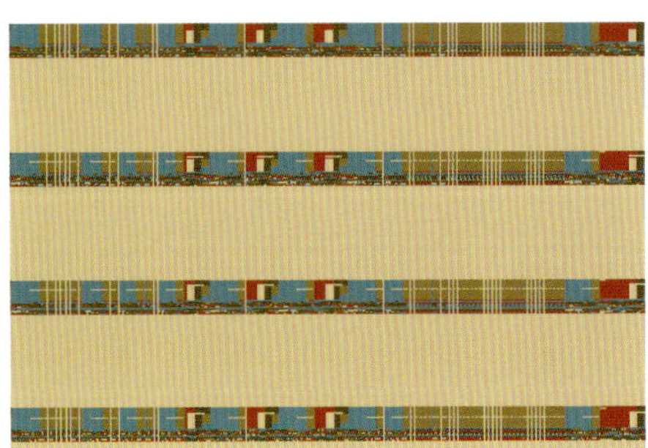

Ant Scott
Gique
Screenshot
2001

067.005

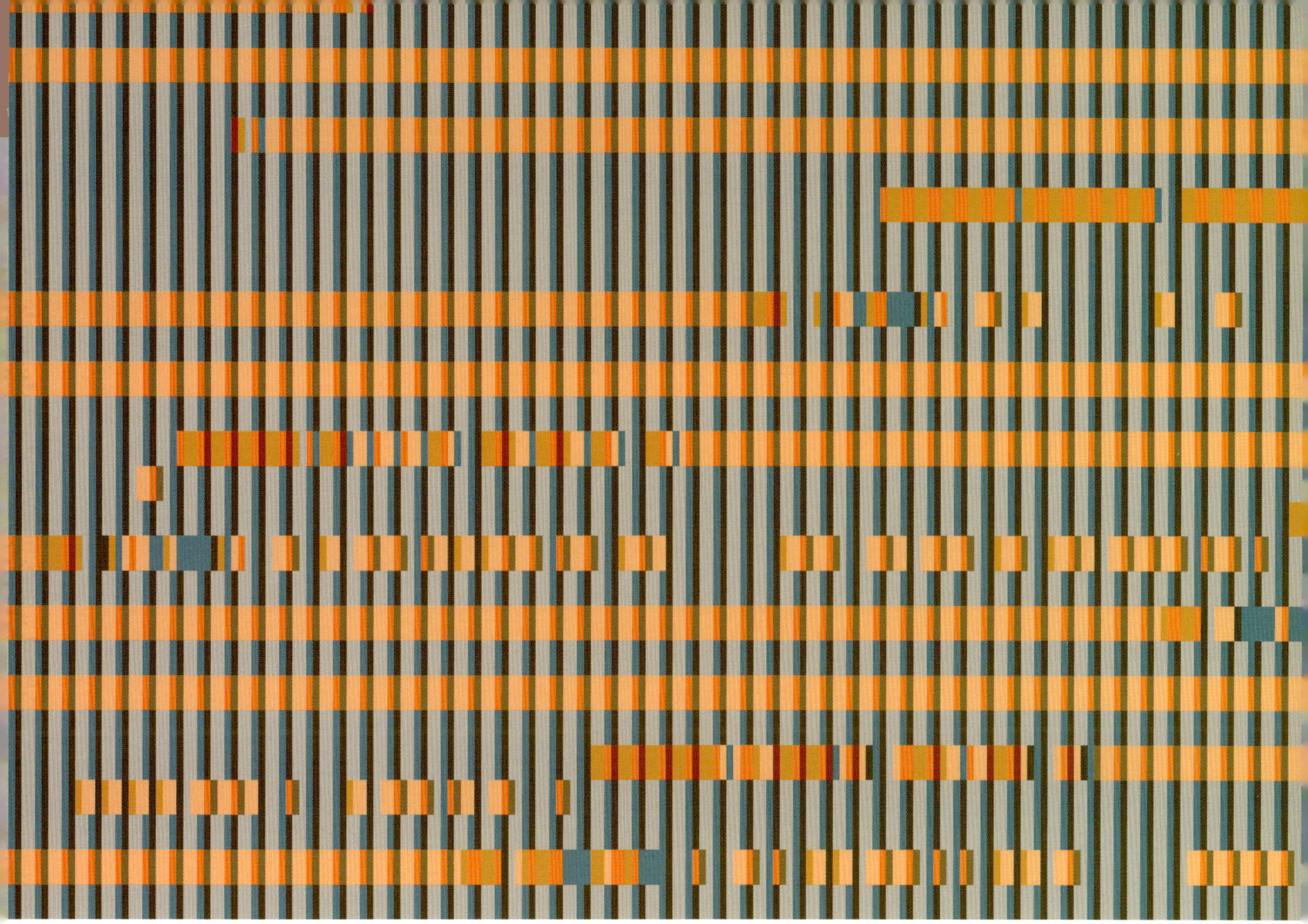

Ant Scott
Endemerol
Screenshot
2002

067.006

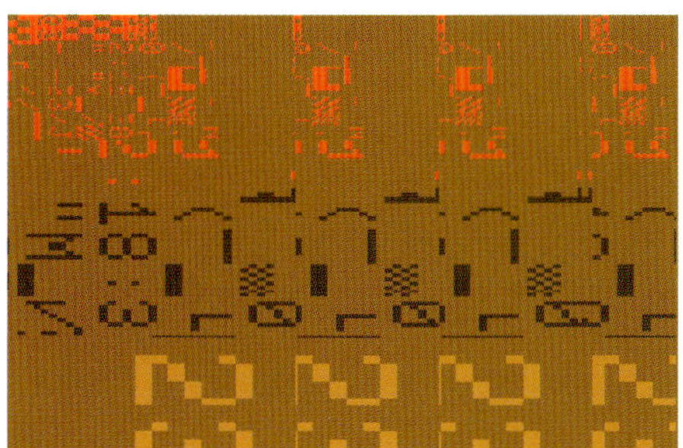

Ant Scott
Un Reith Flat Sip Peb Lyn
Screenshot
2003

067.007

Daniel Stanciu
Lake of Sound
GIF
–

074.002

Akihiko Yoshida
jpeg pulse #02
JPEG
–

086.002
086.003

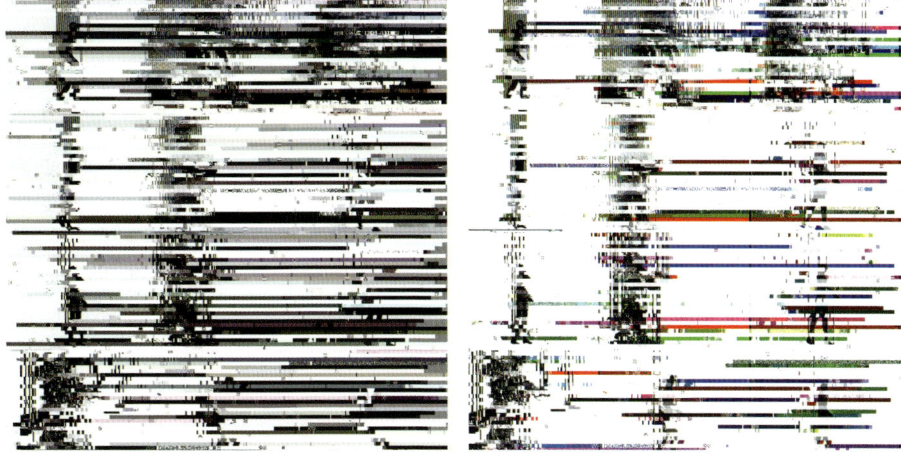

Kristiano Pronin
Warhol Failure (detail)
JPEG
2004

059.001

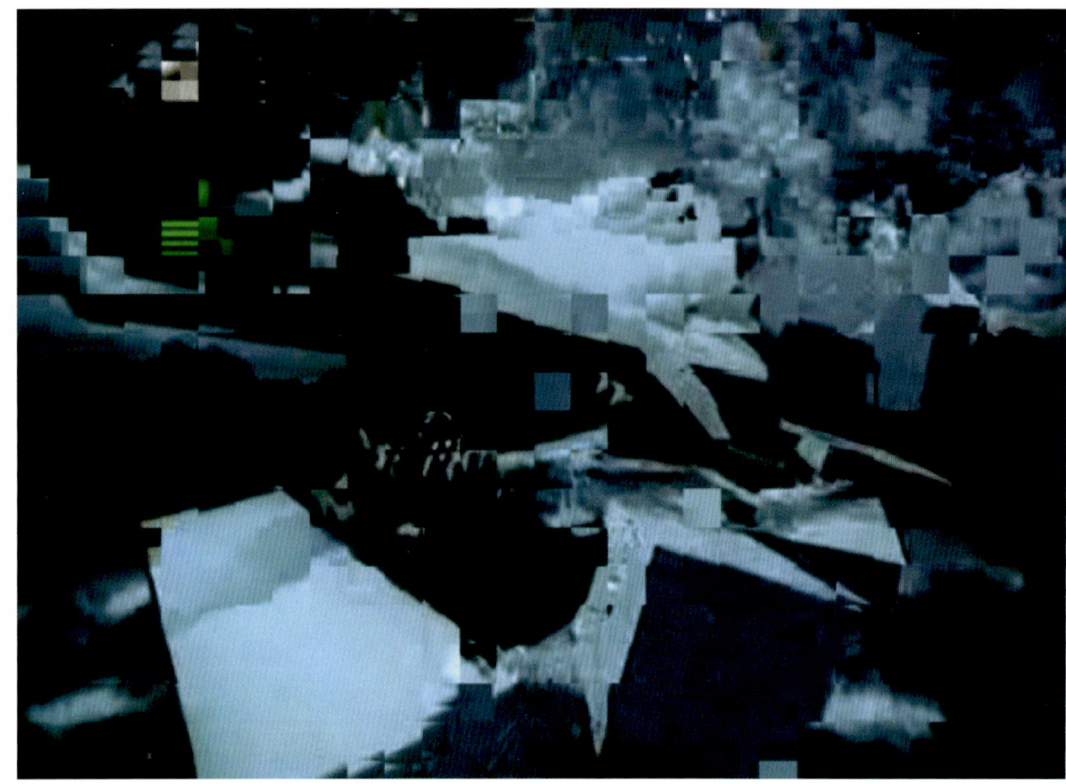

Roger Cosseboom
Untitled
Max/MSP/Jitter
–

013.003

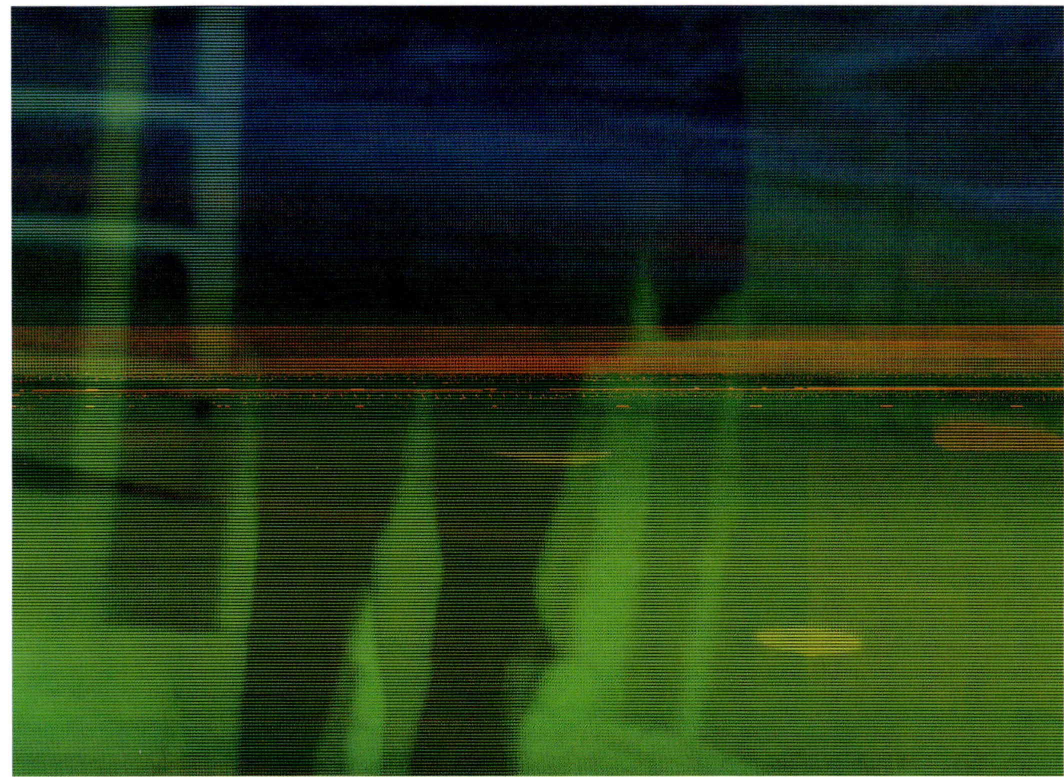

Rob Lycett
Intersculpt
Digital Image
2003

046.001

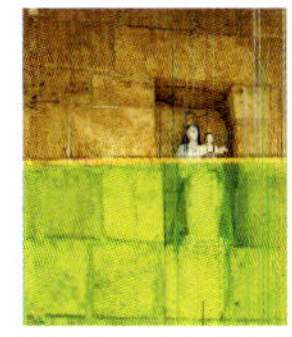

Hamish McDougall
Mary
Digital Photograph
–

049.001

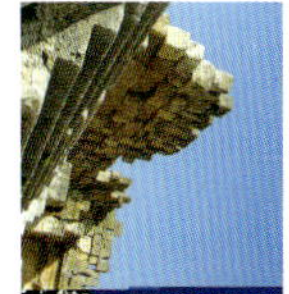

Hamish McDougall
Mountain
Digital Photograph
–

049.002

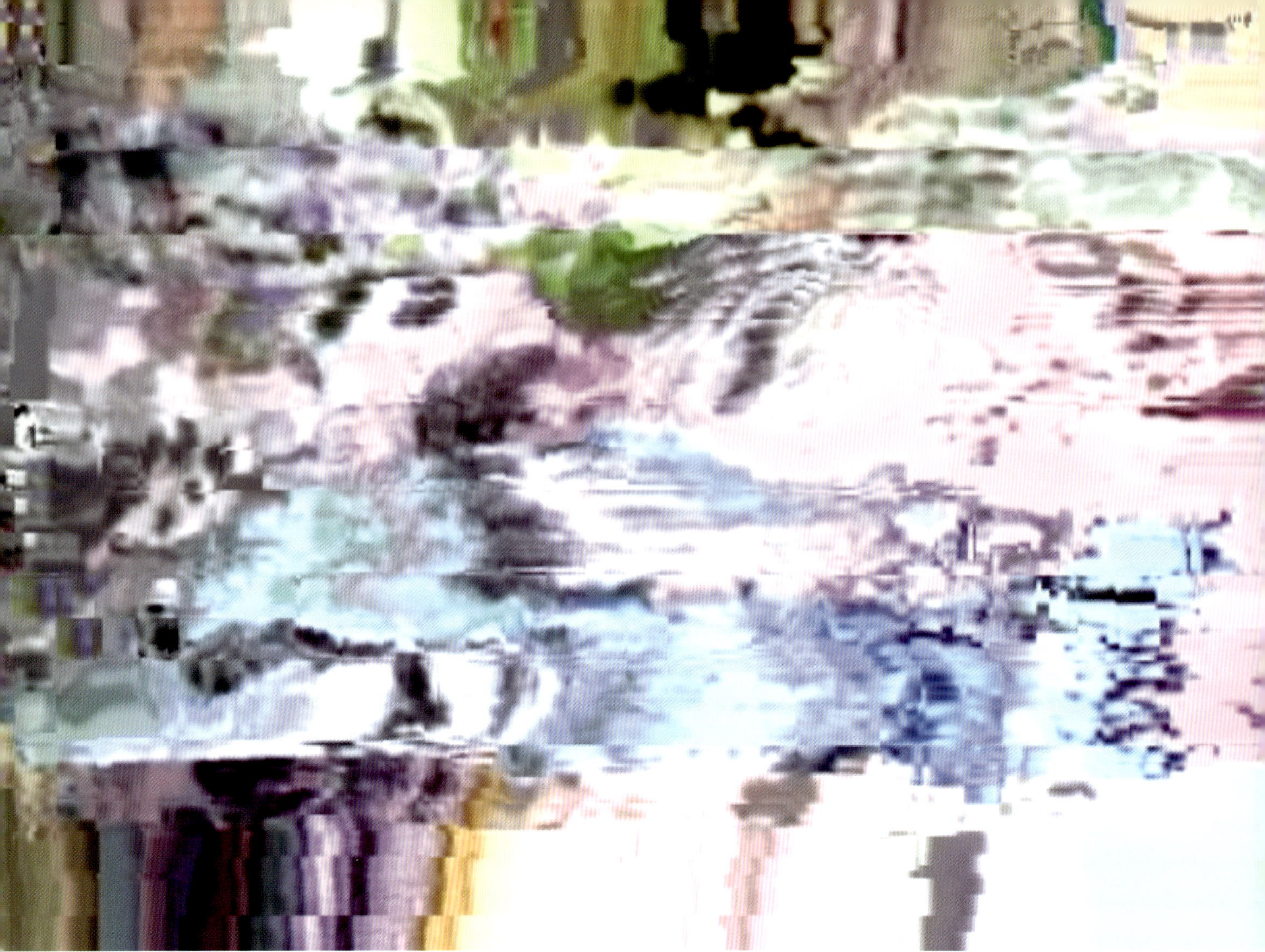

Roger Cosseboom
Untitled
Max/MSP/Jitter
–

013.004

Alessandro Canova
Glitch Runner (detail)
Video Still
2004

009.001

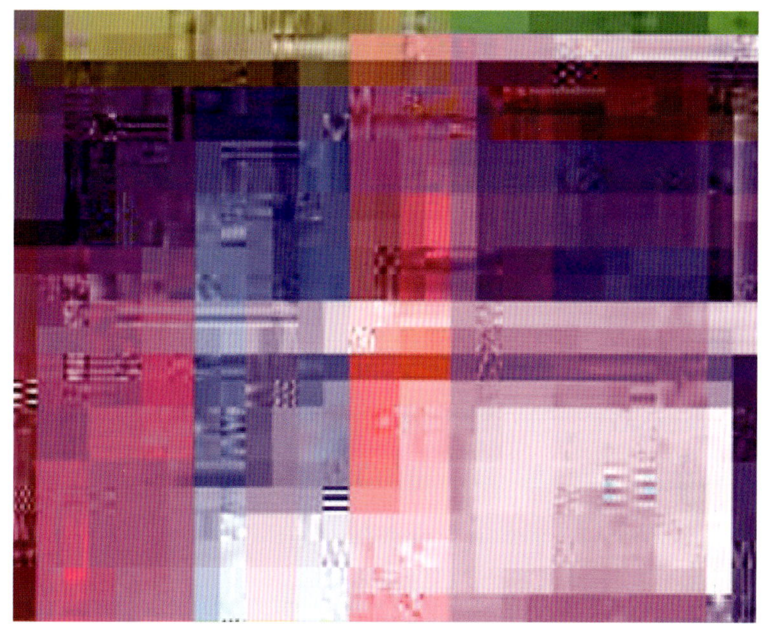

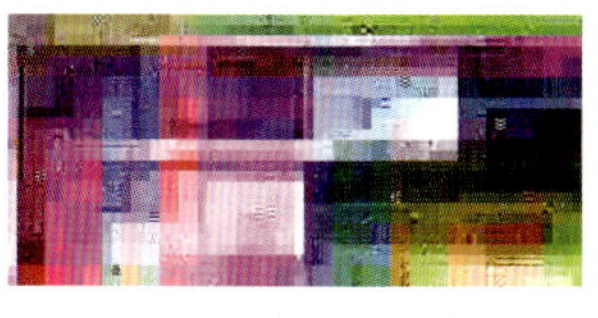

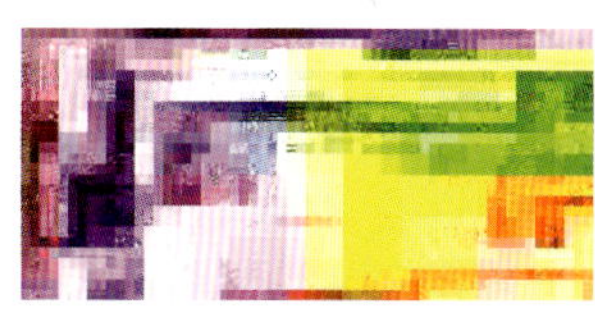

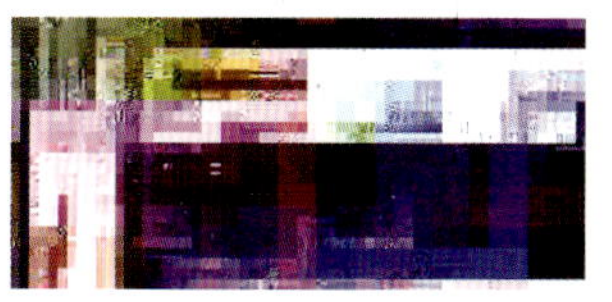

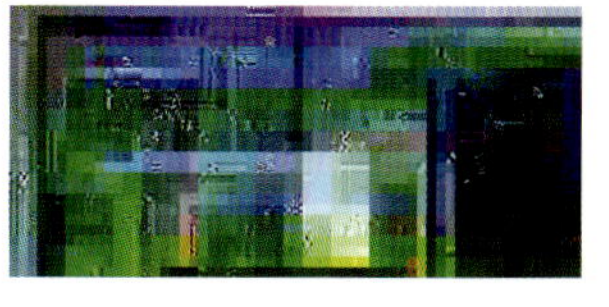

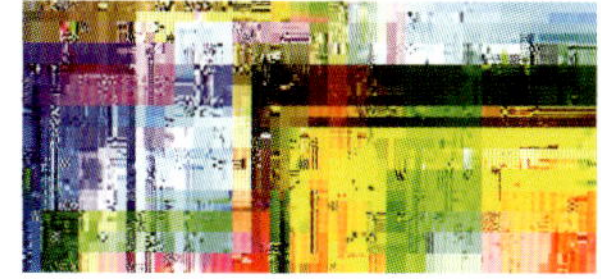

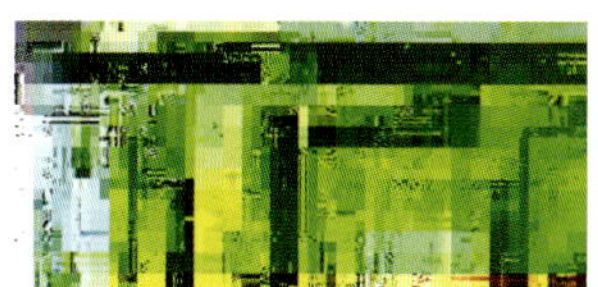

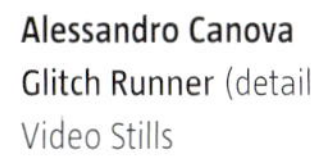

Alessandro Canova
Glitch Runner (detail)
Video Stills
–

009.002
009.003
009.004
009.005
009.006
009.007

Chad McKinney
Deconstruction 1
Screenshot
–

050.001

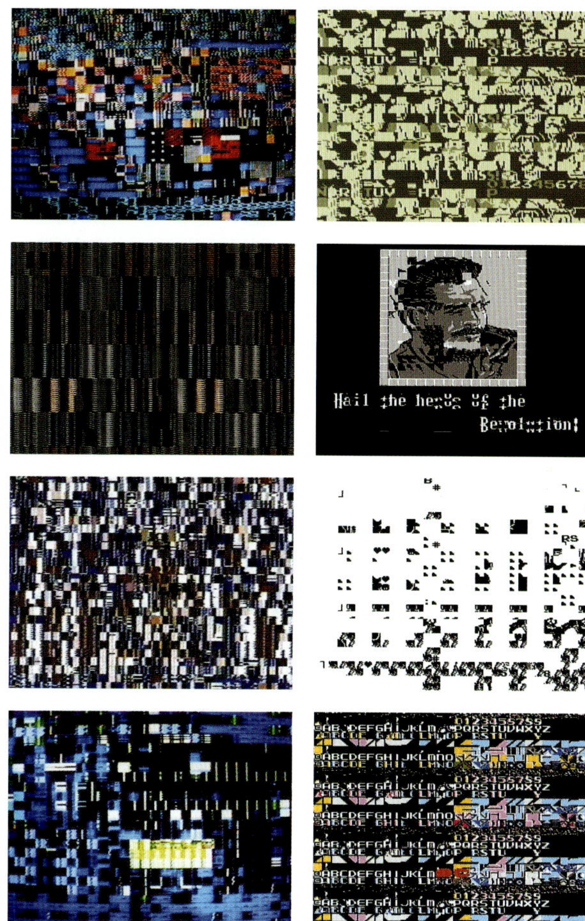

Jeff Donaldson
noteNdo
Video Stills
–

017.001
017.002
017.003
017.004

Tim Johnson
Untitled
Screenshots
–

035.001
035.002
035.003
035.004

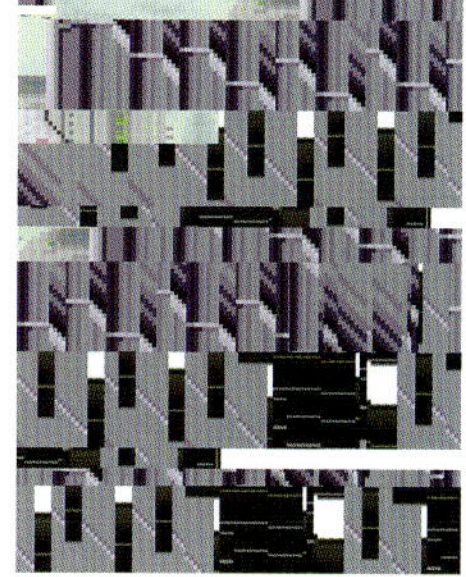

Chad McKinney
ROM
Screenshot
–

050.002

Norbert Pfaffenbichler
Notes on Mazy
Video Stills
2003

056.001
056.002
056.003
056.004

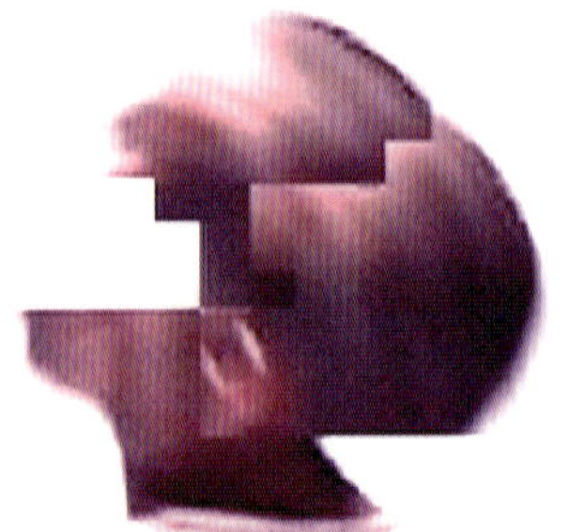

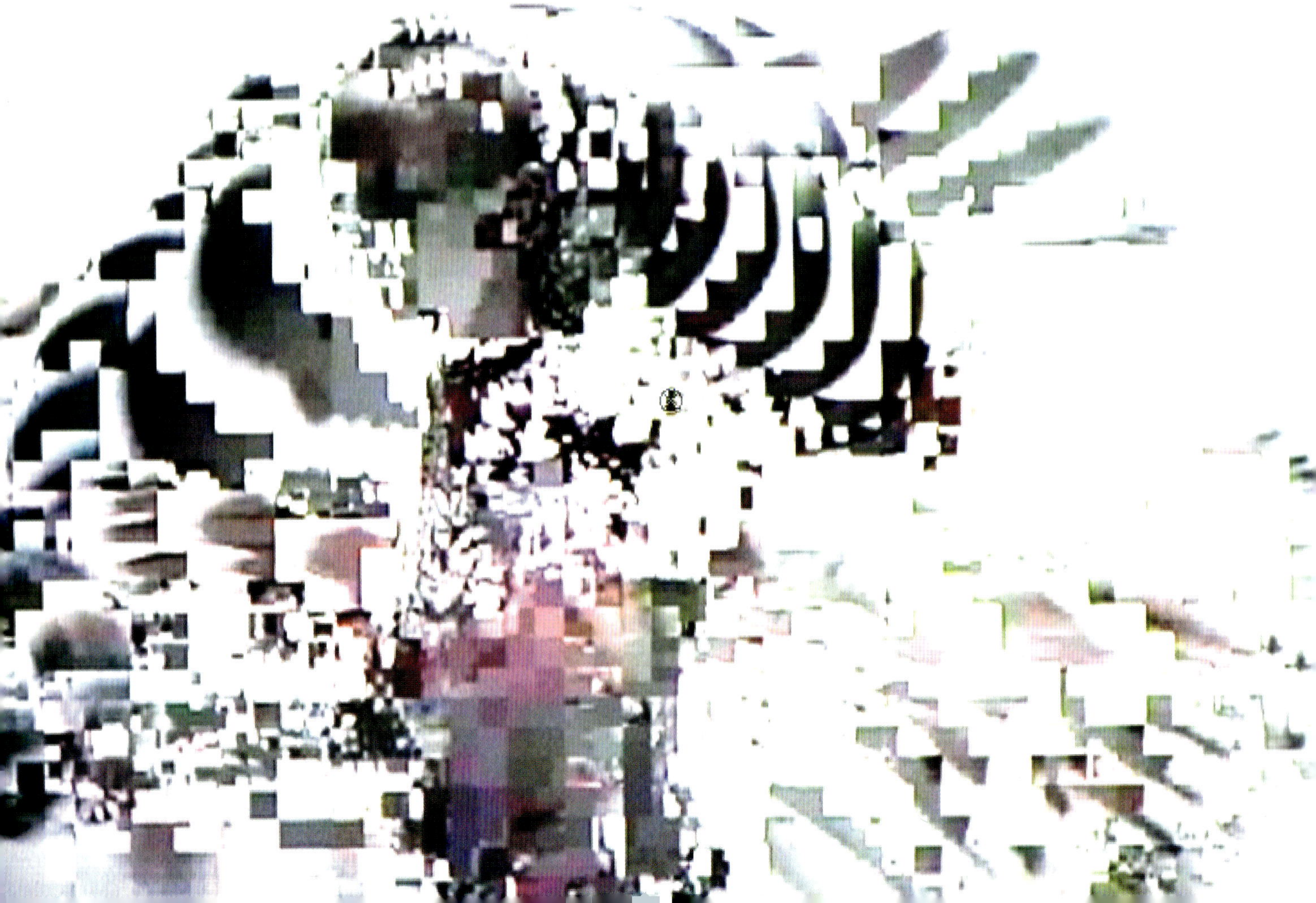

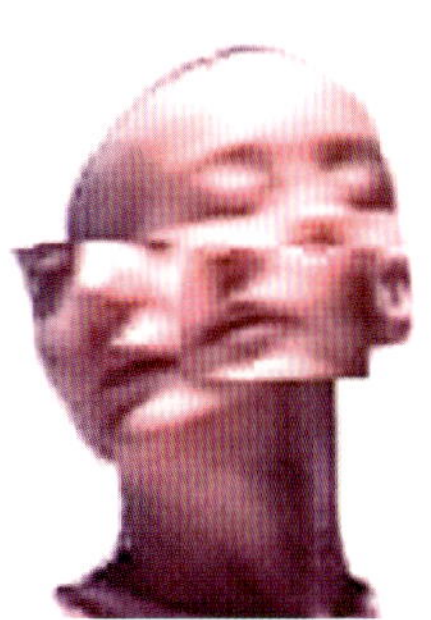

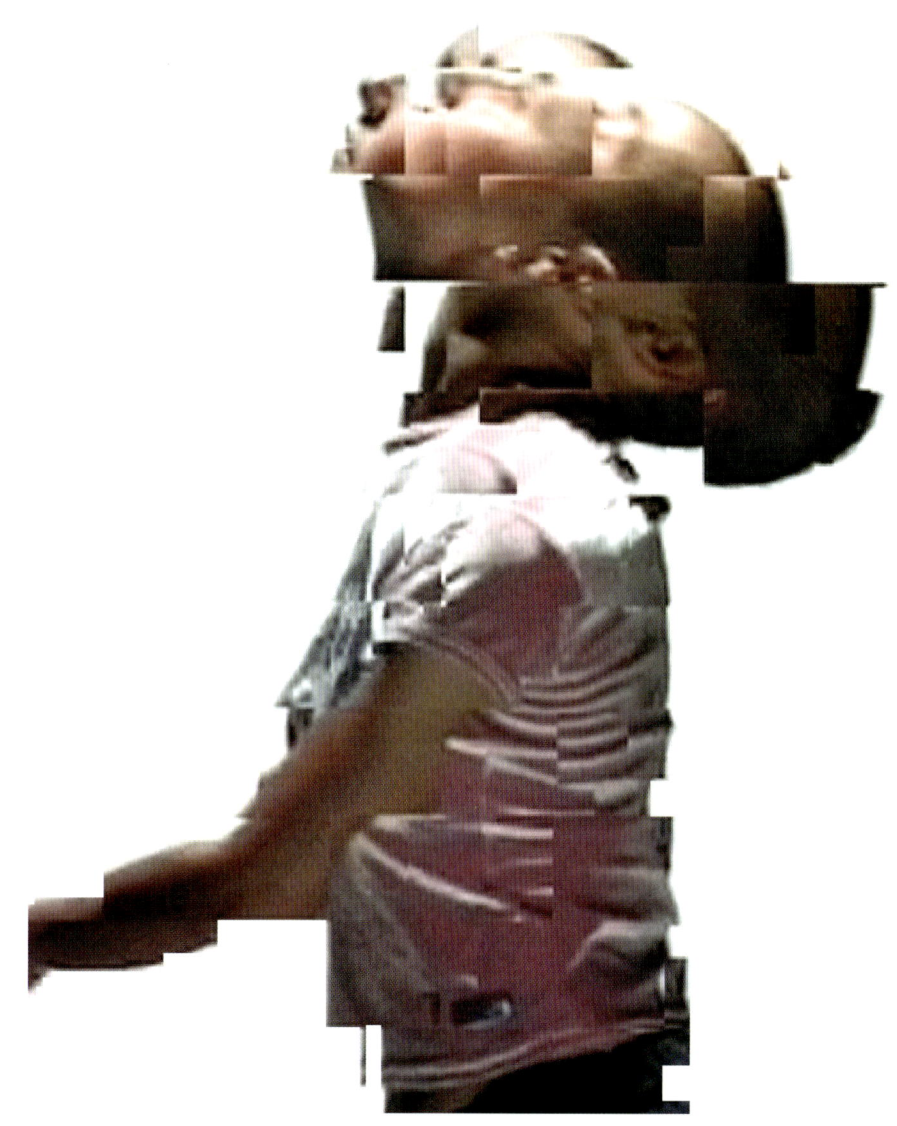

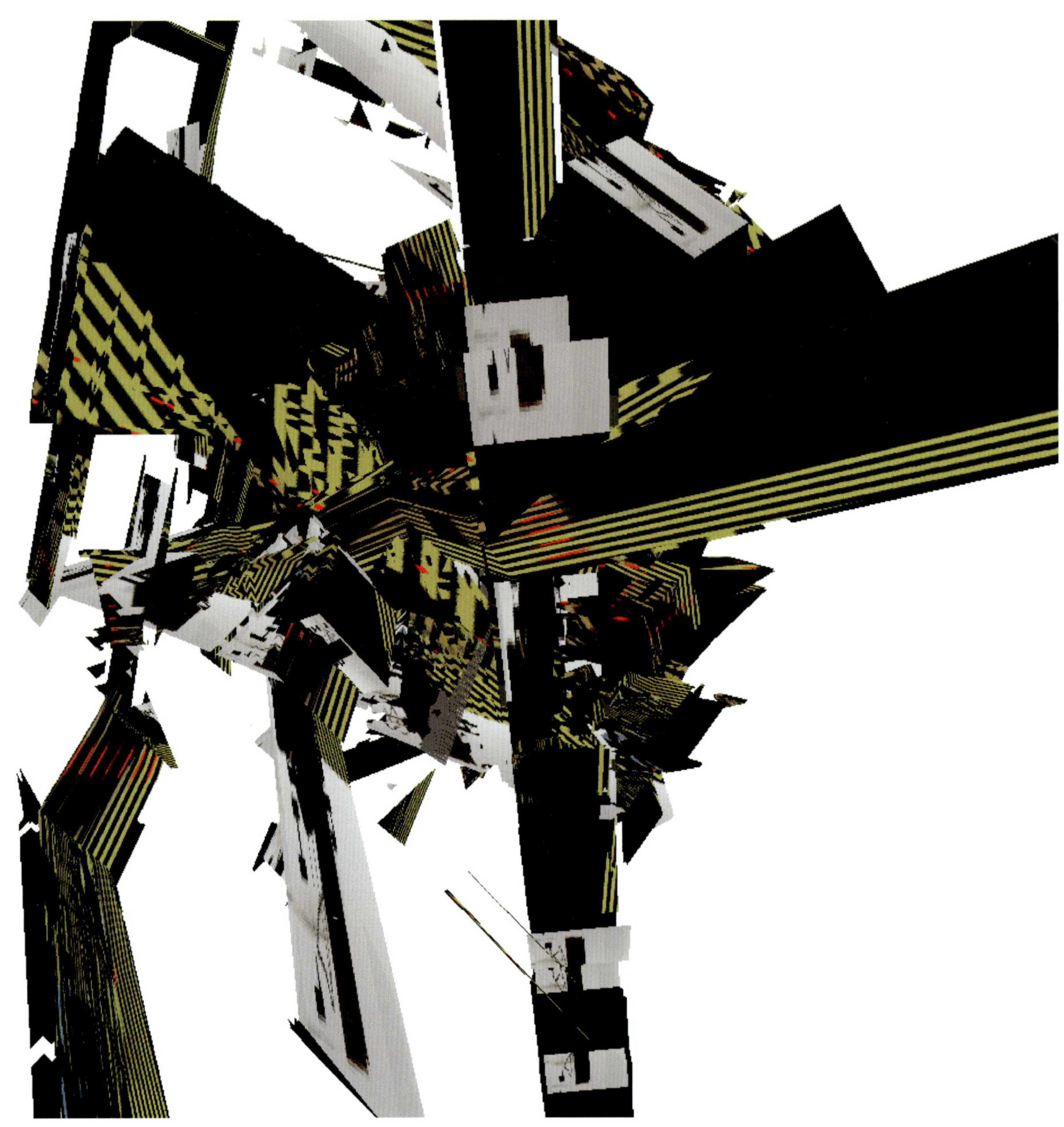

Sincretic + Vasco Godinho
Untitled
Flash
–

071.001

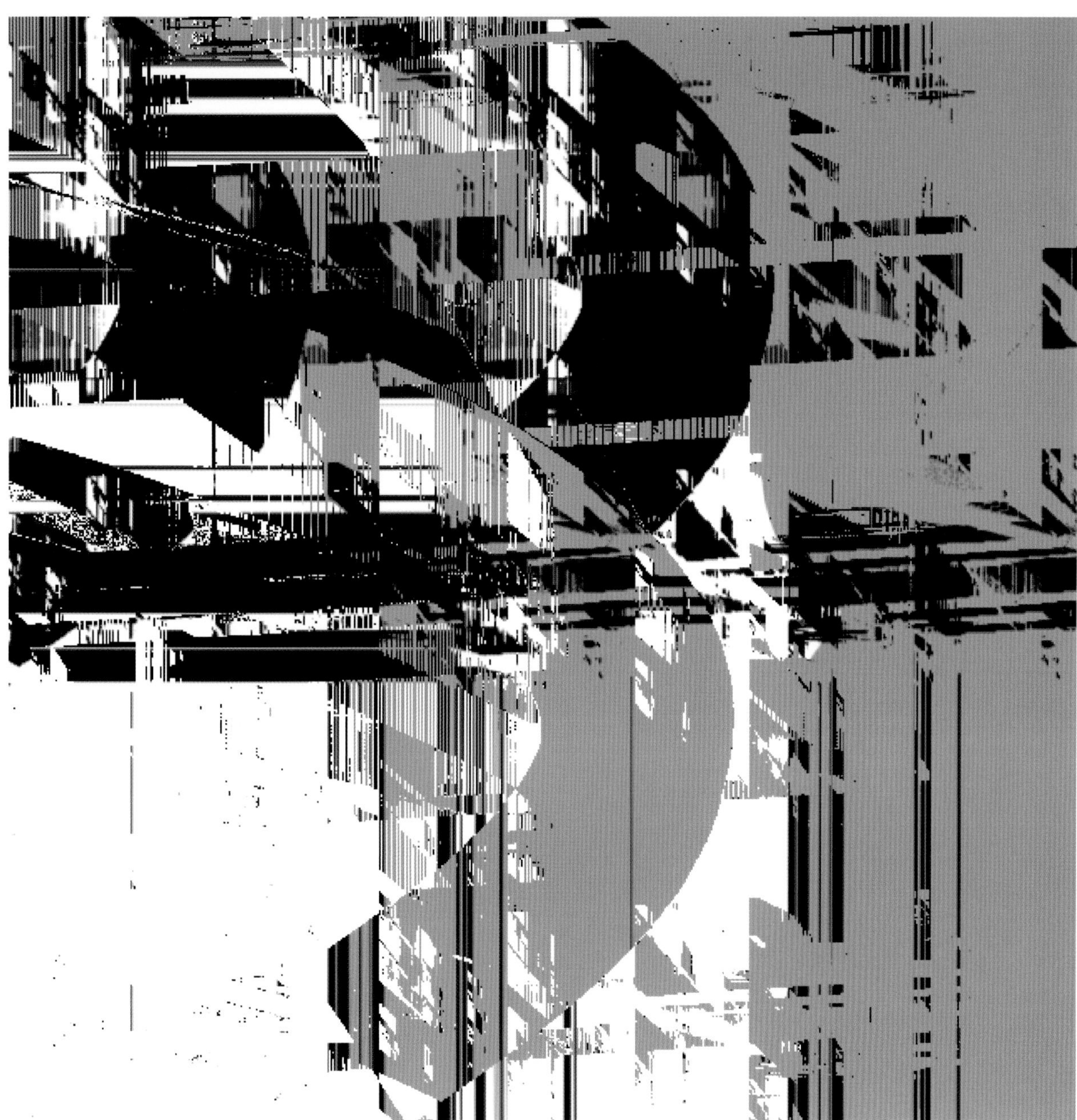

Mario Klingemann
Glitch Architecture I
Flash
2006

038.001

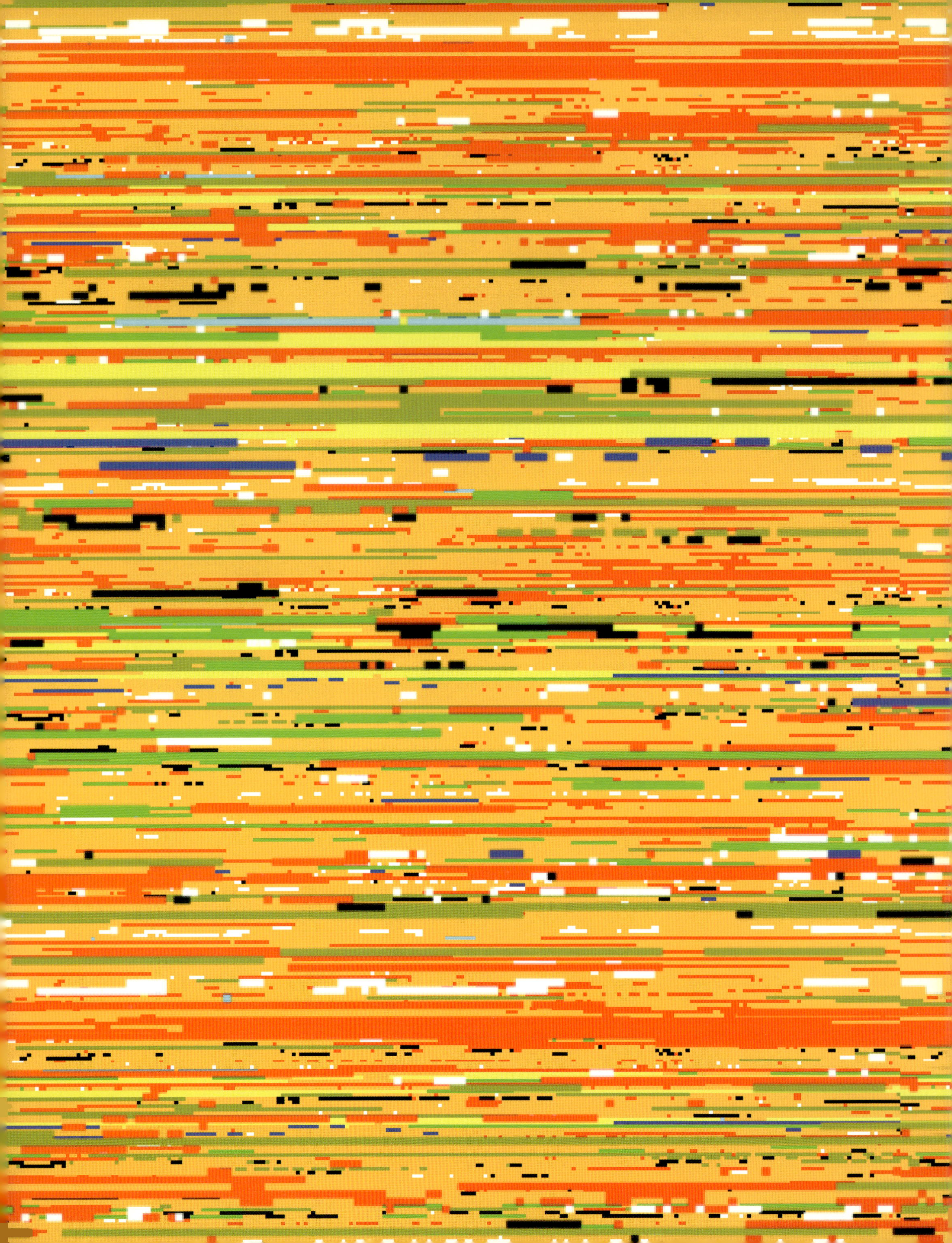

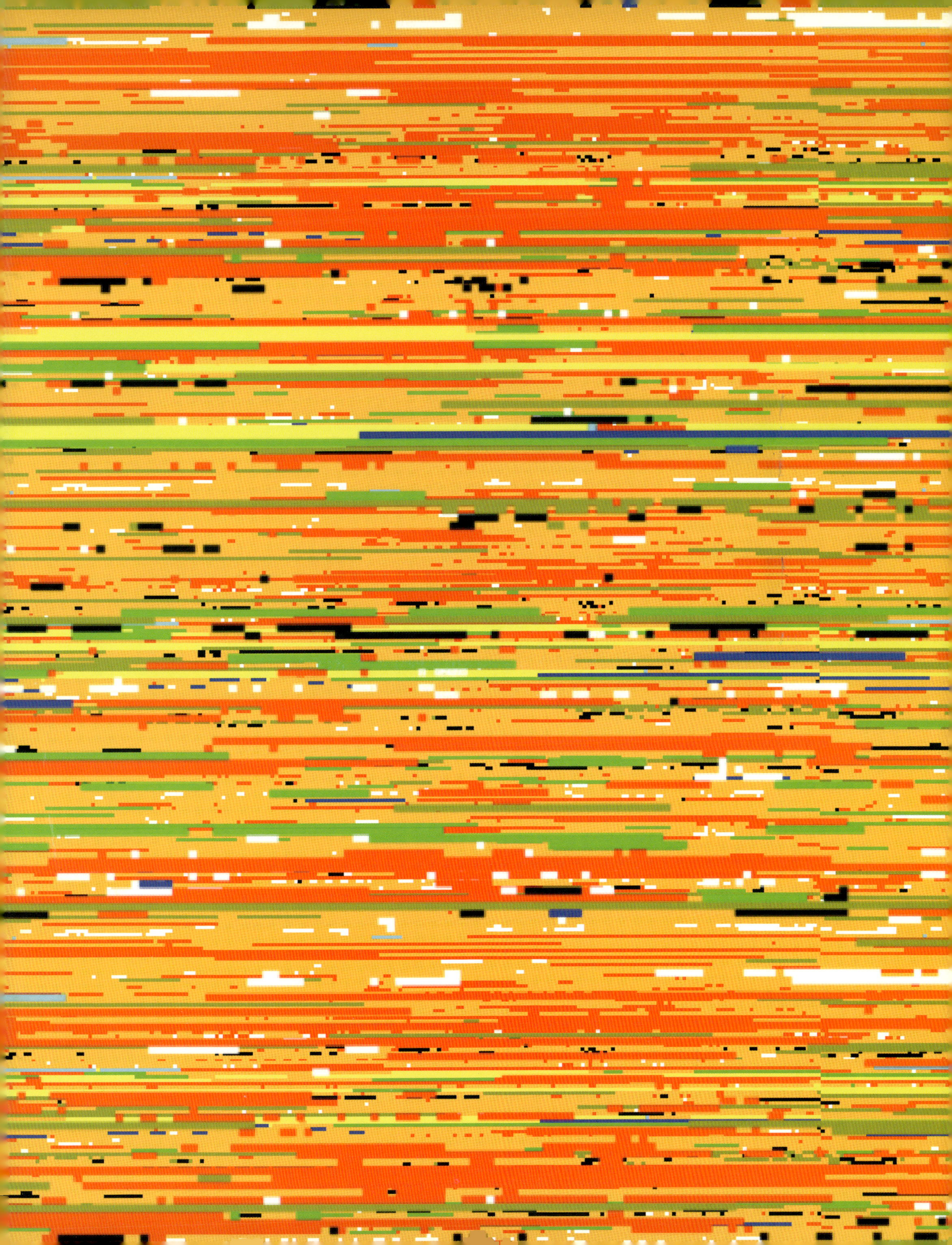

Image Credits

alorenz

A random binary converter: the program grabs random parts of a computer's memory and displays whatever it gets converted to black and white pixels (001.001, 001.002).

Bitmaps derived from the same PICT file using repeated bitmap conversion combined with the screen interference as remix engine (001.003, 001.004).

www.alorenz.net

001.001 pp88
001.002 pp88
001.003 pp96
001.004 pp97

Daniel Althausen

Two differently colored copies of a glitch are misaligned in the same image.

www.trashyard.de

002.001 pp84
002.002 pp84
002.003 pp84
002.004 pp84

Cory Arcangel

A data file of the computer's memory is forcibly played as a QuickTime video file. Each video documents a new day.

www.turbulence.org/works/arcangel

003.001 pp41

Scott Arford

Visual static, granulated washes and pixel fragments are run through the audio input to generate an equally noisy audio component in this AV piece.

www.7hz.org

004.001 pp74
004.002 pp89

Christophe Behrens

Images are repeatedly compressed using lowest quality JPEG compression settings to create impressionist portraits.

www.christophebehrens.com

005.001 pp78
005.002 pp78
005.003 pp79

Michael Betancourt

These glitches were produced using custom-built analog-to-video synthesizer hardware. They resulted from electrical shorts that happened while switching between different settings.

www.cinegraphic.net

006.001 pp93

Enrico Bravi

Images created through the movement of a single one-pixel line, using various simple applications programmed in Shockwave.

www.graphica-programmata.com

007.001 pp66
007.002 pp67
007.003 pp67

brianelectro

Feeding DivX files and NES and Gameboy Advance ROMS into the Atari 2600 emulator Stella 1.4.1, a version that accepts any type of file. The resulting glitch stills have not been altered.

www.flickr.com/photos/brianelectro

008.001 pp32
008.002 pp33
008.003 pp33
008.004 pp33
008.005 pp33
008.006 pp33
008.007 pp33

Alessandro Canova

Stills from a corrupted MPEG file of the film *Blade Runner*.

www.pachinkostudio.com

009.001 pp115
009.002 pp115
009.003 pp115
009.004 pp115
009.005 pp115
009.006 pp115
009.007 pp115

Yve Choquard

The raw data of an image was opened with wrong parameters for its width and height, turning it into a complex pattern.

www.yve.ch

010.001 pp84
010.002 pp84

Curt Cloninger

Source images were taken from Bruce Conner's *Ten Second Film* and processed. Screen captures were turned into nineteen transparent animated gifs, then tiled, layered and randomly remixed using HTML, CSS and JavaScript. Further screen captures of this animation were taken, but the capture software was not fast enough to keep up with the animation, introducing further anomalies.

www.lab404.com

011.001 pp104

Derek Collie

Images taken with a certain digital camera sometimes had a single dead pixel, which always came out white, and blended with the surrounding colors. The effect is most concentrated within a 5 x 5 square of pixels surrounding the dead pixel; these areas were cropped and composited to form the final image.

www.derekcollie.com

012.001 pp77

Roger Cosseboom

Clips from searches for "war," "sex" and "time" on Yahoo Video Search were combined and altered through an autonomous video feedback system. By charting only formal elements within each video, such as contrast and motion, frames were pooled and played back with automatic filtering processes applied recursively (013.001, 013.002).

Video clips with codec errors are processed using a "stuttering" technique in Jitter (013.003, 013.004).

www.thesocietyforpotentialliteratures.com

013.001 pp105
013.002 pp105
013.003 pp112
013.004 pp114

Taylor Deupree

An error occurred while exporting a PDF from Microsoft Excel. This was the resulting file. The Excel document was the digital royalty statement for artist Piana.

www.12k.com

014.001 pp70

Dextro

A software error caused an overflow of the computer's floating-point representation of numbers. Starting from a simple 3D model, this made spikes grow at the edges and corners, similar to an ice crystal.

www.dextro.org

015.001 pp75
015.002 pp75
015.003 pp75

Manuel Dilly

Crash occurring with the WinUAE emulator and edited for color reduction, brightness and contrast.

http://mitglied.lycos.de/tumiki/

016.001 pp42

Jeff Donaldson

Modified NES console used to create forced glitches through bad electrical contacts, system crashes and improper game loading.

http://audiovideo.sevcom.com

017.001 pp117
017.002 pp117
017.003 pp117
017.004 pp117

Paul Emery

A simple rectangle, half black and half white, is fed into a tiling algorithm that duplicates the shape to create an array. A second system then processes the texture map on each tile adjusting the position and scaling with each iteration. The system utilizes a perlin function to introduce a random element across the array. Programmed with vvvv.

www.studioseen.co.uk

018.001 pp44

eNo

–

www.weirdcore.tv

019.001 pp46
019.002 pp76
019.003 pp76

Adam Farcus

A photograph of a television screen taken during a storm causing cable transmission interference.

020.001 pp46
020.002 pp76

Jerome Faria

The MP3 soundtrack to a movie promo was manipulated in a photo editor.

www.nothing.scene.org/nny/

021.001 pp72
021.002 pp73

Fehler

Broken GIFs utilised for trash section of Bremsstrahlung Recordings website.

www.fehlr.com

022.001 pp98

Benjamin Fischer

Source code manipulation of images without use of classic image editing applications.

www.typedown.com

023.001 pp68
023.002 pp69
023.003 pp69

Scott Fitzgerald

A video generator made from a pair of PIC microcontrollers. Long lines of text scroll past the edge of the screen and cause distortion by breaking the horizontal sync.

www.ennuigo.com

024.001 pp105
024.002 pp105
024.003 pp105

Tim Fox

A static image of vertical lines is recorded onto video tape and played back on televsion while adjusting the tracking on the VCR. This is filmed through a DV camera to create the interlacing effects.

www.cultlovesyou.com

025.001 pp36
025.002 pp37

Nik Gaffney

–

www.f0.am

026.001 pp77
026.002 pp77
026.003 pp77

Iris Garrelfs

Audio-Visual interactive installation based on recycling issues.

www.irisgarrelfs.com

027.001 pp52
027.002 pp52

Joe Gilmore

A Max/MSP crash is captured by video and reworked to create the final work.

http://joe.qubik.com

028.001 pp60
028.002 pp60
028.003 pp61

Mathias Gmachl

A short video sequence of a heavily-tattooed individual rubbing his hands across his face is processed using a slit-scan technique to create a facial mutation.

www.live.fm

029.001 pp100

Brent Gustafson

When arcade machines boot-up, many will perform a self-test, part of which is visual in nature. Some are for video callibration (e.g., convergence grids and color patterns), some show a tile map of sprites used in the game, while others show video RAM flushed from memory. 128 captures of various arcade test screens were made and randomly combined.

www.assembler.org/axbx/

030.001 pp45

Alex Horber

Composite image from multiple print-head cleaning cyles, generated by an Epson PRO4000 printer. It is the trace of a physical glitch – a blockage in the ink delivery system.

031.001 pp77

Will Hurt (glitchCORD)

Highly compressed video files are layered, streamed to the internet, transmitted down the telephone line, recorded onto VHS tape and screen-captured using various video settings. The whole process is repeated several times.

www.willhurt.net

032.001 pp50
032.002 pp51
032.003 pp51
032.004 pp51

Eddy Joaquim

Corrupted photos created during faulty upload to photo-sharing website Flickr.

www.flickr.com/photos/aqui-ali/

033.001 pp34
033.002 pp35

JODI

Contrary commands are given in HTML to place the same image again and again in the same place.

www.jodi.org

034.001 pp122

Tim Johnson

NES cartridge loading glitches created by shifting the cart around slightly and changing pressure.

035.001 pp117
035.002 pp117
035.003 pp117
035.004 pp117

Daniel Julià

–

www.pimpampum.net

036.001 pp40

Jason Kahn

Small details are magnified and their importance inverted in our field of perception: going down to the pixel level in an image and using these details as the basis for a new image.

www.jasonkahn.net

037.001 pp43

Mario Klingemann

A user-controlled evolutionary process selects the "fittest" image from a breed of different assembled pieces. The pieces themselves are created randomly by applying a series of filters, transformations, blend modes or paint strokes.

http://incubator.quasimondo.com

038.001 pp121

Karl Klomp

Hardware hacking with digital projectors and a sync pulse generator.

www.karlklomp.nl

039.001 pp85
039.002 pp85
039.003 pp89
039.004 pp89

Rainer Kohlberger

Logo on shop receipt was mis-printed.

www.kohlberger.net

040.001 pp90

Lia

Generative application coded in Director.

www.re-move.org

041.001 pp80

Lia + Miguel Carvalhais

Generative application coded in Director.

www.strangethingshappen.org
www.carvalhais.org

042.001 pp80

Jan Robert Leegte

The work was created as part of a series, named "netsquats." By roughly chopping out the content of a well-known web page by hand, the space was left empty, with just some characters or punctuations left, as scraps and dust in an abandoned building.

www.leegte.org

043.001 pp56

Dimitre Lima

–

www.dmtr.org

044.001 pp30

LoVid (Kyle Lapidus / Tali Hinkis)

Stills from Beta video recording of Sync Armonica, a custom analog hardware video instrument, recorded with damaged sync.

www.lovid.org

045.001 pp85
045.002 pp85

Rob Lycett

Images are opened in a text editor, altered, and then opened in Photoshop in RAW format. The red streaks are created from expired domain names.

www.da-n.org

046.001 pp113

David Lu

Drawing software tools were ported from Processing to C#/GDI+, running on a TabletPC. The pen pressure data was too dense for GDI+ to render quickly, creating long lags between moving the pen on the screen and seeing marks appear. This mode of interaction produced unexpected drawings.

www.velluminous.org

047.001 pp103

Stephan Maich

–

www.latona.us

048.001 pp47

Hamish McDougall

Images were opened in a text editor and altered, before being converted into various image formats (TIFF, JPEG, PSD, GIF) and the process repeated. Further design elements were added with Illustrator.

www.visualastronaut.com

049.001 pp113
049.002 pp113

Chad McKinney

–

050.001 pp116
050.002 pp117

Meta

–

www.meta.am

051.001 pp57
051.002 pp58

Iman Moradi

–

www.organised.info

052.001 pp86
052.002 pp87
052.003 pp87

Michael Norris (Spiketrain)

Shots taken with a malfunctioning Canon PowerShot A6 camera.

053.001 pp51
053.002 pp53

O.K. Parking

A monitor cable was split into separate wires which were individually switched in and out.

www.ok-parking.nl

054.001 pp92
054.002 pp92
054.003 pp93

Alex Peverett

Hand-drawn using a mouse and mainly preset gradient fills. Produced within a primitive paint software application on a mid-1990s PC.

055.001 pp28
055.002 pp29

Norbert Pfaffenbichler

The more intense the dancer's movements, the greater the image interference. Several methods of visual manipulation were combined, such as operating the fast-forward and rewind on a digital video camera, and applying excessive video compression.

www.vidok.org

056.001 pp118
056.002 pp118
056.003 pp119
056.004 pp119

Andrea Polli

Ten minutes of motion self-portraits in which a portion of a live image is drawn on the screen in the approximate area of the motion.

www.andreapolli.com

057.001 pp45

Nicky Proniewicz

A Photoshop brush set was created from sections of the Microsoft Windows GUI and then edited to create the main elements of this design.

www.nickyp.co.uk

058.001 pp39

Kristiano Pronin

–

059.001 pp111

Paul Prudence

The "alpha exploit" is a bug in Flash as it incorrectly tries to handle the transparency of many layered alpha-blended animations while it tries to conserve processor load.

www.transphormetic.com

060.001 pp73
060.002 pp73
060.003 pp73
060.004 pp73

Tim Redfern

Stills generated by hacked screensaver software.

www.eclectronics.org

061.001 pp62
061.002 pp63
061.003 pp64

reMI

–

www.remi.mur.at

062.001 pp81
062.002 pp81
062.003 pp81
062.004 pp81
062.005 pp81
062.006 pp81
062.007 pp81
062.008 pp81
062.009 pp81
062.010 pp81
062.011 pp81
062.012 pp81
062.013 pp81
062.014 pp81
062.015 pp81
062.016 pp81
062.017 pp81
062.018 pp81
062.019 pp81
062.020 pp81
062.021 pp81
062.022 pp81
062.023 pp81
062.024 pp81
062.025 pp81

RetroYou

Game modification.

–

www.retroyou.org

063.001 pp102
063.002 pp102
063.003 pp102

Johnny Rogers

Stills from a film compilation of NES glitches. The electrical contacts on a game cartridge are sensitive and often askew, resulting in a collage of that particular game's sprites. By carefully jostling a cartridge, the glitches can be modified in real-time. The objective is to document these formally beautiful designs. Viewers of this piece often see a favorite game from their past, which is not actually there, in these glitches.

www.geojedi.org

064.001 pp38
064.002 pp38
064.003 pp38
064.004 pp38
064.005 pp38
064.006 pp38

Billy Roisz

–

http://gnu.klingt.org

065.001 pp101

Michael R. Salmond

Source material is a travelogue from Hong Kong to China. Digital transfers from DV are played back using the DivX codec. Various settings of the codec create different aesthetics. There are geographical and spatial glitches in the system, part communist, part capitalist, part human and part social machine.

www.stresspuppy.net

066.001 pp48
066.002 pp48
066.003 pp48
066.004 pp48
066.005 pp48
066.006 pp48
066.007 pp48

Ant Scott

Dragon 32 RAM visualization (067.001). Visualization of internet cookie database (067.002). Long-exposure photographic contact print of glitch animation on computer monitor (067.003). Visualization of operating system temporary file (067.004). Computer screen redraw error (067.005).

www.beflix.com

067.001 pp106
067.002 pp106
067.003 pp107
067.004 pp108
067.005 pp108
067.006 pp109
067.007 pp109

Mike Scullen

A photograph taken of a damaged 13-inch IBM monitor with a Polaroid SX-70 camera fitted with close-up filter.

068.001 pp76

Fairchild Semiconductor

Work from a series of Giclée prints which feature unaltered OS X application crashes.

www.fairchildsemiconductor.org

069.001 pp99

Steven H. Silberg

A greyscale image is read by a computer, one pixel at a time, and translated into sound. A microphone receives the sound and transmits that to another computer where the frequency is translated back into an image. Both the installation space itself and the viewer manipulate the sound, thereby manipulating the image during its transmission. Max/MSP/Jitter is used for the translations between image and sound.

www.shsarts.com

070.001 pp37
070.002 pp37
070.003 pp37
070.004 pp37

Sincretic + Vasco Godinho

Loops of various software processes, including abuse of an Avis|DS, a non-linear editing system that was extruding objects in 3D using vector meshes, on top of which textures were painted. All pixels within the image originate from itself, creating a "meta-image."

http://metaphsk.com

071.001 pp120

Skot (Tina Frank + Mathias Gmachl)

This video uses agitation as well as emphasized scratches and the graininess of found Super 8 footage, as a means of plastic "extensibility" or "liquefaction" of old movies with the help of computers.

The images are synchronized with the music moving forward and backward in single frames like being "scratched."

www.frank.at

072.001 pp101

Megan Sproats

A wireless camera's signal is deliberately mistuned at the receiver.

www.spek.com.au

073.001 pp34
073.002 pp34
073.003 pp53

Daniel Stanciu

–

074.001 pp45
074.002 pp110

Steinbrüchel + Brusa

Randomly generated audio-visual installation and mini CD-ROM.

www.synchron.ch

075.001 pp101

Telcosystems

–

www.telcosystems.net

076.001 pp62

Luciano Testi Paul

–

www.100luz.com.ar

077.001 pp76
077.002 pp91

Dan Tombs

Stills taken from the output of modified video games consoles. The consoles are dismantled and have custom circuit paths added, which continuosly adjust the data flow in and out of the graphics processing chips.

www.dantombs.net

078.001 pp71

Andrew Townsend / Wig-01

–

www.wig-01.com

079.001 pp78
079.002 pp78

Kentaro Tsuji (Nek)

An animation file was opened in a text editor, and the resulting text edited, before converting to a still image.

080.001 pp49
080.002 pp49

Ben Ullman

Corrupted JPEG files are opened in Photoshop. By opening additional images, and scrolling and zooming, further distortions are created.

www.budesigns.com

081.001 pp83

U-Sun

Image is converted to sound, and back to image, using Open GL with Max/MSP and Jitter. The movement of particles is a simulation of a behavioral system.

www.ecolocation.info

082.001 pp90
082.002 pp90

James Warfield

–

www.wig-01.com

083.001 pp82
083.002 pp83

Marius Watz

–

www.unlekker.net

084.001 pp46

Kate Wintjes

Video effects obtained through hex editing, data transfers, DivX encoding, corruption and repair.

www.karmaintakt.com

085.001 pp71

Akihiko Yoshida

When a Nintendo game cartridge is accidentally pulled out while playing, grotesque and beautiful audio-visual errors are created.

http://members.jcom.home.ne.jp/kick.snare.kick.snare/

086.001 pp27
086.002 pp111
086.003 pp111